THEY CALLED US RIVER RATS

THEY CALLED US
RIVER
RATS

The Last Batture Settlement of New Orleans

MACON FRY

University Press of Mississippi / Jackson

The University Press of Mississippi is the scholarly publishing agency of the Mississippi Institutions of Higher Learning: Alcorn State University, Delta State University, Jackson State University, Mississippi State University, Mississippi University for Women, Mississippi Valley State University, University of Mississippi, and University of Southern Mississippi.

www.upress.state.ms.us

Designed by Peter D. Halverson

Frontispiece photograph by Macon Fry

The University Press of Mississippi is a member of the Association of University Presses.

First printing 2021
∞

Library of Congress Cataloging-in-Publication Data
Names: Fry, Macon, author.
Title: They called us river rats: the last batture settlement of New Orleans / Macon Fry.
Description: Jackson: University Press of Mississippi, 2021. | Includes bibliographical references and index.
Identifiers: LCCN 2020048224 (print) | LCCN 2020048225 (ebook) | ISBN 978-1-4968-3307-5 (hardback) | ISBN 978-1-4968-5212-0 (trade paperback) | ISBN 978-1-4968-3305-1 (epub) | ISBN 978-1-4968-3308-2 (epub) | ISBN 978-1-4968-3309-9 (pdf) | ISBN 978-1-4968-3306-8 (pdf)
Subjects: LCSH: Community lifeLouisianaNew OrleansHistory. | New Orleans Batture (La.) | New Orleans (La.)History. | New Orleans (La.)Social life and customs. | New Orleans (La.)Social conditions.
Classification: LCC F379.N5 F79 2021 (print) | LCC F379.N5 (ebook) | DDC 976.3/35dc23
LC record available at https://lccn.loc.gov/2020048224
LC ebook record available at https://lccn.loc.gov/2020048225
British Library Cataloging-in-Publication Data available

CONTENTS

Dedicated to my ninety-three-year-old father Ernest William Fry, who embraced a son who built a house not just on shifting sand, but on a flooded and fragile fringe. Dad wisely realized this story might be as endless as the flow of the river. He always gave the same advice—"Wrap that thing up!"

ACKNOWLEDGMENTS

During twenty years between inspiration and book I was buoyed by the kindness and support of hundreds of people, but my greatest debt is to the dozens of old river rats and batture folks like Joe Judd and Georgie Dumser who told me their stories. They are the heroes of this tale.

The memories of batture folks would never have been published if not for the guidance and encouragement of Dr. Martha Ward. She convinced me that the stories were worth telling, showed me how to ferret them out, and most importantly how to find the heart of those narratives. Long after tapes and notes were consigned to a crate in my loft, Martha never lost faith that I was the person to write this.

A decade after Hurricane Katrina, I found Dr. Richard Campanella in his office at Tulane University. Richard's books had inspired me with their detailed geographic forensics and tales from the intersection of people and place. Richard paused from his own manuscript on that late winter afternoon to give me research advice that energized a new start.

The Louisiana Endowment for the Humanities endorsed my research and provided grant money to develop maps and secure images. The staff at the Louisiana Research Collection, the Hogan Jazz Archive, and the Southeastern Architectural Archive at Tulane University provided patient access to maps, images, and documents. The Historic New Orleans Collection and the Louisiana Collection at the University of New Orleans worked to find and contribute photographs. The US Army Corps of Engineers and Orleans Levee District each opened their archives and images to me.

The line between critical reading, editorial advice, and friendship blurred repeatedly, but the patience of loved ones was most important in completing this multi-decade endeavor. Thank you: Cathryn Abbott Jones, Joe Sasfy and Marianne Mooney, Steve Schweitzer, Marie Isabelle, Liz Calabrese, CW Cannon, Archie, Rose, and Frank.

Nothing between us and the tankers. Photo courtesy of Edward Neham.

PROLOGUE

In the early morning darkness of February 2, 2016, a straight-line wind blasted across the swollen channel of the Mississippi River just above New Orleans at Nine Mile Point. I woke to the crashing of porch furniture hurled into the river below, followed by the deep, thundering, repeated blast of a ship's distress signal. It echoed over the mile-wide river and resonated in my chest. The 816-foot Nordbay Tanker was heading downstream empty and riding high. As it navigated the bend, the starboard flank, half a football field of metal, caught the driving wind like a sail.

I ran out on my deck and watched the 116,000-ton vessel graze the Jefferson Parish water intake upstream. It obliterated the steel tripods, known as "dolphins," that are deployed to stop small things like runaway barges. With quiet grace the ship crushed a disused oil pier that jutted in front of our dozen riverfront homes—like a garbage truck flattening a tissue box. Then the ship was abreast of us, parallel to the bank but too close. The Nordbay's hull scraped the concrete riverbank as its port side encompassed the entire colony. The river, the lights of the Entergy power plant on the west bank, the clouds and fleeting stars were obscured by a towering wall of steel close enough to smell its oil and rust.

Moments later the ship glanced off the New Orleans water intake downstream. The retreating silhouette and throb of engines disappeared around the bend. The waves subsided. My neighbors, dozens of riverbank dwellers who had fled to the levee, muttered "holy shit." Everyone went back to bed.

My first river had been the Rappahannock, a wide tidal stream off the Chesapeake Bay in Virginia, a place that would seem to give little preparation for a life on the Mississippi. My brothers and I spent every summer there in the 1960s, from grade school through high school. In early June every year Dad drove us three boys and our mother two hours down from the Washington, DC, suburbs to the tiny cabin my mother's parents built for $400 during the Depression. We left behind the smell of fresh-cut lawns and, as we crossed the Capital Beltway, shed all the interstate traffic. When we got close and the road turned to dirt, my father drove so slowly it felt like the earth had changed its directional rotation.

Mom rolled down the window to smell honeysuckle and pine needles and finally the sulfur of marsh and river saturated everything. When we pulled into the clearing and the river came in sight, she began to sing "Happy Days Are Here Again." Dad shooed snakes from the outhouse, primed the pump, and then left us behind to return to his job in the city.

My older brother Billy and I were assigned the task of opening the windows, which we loved. The cottage was constructed of odd materials my grandfather bought from salvage yards in Richmond, the closest big city. There weren't enough matching window-sets to place top and bottom sashes in each frame, so he designed a system on the back of the house where the windowsills could be lifted out and the single sash dropped into the wall. On the front of the house the windows lifted straight up into the wall above, where they were cocked at an angle to hold them up. This created large screened openings for river breezes to gust through the cabin. Despite the inevitable mashed fingers, the system seemed miraculous to a preteen boy.

There was no phone at the cottage, and after dad dropped us off, no car. When we needed to go into town, we walked to the edge of the surrounding marsh and looked over at our cousin's farmhouse on the other side. If their car was in the driveway, we set about hollering "yoooo-hooooo," until an aunt or uncle would come out to the opposite bank and commence "yoo-hooing" back. Once the correspondents had one another's attention, a short conversation at high volume commenced over the waving field of marsh grass.

The Rappahannock taught me that rivers are places where days are long and punctuated by the rhythm of waves and storms. The changing seasons expressed themselves in the movement of sun over wide horizons. Riverbanks and mud flats were places to find and catch things and sometimes eat them. My brother and I caught fish under a cork, foraged late-June blackberries and netted August crabs. We shot guns and burned our shoulders in the sun. Our heads hung down looking for arrowheads and barnacled bottles at low tide.

We wandered far but were never lost because the sky was open, and the river was our GPS. It was always nearby, and the land sloped down to it. Some afternoons we walked back through a pine plantation to the hardtop picking up pop bottles with labels like Brown Cow, Orange Crush, and Chocolate Soldier. At Segar's Country Store, we redeemed them for two cents each. Twenty-five bottles bought a card of pre-strung fishhooks or a couple six-packs of tiny wax containers of colored sugar water called Nik-L-Nips. On the way back to the cottage we somehow got laughing-drunk on the stuff.

My nieces now spend their summers in soccer camp and pony camp, places with rules to teach kids how to do things. Our "camp" was a place where there were endless opportunities for misadventure and countless ways to screw up. We suffered poison ivy and chiggers, stepped on rusty nails, pulled fishhooks through our fingers, shot BBs into each other's legs, puked saltwater, and blew bits of flesh away with fireworks. The riverfront porch became a clinic where mom applied disinfectant and bandages, swabbed sand from our eyes, and poured vinegar over jellyfish stings.

My cousins built rafts of rope and logs that disintegrated at the first wave. Billy and I caulked cracks in the bottom of the rotten wooden skiff my mother bought us—aptly named "Scoundrel"—rigged it with a bedsheet sail, and watched it sink to the bottom. We tried to make beer by fermenting sassafras roots and sugar water in jars buried in the woods and ended up dizzyingly sick.

I always wanted to live in a place where I could imagine, find, and forage everything I wanted. I can't remember not knowing that I would live on a river.

THEY CALLED US RIVER RATS

Chapter 1

The Shack

In 1981 I finished graduate school in Virginia, ready to leave the East Coast forever. The suburbs had become a suffocating place where one town ran indistinguishably into another and long, unmoving strands of traffic connected all. Recently vacant lots in modest neighborhoods and exurban fields sprouted identical boxy mansions. I had to decide early whether to buy in. I chose to sell out, step on the economic "down" escalator and move to the country's easiest economy. I bought a '64 Newport with a push-button transmission and drove it down to our most un-American city, New Orleans, a place of warmth and decay on the nation's greatest river.

I approached New Orleans on the straight flat interstate over Lake Pontchartrain. Weeds grew through the road. A monolithic stone marker—NEW ORLEANS EAST—sank in mud and marsh grass beside a freeway exit that abruptly ended in ponds where guys in hip boots hunted snakes, alligators, and wild hogs. Suburban parking lots were virtually deserted; resting seagulls outnumbered cars. A few miles further, I found the city's cars were mostly abandoned and rusting, beached on uptown curbs. Ferns grew from gutters and moss hung overhead from the branches of live oak trees. New Orleans was watching the exodus of its life-blood, the oil industry. The economy had tanked and the place looked more like the "city that forgot to care" than its nickname, "The City that Care Forgot."

Escaping the suburbs was easy but dipping my feet in the Mississippi River was not. Unlike the Rappahannock River, open everywhere along its bluffs, this big river was obscured by miles of flood walls, commercial docks, warehouses, and railroads. Where the docks ended, earthen levees built by the US Army Corps of Engineers (known to locals as *the Corps*) ran high above adjoining neighborhoods. There were only a few obvious windows on the water: bridges, ferries, Audubon Park, and a small boardwalk by the French Quarter known as the Moon Walk.

I rented a dilapidated shotgun house in Riverbend. The neighborhood near Tulane University is named for a curve in the Mississippi that forms the upstream portion of the looping bend that earned New Orleans another nickname, Crescent City. For five years I watched the tops of ships glide past over the green swell of levee. The only life I found on the river was an old man fishing by Audubon Park. He sat on a bucket and threw a line weighted with spark plugs into the current.

One cool fall night in 1985 I sat, beer in hand, at the Maple Leaf Bar, a neighborhood watering hole a few blocks from my house. Local soul singer Johnny Adams had just finished a set when a stout guy, maybe twenty-three years old, in an aviator hat, leaned back on the bar and began spooling theories about local Mafia ties to Lee Harvey Oswald and the assassination of President John F. Kennedy. I bought him a beer and he paused to introduce himself.

"I'm Rob. Where you from?"

Quick to disown my suburban heritage, I replied, "I pretty much grew up on the Rappahannock River in Virginia."

Rob grinned and downed his beer.

"Really? I live in a camp just over the levee here on the Mississippi."

Four years in New Orleans and I had heard of no one living on the big river. I dumped my Bud in a go-cup and followed Rob six blocks up Oak Street, across the Public Belt Railroad, past the horse stables and the stucco turn-of-the-century Sewerage and Water Board intake station. We went through the River Road cut in the levee that separates Orleans from Jefferson Parish and ascended a steep shell driveway. And there it was, that familiar, faintly sulfurous and fishy smell. The river.

A clutch of thirteen stilt houses floated among willow trees in a chill November fog. At the end of a plank walkway, Rob pushed open an unlocked door and lit an oil lamp. There were no sashes or screens in two window casements and fog swirled in the flickering lamplight. The single twelve-by-fourteen-foot room contained a sleeping pallet, a crate of bike repair tools, and a wooden spool-table served by one rusty lawn chair. Rob's chaotic library of environmental writings, conspiracy theories, and Louisiana political history spilled onto a burnished bare wood floor. A plywood countertop supported an unplumbed sink and a two-burner Coleman stove. The tiny gas oven had no supply line. No electricity. No water. No gas. No toilet. Perfect!

The Shack. Photo courtesy of David Ellsworth.

We walked through another door and here, just past the edge of a sagging deck, was the Mississippi itself. Lights from a grain elevator across the way and the "whomp-whomp" of a ship's propeller penetrated the billowing fog.

Rob soared in my estimation. After all, this was the eighties, an era of consumptive capitalism. "Downsizing" would not become a buzzword for another decade. The "tiny home movement" was waiting for the advent of the next century. But here he was in a timeless one-room shack, next to the greatest river in the world. We settled on a three-legged garden bench propped on cinder blocks. Rob lit a bowl of weed and laid out his plan.

"I've got this idea for a jump rope. I mean it's revolutionary and I know Nike is gonna want it. I just need to get together dough to build a prototype and buy a used car to drive out to Nike headquarters."

Rob's camp, known as "The Shack" to all who visited, had been his first foot on the ladder of success. He paid the $75 a month rent from his pizza delivery income and earned grocery money doing bike repair, leaving just enough cash to develop the jump rope. But the rent had gone up to $100 a month, and Rob hated Domino's. He gestured at the orange and blue uniform tossed on his deck, "I gotta quit wearing the shirt of shame."

I jumped in: "Rob, I would do anything to live here."

"If you want it, you need to talk to the landlady, Mrs. Hendrix, and convince her you will pay the rent. She's pretty old and she might want you to do a few repairs."

The deck was falling off, the windows were gone (or had never existed), and I could see a flicker of lamplight through the cracks in the wall . . . but I was sitting on this guy's deck, breathing rich river air. No levee, no dock, no warehouse, nothing between us and the supertankers except fish to catch and driftwood to fashion into furniture. There was no street and thus no noise of street traffic or glare of streetlamps. There was no mailbox for unwanted utility bills; but then, there were no utilities either. Rob got quiet a moment and looked out into the fog, "Well, you might need to pay her a couple months back rent, too." My life in the last river community on the lower Mississippi began that damp fall night.

Undoubtedly, Rob was an outlier among outliers, perhaps the only person to leave the river in a bizarre reverse migration to seek more affordable shelter in the city. He was my introduction to a long line of idiosyncratic characters and refugees, some washed up and others born along the river: drifters and dreamers, artists and writers, kooks and craftsmen, hardworking folks who helped build the city and retirees drinking beer and loafing over fishing lines.

That first night on the river, I laid awake listening to ships and towboats and watching their lights flash through the open shutters. The little house exhaled an odor of water, mud, and old wood. In the morning I biked to my teaching gig at Fortier High School, eager to tell colleagues about this incredible new river home. My teaching assistant, Colleen, sat in our classroom, blowing cigarette smoke out a window and gossiping with Mrs. Henderson, the school librarian. Colleen lived in Pigeon Town, a neighborhood just over the levee from "the Shack." She was about my age, a graduate of Fortier in 1973, two years after it "integrated" and instantly became an all-Black public school. Mrs. Henderson looked like she had been in the school system since before Dewey created his decimal system.

The ladies leaned forward and squinted in obvious incomprehension as I described "the Shack." Colleen inquired, "Baby, you gonna have to take a boat to get to work?" Feigning familiarity, Mrs. Henderson warned, "Be careful around those Cajuns." Neither of these lifelong residents of New Orleans had a clue that the river colony existed right beside the neighborhood where they grew up and worked.

The inscrutability of the river colony begins in its hidden site. The river houses rest on the water side of a twenty-four-foot tall earthen levee, propped up on pilings over a narrow ribbon of sand and silt, known throughout Louisiana as the *batture*. The *Oxford English Dictionary* confusingly defines batture as "a river or seabed elevated to the surface," as if seasonal stages of the river actually raise the height of the land beneath it. Some trace the word to a French nautical term referring to shoals upon which water breaks, while others suggest it derives from the French verb "to beat" and refers to settlers washing laundry in the shallows, or waves beating on shoals.

The Louisiana Civil Code tried to sort out the meaning, defining the batture as "Accretion formed successively and imperceptibly on the bank of a river or stream...." The legislature clarified that "accretion" as a place between the "ordinary" high and low water marks. These definitions have provided personal enrichment for centuries of riparian lawyers who enjoy operating in what a friend called "a gray area within a gray area," arguing over what constitutes the "bank," what the "ordinary" high water mark is and how to measure it. To either further understand or become totally confused, you may consult a definitive entry on the subject in the *Louisiana Law Review*, by A. N. Yiannopolis.[1]

For everyone but lawyers it is enough to say the batture is the area between the river side bottom of the levee, the "toe," and the edge of the river when it is low.

The batture colony wouldn't exist but for the river, the city, and the levee builders—any one of those things, however, might yet destroy it. The river built all the land under the city of New Orleans during the millennia before European settlement, casting about its low floodplain and depositing sediment. It built a natural levee of sediment along its edge and formed the low seasonally flooded batture within its flanks.

New Orleans was founded and grew on the landward slope of the natural levee. The land was soft and low and prone to overtopping in the spring. French colonists who founded the city in 1718 watched it fill with muddy water the following year. By 1727 they had built a three-foot-tall, mile-long berm atop the natural one.[2] Thus began a three-hundred-year struggle in which levee builders have raised and hardened walls around the city and the river has continued to threaten and occasionally to breach and overtop them.

The river still has agency between its levees, where my batture camp rests. On the outside of bends, it swings hard against the shore and creates a constantly eroding *cut-bank*. Opposite, on the inside of bends the current slows, deposits sediment and creates a wider batture or *building-bank*. At building-banks the batture can grow to thousands of feet wide. In south Louisiana, where there is so little high ground, the wide battures became valuable real estate.

The harrowing battle between the river and levee builders didn't forestall a secondary contest on the batture. Ordinary citizens, colonial powers, wealthy landholders, barons of commerce, local governments, and even a United States president fought for control of the water's edge. Rails, wharves, warehouses, and shipping terminals came to mark the winners in this battle for the batture, but they would also hide another wave of claimants.

In a stroke of linguistic hubris, the levee builders and economic elites who walled off the waterfront described the area occupied by city folk as "inside" the levees. This rubric established the batture as an unprotected no-man's-land where the river was a permanent frontier. By definition, batture dwellers would be outsiders living in an ephemeral wilderness at the city's edge, built by the river and shaped by the city and eventually by the all-powerful Corps.

Batture dwellers weren't lured to the river frontier by colonial land grants or state-sponsored homesteading. There was no land rush among river folks for a fortune to be made on the wave-swept silt. They took root in the same manner as the seeds of willows and buttonbush, carried by the current and winds of the river valley. They wafted over the levee, drifted from the wintry north, and fled the storms that rolled across the Gulf of Mexico and Cajun prairie.

Today's twelve batture camps—Rob's Shack was lost to fire in the 1990s—are a window into the untold story of New Orleans' 140-year-old outsider community, a line-village that once extended over much of the city's river-front.[3] It is a narrative that telescopes to farms and cities and mountains far upriver and periscopes to battles fought with city folk just over the levee. It is a tale of wharf rats and river gypsies; of shantyboaters and stilt house people; of frontiersmen and refugees fleeing fires, floods, and economic hardship. It's my story, too.

Chapter 2

Mile Marker 104

My batture colony can't be found on Google Street View; it is not a city place, but a river place. Consult a harbor map or the US Army Corps of Engineers Navigation Chart for the lower Mississippi and between mile marker 103 and 104—one hundred and four river-miles above the Gulf of Mexico—you will see it, a gaggle of twelve unlabeled, tiny black rectangles nestled in the outside curve across from Nine Mile Point.[1] The curve is depicted as two conjoined bends, Southport and Greenville, but the entirety is commonly referred to by the name of the community at its heart, Carrollton Bend. In river pilot language, today's batture houses are on "the left bank descending," near Southport, where the parishes of Orleans and Jefferson meet.

The river at Carrollton Bend has dramatically shaped the lives of batture and city folks alike. The Mississippi forms a six-mile crescent that begins just above the colony and circumscribes what locals call Uptown New Orleans in a bulging peninsula of sorts. The city is pinched at its upriver extreme, across from my camp by the finger of Nine Mile Point, and downriver, across from the French Quarter, by the thumb of Algiers Point.

For river pilots and levee builders, Carrollton Bend is one of the most dangerous compound bends below Baton Rouge. The current hurtles around Nine Mile Point and swings with centrifugal force on the cut-bank where my colony stands. The river pushes ships and barges against this bank and at times has undercut slabs of batture, wharves, and levee. It has claimed the lives of fishermen and swimmers and caused the surrender of entire city blocks. Amidst all of this mischief, the bend became a refuge for stilt house folk able to adapt to the river's vagaries.

"Shanties," "shacks," "hovels," "huts," and "dens." Local newspapers could never settle on what to call the homes of batture dwellers, but they obviously did not resemble city houses. For a century, batture residents have

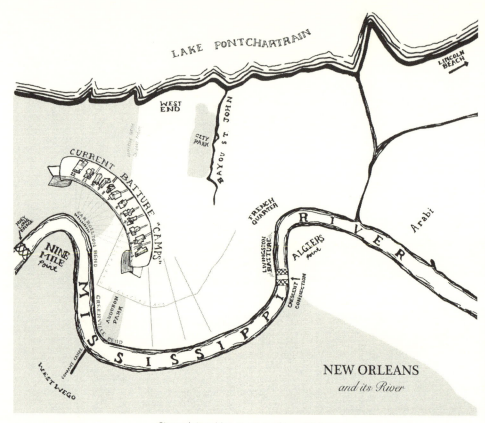

City and river. Map courtesy of Sara White.

referred to their homes as "camps." Stretching upriver from Camp 1, directly on the Orleans-Jefferson Parish line, the twelve remaining camps are attached to about three hundred yards of shore by fifty-foot-long catwalks. In an odd bit of symmetry, either end of the colony is embraced by a city water intake and marked by 150-foot-high steel towers that carry electricity across the river from the Entergy power plant visible on the opposite bank.

The camps have always been continuously occupied; they have never been part-time hunting, fishing, or vacation cottages, as the epithet might imply. The name "camp" springs from their informal, whimsical design. Batture camps are to contemporary housing what outsider art is to motel prints. Because they are self-built, not subject to common rules, covenants, or codes, and have been wildly modified by successive generations, no two

Notable Sites and People of

Carrollton Bend

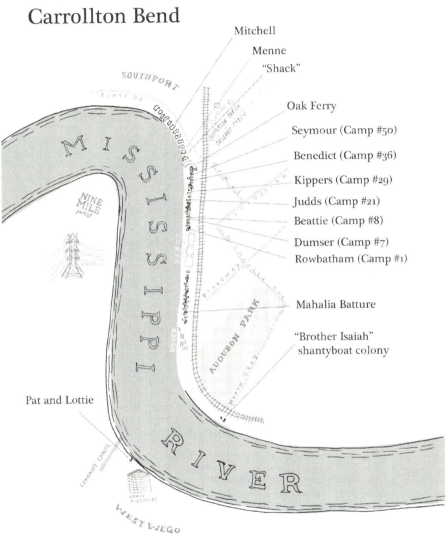

Notable sites and people in Carrollton Bend. Map courtesy of Sara White.

batture houses are ever alike. The guiding precepts of architecture outside the levees have always been affordability and the eccentric whims of their inhabitants. Combine these with an affinity for found or repurposed materials, and untrained builders, and you have a classic camp. A writer who visited the Carrollton Bend settlement in 1937 noted:

No two batture houses are ever alike.
Photo courtesy of State Library of Louisiana Historic Photograph Collection, hp006431.

A man can build himself a home for nothing more than the cost of a few nails in this city if he has a skiff and patience. Out at the end of Magazine Street and across the levee there's a little settlement of such homes, built mostly from lumber salvaged from the river after being discarded by workmen and repairmen upstream.[2]

Laborers and artists looking for affordable digs, fishermen and maritime folks who preferred life on the water, and refugees of all types built camps—they weren't the martinis-at-sunset crowd. Maybe this is why residents have always referred to the river side of their houses as "the back"—a notion that seems totally perverse to me—and to the levee side as "the front." This may also be why so few houses had windows, much less decks overlooking the river. The batture of 1986 was not the plantation South of tidewater Virginia, where my family had "riverfront" property.

I didn't get inside all the homes of my neighbors right away, but the old ones still haven't changed much. A quick inventory produced no "typical" camp. Camp 11 was home to Mary, whose two husbands had lived and died there of mysterious causes. There were no windows on the river side and

Mary's garret had no windows. Photo by Macon Fry.

only one facing the levee, and nothing to see if there were; the structure was smothered in vines. Its architectural signature was a ten-by-ten-foot "room" protruding from the barely sloped roof. In a harbor town this tower might be a place to gaze out and await the return of an oceangoing loved one. But Mary's garret had no windows, just corrugated metal walls and a sagging "suicide-door" opening into thin air. Inside, the place was a maze of rooms cobbled together in indeterminate order. The walls and ceiling were—and still are—covered in a suffocating mismatch of one-foot-square carpet samples.

Next door, Camp 10 stood in contrast to its neighbors. The cute cottage had been brought over from the city side of the levee and set on pilings. The owner, Robert, and his adult children were second- and third-generation batture dwellers. They had lived in six different batture houses and were proud to have finally carved a sliver of order out of the wilderness. Robert was a housepainter. Every summer he and his son Daryl painted the metal roof, the walls, the pier, the deck, the creosote pilings, the fence posts, and even the Blessed Virgin Mary statue. After forty years, the layers of pigment weighed more than the decaying wood beneath.

Daryl was the colony's most recognized and beloved resident. He spent his days on the levee mowing in front of everyone's camp, pulling weeds, and raking grass clippings. He manicured a perfect rectangle around his own house, one that extended up and across the levee and twenty feet down the landward side. He befriended all who walked past the camps and paid special attention to their pets. Every morning, he placed a plastic fire hydrant and bowl of water atop the levee for the benefit of rabbits, cats, and canine friends.

Another neighbor, a tugboat and supply vessel captain known to all as Captain Bob, was responsible for the "renovation" of two batture homes. Camp 7 was a narrow "shotgun" house constructed in the 1920s. Bob bought it and pleased his wife by putting a faux-brick veneer around the faux fireplace. He then set to adding a wing to either side. And wings they were. Lacking funds to purchase pilings, Bob used spindly, eight-foot long land-scape timbers to support the additions. They sank quickly in the batture silt. On the levee side, a giant sycamore was in the way. Bob cut the tree six feet above the ground and rested the addition on the stump. The whole thing was still in pretty bad repair when I arrived and the wings of Bob's house never fully unfurled. They sank toward the ground in the partially extended span of a bird balancing on a narrow perch.

Bob's other project, Camp 2, sat immediately upriver from my shack. He bought the place for his daughter, Lil Rita, who moved in with her husband and baby before the renovation was complete; some neighbors intimated that Bob's renovations were *never* complete. When the river rose and spurted through the floor in her front room, Lil' Rita put coffee cans under the table and chair legs and slipped on a pair of boots.

Two months after I moved into the Shack, the root-ball of a sycamore swept under Lil Rita's place and took three pilings out. I heard cursing over the wave-wash, poked my head out and saw Lil Rita on the levee cradling her baby. Her father, Captain Bob, was chest deep, his back against a piling and his bare, tattooed arms—with the names of his first, third, and fourth wives displayed in blue ink—straining against the stump.

The third neighbor up was in a skiff, chaining a "come-along" winch to a willow tree far out in the flood. He delivered the end of the chain to Captain Bob. Within fifteen minutes the men of the batture were all in frigid snow melt, swearing and laughing, grappling to chain the stump to the come-along and dislodge the waterlogged wood. Lil Rita's house was wounded but still standing.

Lil Rita surrendered her back room to the rising river and moved all her things into the higher side of the house. A year later she retreated with her husband and baby to an apartment in the city and sold the place to a couple of young writers who didn't mind wearing rubber boots when the river rose.

My Shack, Camp 1½, owed its fractional address to the ingenuity of builders who added camps between older ones in ad hoc fashion. The most diminutive and primitive of the structures on the batture, the Shack was bravely pushed farther out into the river than its neighbors. A single board-and-batten room without utilities, without window sashes, without even a whole number address, it was the Ellis Island of the batture, the entry point for half a dozen current and former batture dwellers waiting to purchase their own homes.

Lil Rita's near miss gave me a fuller understanding of why upriver neighbors in Camps 3 through 12 maintained an eight-foot river-side fence. The three camps on my end, Lil Rita's, the Shack, and Camp 1 sat exposed to whatever washed up. I don't know what Captain Bob's excuse was, but I had just moved in and had no experience with the threat of waterborne debris.

A few weeks after Lil Rita's brush with disaster, a cottonwood tree floated downriver while I slept. It bumped along the upstream fence like a pinball, careened off Rita's already teetering camp and jammed at an angle under my floor. Glasses crashed into the sink, books fell from shelves, and I bolted for the levee. The leviathan was jammed between two pilings and its branches were lodged in the river silt. Each small wave sent a shudder through the Shack.

I waded out in my boxers, waist deep, and wedged a two-by-four under the trunk for leverage. The tree was at least twenty-five feet long and mostly submerged. It was like trying to lift a school bus. Then the wake from a passing ship rolled in. The ship-swell lifted the cottonwood off the bottom just enough, and I set it free to float toward the Gulf of Mexico. I got my cold body back onto my palette bed, pulled on a blanket, and slept soundly.

I put screens in two gaping window openings and a sash in another and waited for the river to retreat to install a fence. I plugged holes in the floor and stuck a Winnebago toilet in the riverfront closet. My gal rejected these amenities and, after a few months, left me for good. Her parting words: "If

Who doesn't want to live like Huck Finn? Photo courtesy of David Ellsworth.

you want to live like Huck Finn, go right ahead." For people with suburban dreams like my father—who had great expectations after paying for my post-graduate education—batture life was a radical repudiation of values held dear. All I could say was, "What guy doesn't want to live like Huck Finn?"

The Shack became a perfect home. A hose from Lil Rita's "camp" provided water to the kitchen sink, which drained noisily onto the beach below the house. Electricity followed. The interior and exterior walls were one and the same. To keep roaches, mice, spiders, bees, mosquitos, and cold air from infiltrating the numerous cracks, I nailed foil-backed insulation board to the walls. This created a Gemini spaceship effect which I corrected by stapling brown paper and burlap to the inside. The insulation did little to discourage insects and rodents, but it made the place feel cozy. I could open a beer.

After three weeks in the Shack, I woke to a ruckus on the levee side. "Rob's bike ain't here. Let's just go around." Four figures passed the open shutters and skirted the house on a narrow plank walkway. In a shuffling of feet and furniture they settled on my river deck. "I'm going back to get the cooler." Guitars were tuned, beers opened, and the party got underway. As a fifth figure edged past my darkened window, I kicked off the covers and sat on the bed.

The shack became a perfect home. Photo courtesy of David Ellsworth.

The music wasn't too bad: Creedence Clearwater, the Byrds, The Band. I could hear everyone was having fun as I crept to the front door, kicked it open, and demanded, "What the hell are y'all doing on my porch at 1:00 AM? Rob doesn't live here anymore. I do."

My guests slouched on the tiny deck in wide-eyed and stunned silence, clearly shocked that Rob had abandoned the Shack to anyone who would wish to evict them. I felt bad.

"Hey, you guys could at least offer me a beer . . . and call first next time." I forgot the shack had no phone line. People just stopped by.

I never got used to Rob's buddies showing up at night, but loved that they showed up with banjos, bongos, and beer. It was normal to roll in from my day's work teaching autistic students and find an old pal or a stranger crashed in the hammock on the river porch. Sometimes out-of-town guests would gather on the deck, shucking crawfish and tossing the shells in the river. It felt like the Shack belonged to everyone until I biked home one day and found a legal envelope tacked to the screen door.

Nothing could have looked more out of place than that crisp white envelope on my unlocked door, but it wasn't just my Shack. Notices fluttered on the doors of many neighbors. A wealthy attorney in the city claimed to own the land where we lived—which was at that time not land at all but flooded batture. We, the batture dwellers, were hereby ordered to respond.

In those first years on the river, hundreds of people had visited me at the Shack. All my city friends dropped by and a host of relations and school chums from Virginia were curious to see where I had landed. They always had the same question: "Who owns these places?"

I was a renter and assumed that my landlord owned the Shack. I assumed that everyone up there owned their camps. The structures were all at least forty years old, and residents were constantly working on them. Heavy work. Building additions and securing them against the river. This was not the labor of renters. Like everyone up there, my response to the curious was always, "We own them."

A young law student and bird artist living a couple of camps upstream called a meeting. She and her husband—a ballet dancer, decoy carver, and med student—were a new breed on the batture. She was as competent with a law book as with a hammer. He was as likely to be found hatchet-carving a dugout canoe from a salvaged log as performing in *Swan Lake*. In the 1970s they had moved into the most flood-prone camp, cut pilings with a bow saw, and shored it up, just above the highest water. They tarred holes in the roof and applied gym-court polyurethane to the wood floors. At high water, there was no freeboard between the bottom of their house and the river. With the doors open, the high-gloss floors shimmered as if the house had filled with water.

The meeting was the first of only two times in my thirty-five years on the batture when nearly all the residents sat down together. It was my first chance to get to know a few folks. As a renter I didn't belong there, but Jean, my elderly landlady, needed a ride up to the batture. I picked her up at the dilapidated boarding house she owned in the tony University section. Jean happily coexisted there with wild house mice, feral cats, and a few ne'er-do-well short-term tenants.

On the drive back to the meeting, Jean explained that she had inherited the Shack from her son, who'd died over a decade earlier. She seemed not at all worried about legal threats. As we ascended the levee, she proclaimed, "I'm ready to sell my house in town and move out here. You can help add a second room for me." I wasn't about to share a house without plumbing with Jean and cautioned that we better straighten things out with the threatening lawyer first.

I didn't envy our young law student among the old batture dwellers. There is a historic suspicion of officialdom among river folk and a general

There was no freeboard between the house and river. Photo by Macon Fry.

belief that nothing good can come from encounters with the legal profession. Lawyers, and sheriffs are seldom seen and almost never welcome on the batture. No one at our meeting trusted newcomers either. But this gal, who arrived on the batture just before I had, in 1981, studied law and was the only one among us who understood the risk.

We sat in a circle, clutching our letters. Some residents carried scrawled purchase records and receipts dating back fifty years. I sat next to the Gaudet brothers, Shoe and Ferdi, who lived in Camps 6 and 8. Shoe, a retired brewery worker and the fisherman of the batture, identified the person claiming our homes as "a big-shot lawyer whose uncle and great uncle ran illegal gambling houses just over the levee for maybe a hundred years." Ferdi recalled the batture residents hired a lawyer back in the seventies, who "sold us down the river and got his crooked ass disbarred."

Our legal eagle opened with a disclaimer: "I'm here as one of you, a resident. I can't offer legal advice." She suggested not to worry, to pool our meager resources and hire an attorney. There were numerous problems with the attorney's claim. We were in fact owners by dint of purchase records and well over fifty years of documented, continuous occupation. We had a legal claim to our land as well as our homes.

Ownership through prolonged, unchallenged residence was a barely familiar concept to me. I had read about "favelas" and informal settlements of shanties and tin-roof shacks in other countries. Occasionally a news story appeared about individuals found squatting in vacant urban buildings, politically motivated "invasions," or transitional colonies of displaced people seeking affordable housing.

My batture community was established, if eccentric. Working families, retirees, students, and a schoolteacher lived in these houses. Generations of river people had built houses and raised kids there, ignored by everyone. Our "squatting" more closely resembled that of Appalachian homesteaders who had prospered on an earlier frontier until landholders who had never set foot on those slopes realized there was money to be made in the coal-rich hillsides.[3] Now a city lawyer claimed our homes, our very neighborhood.

No one on the batture ever called themselves a squatter. Our informal advisor reached a prescient conclusion: "Fights over ownership and use of the batture date to colonial times. This case could take a long time."

Chapter 3

Becoming a River Rat

In 1985 a writer from the *Times-Picayune* called Shoe Gaudet onto his catwalk in front of Camp 6. She had heard that a prominent local attorney was claiming our batture. Shoe would have ignored a male reporter but in an unguarded moment he explained the batture ethos succinctly: "I don't worry about all that . . . you could get hit by a truck crossing the street."[1] Three years later, batture resident Sigrid Bonner expressed no concern: "If all my dreams come true, I'd be an old lady here. . . . But if I get to live here five years, I'll consider my happiness complete and that I'm a fortunate woman."[2]

The oldest batture dwellers—those who had seen camps washed off the levee and floated down a swollen river—didn't fret about a lawyer's harassing letter any more than they worried about the seasonal inconvenience of high water. No one looked at owning a batture camp as possessing a "piece of the rock." The batture dwellers had turned away from the rat race. They had persevered through peril and threat because the river represented a different way of life. They were as much vested in the place as invested in the property.

In November 1993, Shelton "Shoe" Gaudet, the last fisherman on the batture, died. His people came into town from rural Mississippi and burned his few personal effects. I found the family standing around a smoking fifty-gallon drum by the river and decided not to wait for Shoe's ashes to cool. There were only thirteen camps, all held so dearly that it had seemed impossible I would ever be able to purchase one. I offered to buy Shoe's place right then. A few thousand dollars cash, a handshake, and a bill of sale registered with Jefferson Parish sealed the deal. I had never been inside, but it didn't matter.

In March 1994, I had the key to my new home and could see what I had bought. Shoe loved to fish, drink beer, and watch girls ride bikes on

"Shoe" Gaudet on his catwalk. Photo from *Times-Picayune*.

the levee. His house reflected these interests perfectly. A shed on the river side was the most soundly constructed room on the property. It was filled with fishing gear and mangled tools. When you looked out from the house toward the river, that's what you saw: a shed. Beyond the shed, Shoe's true home lay at the end of a roller-coaster pier; it was a tiny, tin-roofed room with open sides and pulleys to reel in trot lines. During his two decades of occupancy, no improvements were made inside the camp other than the application of a solid coat of nicotine to the walls and ceilings.

Camp 6 didn't sprawl, it hunkered. Generations of occupants had added small rooms onto the back, away from the eyes of permitting authorities. Successive roof additions angled down so low it was necessary to duck going out the river door or you'd knock yourself out on a rafter. I bought a bucket of tar to waterproof the roof and painted the head-knocking rafter orange. It was spring and the river was high. Each time a ship's wake rolled in, muddy water sprayed through cracks in the floor.

I decided that when the river receded in June, I would raise the house. It never occurred to me to rebuild it. I wanted it authentic and original. I wanted to honor the strange aesthetics of the many occupants who contributed to the place with found wood, straightened nails, and buckets of roofing tar. Besides, I had no money, had never constructed anything, and knew that no permit had been issued to build a house on the batture for fifty years.

If people with limited skill and resources could build a structure like this to last over fifty years, surely I could raise it up. So June found my buddy Dave and me under the house in a damp crawl space that varied from three to five feet. It was a little higher under the house where the beach sloped down toward the river. The height of various additions had been dictated by whatever length pilings the owners could find floating in the river or pilfer from the neighboring creosote plant.

Everyone on the river keeps a couple of bottle jacks in case they need to shim up a sill or replace a piling, so I borrowed these from my neighbors. I built three beams the width of the house by laminating salvaged lumber, hauled in some discarded telephone poles and filled a couple coolers with the cheapest beer I could find, a local product labeled "Quittin' Time." We used three truckloads of twenty-four-by-eighteen-inch square bridge-tie cut-offs from the rail yard to "crib" the house as it slowly rose.

The jacks rested on wide wood blocks to keep them from sinking in the soft river silt. We placed a beam across the jacks the length of the house, lifted one side and rocked the house up, getting a couple inches across the front, then a couple in the middle and finally a couple in back. As Dave pumped the jacks, I slipped shims onto stacks of cribbing. We swatted mosquitoes all day and smashed our heads on the variety of uneven floor levels.

Most of the old pilings fell over as the house was lifted, held in place not by their depth but by the weight of the building. Beneath each piling a dozen cans had been flattened and thrown in as a footer. An archaeologist could date additions. The oldest pilings were set atop rusting Jax beer cans, more recent repairs were supported by Dixies, and Shoe's handiwork was built on a foundation of crumpled Milwaukee's Best. Dave and I were not keeping up with the inspired crew that put these in.

The weeks of lifting stretched on as cribbing sank in the sand, rooms began to separate, the plywood floors buckled into skateboard ramps and daylight appeared between the walls and the floor. Thankfully it was cool under the house. We drank more beer as it got easier to move around without conking our heads.

By July, Dave moved on to other projects. The camp was high enough to call the project done and figure out how to repair all the damage we had wrought in the process. But then I noticed the front downriver corner was a little lower than the rest. I got under the sagging corner and gently jacked it up a little higher. The dozen or so six-foot-high stacks of blocks holding

Camp 6 collapsed with a hollow rumble. Illustration courtesy of Elizabeth F. Calabrese.

the house up slowly shifted toward the river and suddenly the house collapsed with a hollow rumble onto the sand. Camp 6 landed across my torso.

To my surprise, batture neighbors rallied around me after the disaster with an odd respect that may have been tinged with pity. I had been baptized in the rubble and walked out a full-fledged resident. Judging from nests inside the roof debris of Camp 6, there would be some homeless rodents that night. Like them, I crawled into the vacant camp next door. I rolled out a sleeping bag. A river rat.

The next day, I sat on the elevated catwalk from the levee to my recently purchased batture camp and looked down on the remains, a collapsed pile of plywood and weatherboard resting on the beach. A few old pilings provided exclamation points. They pierced the floors and in one room pinned a bed against a ceiling. I had masterminded the destruction of one of the last thirteen river camps, nearly a tenth of the century-old batture colony.

No one had built a camp on the batture in forty-five years. Even small exterior additions required permitting by the East Jefferson Parish Levee District and review by the Corps. With trepidation I called the levee board and asked for the boss. A day later a black Lincoln Town Car with official plates stopped on the levee in front of my pile of rubble. Mr. Heitmeyer, the levee board president, shed his sport coat, picked up a clipboard and trudged down to the debris field.

Even with his coat off, this grey man in his early seventies projected authority. Heitmeyer took a long look at the mess by our feet, turned to me and said, "What you need to do is shore it up." He didn't seem like a person to argue with, but I had already tried to shore the place up once, when it was still in one piece. "I think we have some rebuilding to do, Mr. Heitmeyer." The big boss dismissed my words with a single shake of the head and handed me a blank permission form with the directive: "I'm telling you what to *say*. Just keep it in the same footprint as the old one and submit a drawing of what you will build along with your application."

September had arrived. The days were still long, but the sun was kind. Sycamores and willows in full leaf shaded a broad expanse of silt where the river had retreated. My old buddy Dave returned to what he called "the scene of the crime" and cheered me with his greeting, "Let's get started." We posted freshly minted permits from the levee board and plugged a saw into the temporary electric box.

"Shoring up" the camp proved much easier than raising the old one. There was no crawling around on the sand pumping bottle jacks. No floor joists to bash our heads on. Pals came and pulled nails, cleaned and stacked lumber for reuse, and loaded the truck for dump runs. We had bonfires on the beach at night to dispose of rotten wood. The fires turned into parties with flame jugglers and guitars as the unusable remains of the old camp disappeared.

I scavenged old electric poles from a utility yard under the interstate. Cut to fourteen-foot lengths, they barely fit in the old panel truck two at a time. The yard boss saw me chainsawing and turned me loose on a recycle dumpster full of twelve- and fourteen-inch galvanized bolts, nuts, and washers. The river helped, too; a couple long creosote timbers washed up on the beach our first day of work. They would be half the beams needed to start construction. From a neighborhood being torn down out by the airport, I pried loose four double sash windows and two interior doors with frames. Everything was coming back together.

I bought an old fashioned scissors-style post-hole digger from Lowe's to set the electric pole pilings four feet deep. Tree roots cut easy, but previous batture dwellers had used the beach as a personal dump. Buried mattresses, appliances, and sand-embedded carpet had to be dug out by hand. The entire beach seemed to be laced with buried nylon ship rope, three inches in diameter. Rather than dig hundreds of feet of ditch to remove the rope,

Dave examines our "tarpaper shack." Photo courtesy of David Ellsworth.

we got on our knees and hacksawed through it. Some of the holes took half a day to excavate. Finally we poured eight inches of concrete into the finished holes and dropped the pilings in.

Batture neighbors came to watch and teach a few tricks: "Paint the pilings and beams with old motor oil to discourage termites." "Pour some oil into those holes, too." "Put the narrow end of the pilings down. Friction, not the width of the base holds 'em in place." "Bolt long boards onto the bottom of the pilings, against the sand, that way for one piling to sink, they all have to sink and drag down the connecting timber, too." With the remains of the old camp and scrounged stuff, we had enough lumber to reconstruct almost everything on a slightly smaller footprint.

One morning in late September I left for my teaching gig with instructions from Dave: "Don't come back without a floor." Halfway to work, a recreation department crew was renovating a ball field, replacing beautiful old wooden bleachers with flimsy aluminum ones. There were over one hundred twenty-foot-long two-by-twelve-inch fir boards, layered with hardened chewing gum and carvings such as "Shayna luvs Wayne" and "Go Fortier Tarpons." It was more than enough material for a solid floor, and if we ripped the extras down the middle, half the rafters.

Dave and I were standing high above the beach on the bleacher floor with no walls or roof when he broke the news, "I have no idea how we are going to raise that center beam we just built."

The roof beam had three layers of bleacher boards sandwiched with two layers of three-quarter-inch plywood. It was twenty-eight feet long. Heavy. It rested on the deck at our feet and belonged atop two fifteen-foot-tall posts. Over a protracted lunch break we contemplated platforms, winches, and amateur solutions too ridiculous to detail.

We were stuck and in a funk. We cleaned the work site, organized our tools, stacked and covered lumber. Dave was ready to head home, when a full-size Winnebago with Ontario tags backed into the driveway and blocked him in. A sinewy senior in clean work denims climbed out.

"I'm a friend of your neighbor, Jules, down from Ontario. Mind if I park in your driveway?"

The last thing we needed was a decrepit mobile home jamming the work site.

"How long?"

Walter smiled. "Just 'til I find a little job. I frame summer cottages in Northern Ontario and come down at this time every year to find warm weather and work."

Walter's Winnie found a home in the driveway and we had a crew chief. No nail gun on this job. Dave and I tapped away and Walter swung his thirty-six-ounce framing hammer. We followed Walter's advice, covered the entire camp with salvaged plywood, then stood back when he grabbed a chainsaw from the Winnebago and cut openings for the doors and all the windows. Within three weeks the beam was up, the house was framed and sheathed, and a tin roof was glinting in the fall sun.

I wanted to cover the camp in something easy to install, something that would last forever and not need painting. Camp #5 was covered with green-gravel roof-felt in wide strips running vertically on the sides. Narrow wooden battens were tacked over the seams and down the middle of each three-foot-wide strip. By my neighbor's estimation, the stuff had been on the house for fifty years and still looked decent. The effect was campy but super cheap and easy to put up.

At Christmas my father came down from the Virginia suburbs, excited to see what we had built. He stood at the top of the levee and assessed my new home. He stared and shook his head in dismay.

"You spent the last eight months building a tarpaper shack!" He moaned. I tried to point out that the roofing supply outlet called it "gravel aggregate," but you can't fool a child of the Depression when it comes to tarpaper.

I needed to leave my temporary shelter in Captain Bob's vacant camp next door. Bob and Rita had retired to Arkansas and their place was a wreck. My sleeping bag and hot plate occupied the only dry spots between roof leaks. If I left my shoes beside the sleeping bag on a rainy night, they filled with water. Even before the paint dried on the walls, I moved into my tarpaper home.

The new camp felt and looked like it grew there. It had contemporary touches like a river view and a shiny tin roof, but most of the stuff under that roof was found. It was more part of the batture than the city. If the pieces could speak, every scrap would tell a different story. Some would call out the names of people who lived in the old camp: "Robert Mitchell," "Marcel," "KY," "Captain Bob." Beams might answer "flood of '93," joists "flood of '54." Window trim would volunteer "barge accident"; the countertop "old

The new camp felt and looked like it grew there. Photo courtesy of Amelia Graham.

streetcar barn"; floors and rafters "playground bleachers." To this day, people visit my camp and say, "I love the way your house smells." I was proud to walk inside and savor the aura of old wood.

I put a bed on the gleaming bleacher floor and woke up in the new camp, looking out through a wall of trash-picked jalousie windows. A tanker rounded the river bend at 9 Mile Point. Home.

Chapter 4

Batture Wilderness

M̲ost people no longer think of the Mississippi River as a place, much less one that is special, spiritual, or natural. Almost no one could imagine it as a home. Even though I have indoor plumbing and electric lights, people ask me, "Why do you live here?" To many New Orleanians the lower Mississippi River held all the cache of a giant sewer or commercial viaduct—dirty, dangerous, and degraded.

I always loved the openness and possibility expressed by flat water, big rivers, and wide horizons. But the pull of the Mississippi is elemental. The land between the levee and the river has its own rhythms, its own microclimate, its own cycle of flora and fauna. Step over the levee from the stagnant air of the city and everything is moving and changing. It is a living edge.

Paul Hartfield, a marine biologist with the United States Fish and Wildlife Service who grew up on the Mississippi, raised eyebrows among naturalists but got it exactly right when he called the river "an engineered wilderness."[1] Hartfield points out that despite a reputation for pollution and industry, there have been surprisingly few extirpations of species in the lower river. Most of the plants and animals that explorers found in the lower Mississippi are still there today, living beside dams, levees, and revetments. To Hartfield, the river is a place that "emanates wildness." Even John Barry, the methodical historian of the Great Flood of 1927, rhapsodized that "the Mississippi River is wild and random."[2]

Cold water from the north courses downriver from the Northern Plains and Ohio River and braces the batture with its chilly breath. Today, February 15, the river is forty degrees and the thermometer on my door registers sixty-two degrees. A thick layer of advection fog, generated by the collision of warm air and cold water, is piled against the levee; it spills over into the city in freshets that dissipate when they hit the seventy-degree temperatures hovering over urban asphalt. A zephyr swirls on top of the levee and spirals currents of warm and cool around joggers and bicyclists. In thirty years on the batture, I have never needed air conditioning.

Powered by the flow of the world's fourth largest river, movement is the basic condition of batture life. A famous song proclaims, "Ol' man river, he just keeps rolling along." But the river doesn't just roll. When a storm comes off the Gulf of Mexico, the wind careens over the wide expanse; waves start up against the current in violent protest. Seventy-mile-per-hour straight-line winds recently charged downstream and blew a train car off the nearby Huey P. Long Bridge.

In the spring the Mississippi can carry 1.25 million cubic feet of muddy water per second past the Carrollton Bend camps, enough to fill the Superdome in less than two minutes.[3] It affects how plants and creatures make their homes and how rooted they become. When it rises, the river makes every batture camp an island, moves through our foundations and yards, laps at our pilings, and can be heard sloshing under the floor. The river changes batture flora and fauna from terrestrial to riverine and back as a season's work.

In winter and spring, storms from the west deliver deep snow to the Rockies, the Great Plains, and the Ohio Valley. Cold rains blow through the mid-South and western slopes of the Alleghenies. The precipitation from over a third of the country flows into the lower Mississippi. Typically beginning in late December or January, batture dwellers watch the river rise. River stages are not an abstract measurement here. A vertical rise of two to four feet in late winter translates to water covering perhaps forty horizontal feet of batture, flushing out wildlife, sending roaches and centipedes and mice crawling up the stilt legs of camps and drowning small annual plants.

The Lower Mississippi River Commission and US Weather Service measure the relative height of the river above "mean gulf level," which approximates sea level.[4] One river gauge is located at the Corps' district headquarters in the heart of Carrollton Bend. The National Weather Service posts seven-day and twenty-eight-day forecasts on the internet for major cities up and down the river. It is now possible to see a flood coming weeks in advance.[5]

Most batture dwellers eschew computer reports and simply wake up in the morning and look at the previous night's rise. Decades ago my neighbor

Tying off logs under Camp 1. Photo by Macon Fry.

in Camp 5 sculpted a life-size nude and propped the figure against a camp piling. We call her "Our Lady of the River," and when the water reaches her thighs, it's time to bring junk stored in our yards up to higher ground. The river's stages can also be read in its flotsam. As backwaters overflow, water hyacinths bob past in midstream. A rapid rise or fall upriver causes banks to crumble and sends entire trees down the channel. When untethered buoys rush past and the water laps at Our Lady of the River's sculpted breasts, it's time to batten down the hatches.

When the river went down in the summer of 1994, my first year in Camp 6, it swept six inches of silt from the beach. Barrels, ship ropes, washing machines, car parts, broken bottles, and rotting truck tires emerged from what had been nearly flat sand and weeds the summer before. I put it together and figured out the source of this accumulation. When the former neighbor, Captain Bob, got home from working on the river, he

Terrestrial castoffs and river-borne refuse. Photo courtesy of David Ellsworth.

repaired appliances and cars. The stuff he couldn't fix, Bob discarded on the "beach" in back of Camps 6, 7 and 8. Judging from the desolate scene on the riverfront, quite a few irreparable items had complicated Bob's life. Three complete car chassis rose from the sand.

The castoffs of terrestrial life joined with river-borne refuse in back of the camps. Three-inch-fat nylon ship rope twisted about the bare roots of willow trees and snaked through discarded car steering wheels. A smashed hardhat reading BISSO MARINE dangled from the low branch of a previously flooded sycamore. Crows picked through an old maritime work vest, tubes of diesel lubricant, an empty plastic gas can, and several bait containers stranded at water-edge.

Within a few weeks, new willows began to grow in the car chassis and wire grass covered the partially buried bottles. A mockingbird nested in the hard hat. The river had receded, and plants and animals were reclaiming their seasonal home.

It was late May and the recently exposed batture was exploding with bird-song and baby willow saplings when a girlfriend brought a former college classmate of hers over the levee to meet me. Billy Finney emerged from a dented Toyota pickup with a bruised canoe hanging out the tailgate and greeted me in competing narratives, one conversational, the other an excited compendium of all he observed. "Hey Macon, I'm . . . Loggerhead Shrike! . . . Billy . . . Phoebe! . . . Finney . . . Downy Woodpecker!"

Finney's curiosity for every plant and creature along the river had earned him the nickname "Hucklebilly Finch." At age thirty-three, the scruffy National Park Service biologist seemed too young to know so much about the flora and fauna of the batture. His knowledge was gleaned more from a riverside childhood than from textbooks, and he seemed equally comfortable picking up a rat snake off my compost pile with his bare hands as teaching a greenhorn a few things about riverbank biomes.

A narrow shell path leads over the levee across the street from the home where the young Finney lived in the suburb of River Ridge. The muddy track descends onto a wide and wooded batture where Billy "grew up":

> That path was our door to the wilderness, our way to get out of the city. Everybody called that part of the batture Charlie's Point, named after an old river rat who once lived there. We'd go back in the woods and get turtles and frogs, then we'd walk the rack line when the river came up and flip the driftwood over to catch snakes: speckled kings, diamondback water snakes, Texas rat and ribbon snakes.

Finney's sharp brown eyes darted among the budding batture willows as he spoke, and he laughed at the intrepid mockingbirds nesting in a hardhat.

> Mom constantly constantly told us "don't go by the river." But we were out there every day. When the water went down, we collected stuff from Charlie's Point with a dip net. We didn't know what they were, but we would take them home and put them in a tank to see who would eat who. It didn't take long to figure out if you put a bass or a goggle-eye in there it was gonna eat everybody else.

Talking to Finney on the batture was nearly impossible. Conversation halted when he sighted a yellow-rumped warbler and again when a Mississippi kite caught a thermal overhead. Gulls, whistling ducks, and chirping frogs—Finney's specialty—all distracted him from his main point.

"This is a fringe. It's where water meets land, the exact place where the biomes overlap. That overlap offers an amazing variety of places for food, perch and shelter. It's a refuge and a temporary habitat for all kinds of animals."

The batture is not only a fringe, it is also a place in flux, and only a temporary habitat for many of its occupants. Finney called on an odd metaphor for a place that is actually under water up to half of the year:

> When the river is high it acts like a burn in a forest, opening a wound on the batture every year. The current drowns or rips up shallow rooted plants and displaces rabbits, armadillos, raccoons, turtles, snakes, coyotes, and other terrestrial species.... Then when the water recedes, the batture is like a flame-scorched hillside, ready for succession on steroids.

The falling river deposits rich silt filled with seeds carried on the water and wind that flow through the valley, and Finney proclaimed, "a new suite of pioneer species colonize that fertile palette." The river can leave a shallow pond of tadpoles and leaping mullet that shrinks in two weeks to become a damp slough. That slough dries and erupts in thousands of black-eyed susans or a forest of small willow switches.

Some plants persist even during high water events. Black willow, sycamore, mulberry, and more recently, Chinese tallow trees tower over the wildest sections of batture. Beneath them and hanging from branches are perennial vines: trumpet creeper, poison ivy, and blackberries.

The levee board keeps a twenty-foot-wide swath of grass cleared and mowed between the toe of the levee and the batture wilderness. Work crews on dozers push driftwood and overgrowth and smash it all in a heap against the batture woods. Robust species like elephant ears and blackberries thrive in the resulting disturbed earth. They quickly punish the levee workers and reward berry pickers with a profusion of new growth by the tree line.

Finney would have gladly spent the day on the batture, reveling in its plant and animal populations and rhythms, but a seminar on frog populations called him away to Lafayette, Louisiana. He left me feeling like one of a cast of pioneer species, a part of the web of batture life, and determined to spend my days exploring that wild fringe.[6]

When I arrived on the batture, only two of my neighbors, the retired brothers Shoe and Ferdi Gaudet, still fished the river. Every year when the water
came up, they went out on Shoe's pier and set lines off the end, which was
covered by a tin roof and provisioned by a dorm-size refrigerator. They
fished until their cooler was stuffed with catfish or they felt they couldn't
drink any more beer; then they went to the levee-side deck to clean the
fish, give filets to pals, and drink more beer.

After Shoe died and I moved into Camp 6, no one else on the batture
was interested in fishing. Most of my pals were deeply suspicious of the
health consequences of eating river catfish. Some of the same people who
wondered why anyone would live on the river also inquired, "What are
you gonna do with those fish?" I often replied, "A river catfish won't be the
thing that kills me."

I grew up catching and cleaning catfish and was inspired by the big wet
pantry out back. There was also Mark Twain's account of Huck and Jim's
fishing exploits:

> ... the days went along, and the river went down between its banks
> again; and about the first thing we done was to bait one of the big
> hooks with a skinned rabbit and set it and catch a catfish that was
> as big as a man, being six foot two inches long, and weighed over
> two hundred pounds. We couldn't handle him, of course; he woulda
> flung us into Illinois. We just set there and watched him rip and tear
> around till he drownded.[7]

Huck and Jim actually could have caught a fish as large as a man. There
are stories of early river explorers whose small boats were nearly capsized
by run-ins with massive fish.[8] In 2005 a fisherman on the river in Alton,
Illinois, landed a 124-pound blue catfish, 58" long and 40" in girth.[9] Old men
bike down the levee past my camp with catfish hung from their handlebars,
tails dragging in the dust.

My first catfishing exploits in the Mississippi, however, were complete
failures. I cast from the deck of the shack and snagged a willow tree; the
line came back minus the lead sinker. I re-weighted the line, cast again, and
hooked another obstruction on the bottom. Again, no sinker.

Brother John Lewis, a gospel singer and avid fisherman, introduced me
to the secrets of fishing in the Mississippi. John had fished the riverbank

for over forty-five years. He gave the catch to his wife, Sister Alberta, who served the catfish fried golden at her Central City home, which doubled as a restaurant and where she hung out a sign, "Alberta's Soul Food." That's where I met John, at Sister Alberta's single dining table over a plate of crispy river catfish.

To avoid the frustration of losing hundreds of dollars' worth of lead weights, John filled a bucket with worn-out spark plugs from a neighborhood service station. He showed me how to tap the contact down on the plug, forming an eye to tie onto. John then examined my line and pointed out, "That piddly little string ain't gonna hold no river-cat!"

John rejected merely "bank fishing," as fishing from the shore is called. He claimed his technique was "as surefire as money in the bank"; thus he called it "fish-bankin'." He would find an open place on the river shore, knock holes in a can of dog food and drop it beneath the branches of a barely submerged willow. As the dog food attracted his bait, John stuck three forked sticks into the sand and propped fishing rods in the forks, ready to bait and cast. He flipped over a five-gallon bucket, sat down, and drank a root beer. When the cold drink was empty, he pulled a dip net below the willow branches and scooped out a half-dozen or so three-inch-long shrimp which had been feeding on the dog food. John always introduced the shrimp to his hooks with a smile that broadened into a laugh and the prediction, "This shrimp is gonna catch a fish or die tryin'."

I might have done well to employ John's technique of "fish-bankin'," but after moving into the new camp, I made the fateful decision to pursue big catfish lurking much farther out, under the flooded willows. I bought a spool of heavy, tarred fishing line and cut it into thirty-foot lengths. At the bottom of each length I tied a five-pound window weight below two #7 hooks. I baited the lines, wound them around the weights and tossed them into my old aluminum canoe.

The trick in securing and running the lines was to paddle out and tie them to small willow saplings and branches, all the while keeping the canoe in the slower current just inside the trees. I dropped the weights overboard where the current grabbed them and pulled the line taut, then returned to my deck to watch in comfort as the saplings and limbs with lines began to shake and bob, a sure sign that a fish had found the bait.

The canoe method worked fine until one afternoon in late July. Clouds had rolled in from the west and crowded the horizon when I spotted a shaking willow sapling twenty yards downriver from my camp; it was bending low in supplication to what had to be a giant catfish. I threw a lifejacket on, put a spare paddle in the canoe, and headed out. The wind was blowing hard downstream, and as I grabbed the line and pulled it up, I lost my grip on the tree. The canoe drifted into the faster current and the fishing line connecting me to the tree slowly played out. I could feel there was some serious weight below.

A beautiful twenty-pound blue catfish broke the surface. I pulled the line high to grasp behind his pointed barbs and a second catfish, bigger than the first, appeared on the bottom hook. Beneath that fish, the five-pound weight swung in the current. Over fifty pounds of fish were pulling in opposite directions. I lunged for the bottom fish and heard a splash. Cheap paddle I thought, as my extra paddle disappeared around the bend.

I kept the good paddle under my foot and lifted the line again. When both fish were onboard and raising hell around my bare feet, I unhooked them. Maybe I spent a moment too long studying the beautiful yellow flat-head thrashing about. Before I could re-bait and toss the weight back over, the wind pulled the last slack out of my line and the bottom hook snagged under a gunnel. I tipped long enough to see the second paddle float away.

I considered letting go of the line and following the paddle into the channel but, in a singular moment of common sense, relented and pulled back to the tree. Being pinned under a fallen batture camp was ignominious enough without also winding up in the middle of the river, in an electric storm, in a metal canoe, with no paddles. The rain drummed on the aluminum hull and lightning illuminated a darkening sky.

My main concern was to look around and see if any neighbors had witnessed the spectacle. The coast was clear. I returned to shore by cordelling from one willow to the next, grasping the dangling fronds, pulling in to the trunk and pushing off again. When I reached the fence line in front of our camps (considerably downstream), I was calm enough to feel cold. I grasped the chain link and hauled the canoe hand over hand back to my gate. It was a humiliating way to catch a couple nice fish and caused me to seriously consider that perhaps my pals were right; a river catfish could be the cause of my death.

Now there are two of us fishing on the batture. My neighbor got tired of watching me pull in catfish, and in the spring of 2019 we teamed up to catch bait and hoist fish too big for any one person to land. We caught 1,300

Time to get the filet knife and heat the oil.
Photo courtesy of Steve Schweitzer.

pounds of catfish from the safety of our piers—a lot more relaxing than fighting the current in a canoe. I tie my lines to a railing, then wrap them around pencils stuck between the deck boards. When a pencil snaps and the line lurches hard against the railing, it's time to get out the filet knife and heat up the oil.

At the time, I gave little thought to the small bait shrimp John Lewis dip-netted. They resembled the brackish water grass shrimp I found in the Rappahannock River as a child. But the Mississippi isn't brackish in New Orleans; it is fresh, and I had never heard of freshwater shrimp.

One of Shoe's old shrimp traps.
Photo courtesy of Edward Neham.

Then I bought Camp 6 and found a stack of wood and wire traps stored in Shoe Gaudet's fishing shed. I showed them to Shoe's brother, Ferdi, who lived upstream in Camp 8, and he explained, "Those are shrimp traps, podnuh. River shrimp are good eating and even better bait. Knock some holes in a can of dog food or put a piece of beef-melt in the bottom and put the trap out there under a willow tree overnight."

Shoe's shrimp traps were in bad shape, but I followed Ferdi's directions and caught hundreds of shrimp the first night. Most were too small to eat, but I was hooked. For the cost of a can of cheap dog food and with no work whatsoever, I caught enough bait to run all my fishing lines.

When I began to read about the pursuits of batture dwellers, I discovered river shrimp were more than a favored bait of old fishermen; they had once been a mainstay of the batture dweller's economy and one of the iconic native foods of New Orleans. Before seine boats sifted lake shrimp

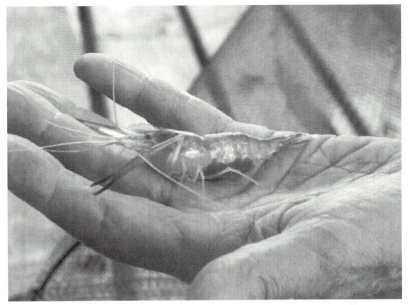

River shrimp, *Macrobrachium ohione.* Photo courtesy of J. Jeffrey Minzey.

from estuaries around the Crescent City and long before deep water trawls found jumbo shrimp in the Gulf of Mexico, river people caught the small arthropods in dip nets and homemade traps. In 1794 naturalist Christopher Hutchins traveled the river and observed: "A dish of river shrimps is easily produced by hanging a small canvas bag with meat in it to the banks of the river, and letting it drop a little below the surface of the water, within a few hours a sufficient quantity will have got in the bag."[10]

Macrobrachium ohione became the original table shrimp of South Louisiana. Served in stews and gumbos or boiled and spiced, it was the favored shrimp in New Orleans' fine restaurants, barrooms, and batture homes. Even as seines took hauls of saltwater shrimp from estuaries around New Orleans, river shrimp were "considered more delectable than . . . lake shrimp, its coarse and inferior cousin."[11] In 1911 they sold for twenty-five cents a pound, compared to ten cents a pound for large lake shrimp.

Trawlers had been plying the deep waters of the Gulf Coast for over a decade in 1929, when a *Times-Picayune* columnist placed the diminutive river shrimp in New Orleans' culinary pantheon: "We have always said that as long as folks in New Orleans drink real coffee, eat crawfish and river shrimp . . . we'll be different."[12]

Unworried by the cost of fuel for boats or nets during the Great Depression, batture dwellers caught, sold, and bartered river shrimp.[13] They constructed shrimp boxes from whatever was free and took their harvest to bars and restaurants near the levee. Refrigeration was nonexistent in batture homes, so shrimp that weren't sold were put on the supper table. In 1938 river shrimp were still selling for twice the price of lake and gulf shrimp.

But *Macrobrachium ohione* occupy a precarious niche along the river shore. The shrimp are amphidromous—meaning they must migrate between fresh and saltwater. Although found as far north as Ohio, the larvae must develop in brackish estuaries near the Gulf of Mexico. In late spring and early summer, the tiny invertebrates cling to the batture as they travel back upstream against the current at a rate of five miles a day.[14] These are the prime months for river shrimp harvest.

Dams, diversions, and revetments intruded on the natural migration of the river shrimp, and water quality deteriorated. At the same time, large gulf shrimp could be caught nearly year round, then bagged and stored in modern freezers for shipment across the country. Whether it was because of environmental degradation or the imprint of wartime standardization, by 1947 the market flipped; river shrimp sold for half the price of jumbo headless shrimp.[15]

In the 1950s, river shrimp disappeared altogether from restaurant menus and grocery store ads. Finally, like the diminished community of batture dwellers, the once ubiquitous river shrimp evaporated from the consciousness of the city. In 1962 a shopper's column in the classified section of the newspaper posted a call: "Up and Down the Street's readers keep asking for river shrimp. Anybody got them this spring?"[16] No answer followed.

As the river shrimp make their journey upstream and water recedes from batture ponds in the early summer, another cousin of the batture dwellers invades the shore. Blackberries cling to the exposed riverbank with the same tenacity as batture dwellers. They are invasive, tough, prickly, and beautiful in spring blossom. They love to have wet feet and if someone thinks that whacking them will retard their growth, think again. Cut the old canes from a wild blackberry plant and the second-year growth will run rampant with fruit.

When I moved into my newly built house on the batture, I tried growing food for market by terracing pots along the slope of the levee, out of the river's reach. I set up a self-serve produce stand and cigar box for customer cash beside the levee bike path. But the small bunches of lettuce and kale wilted in the sun before anyone could buy them.

Then, in March, early dewberries started blooming in the cracks along the concrete sides of the levee. They covered my cultivated pots. When the fruit matured, there were just enough for me to eat a few every day but their appearance alerted me to a bounty emerging in the woods on both sides of the colony.

In places where the levee board bulldozers had been hard at work the year before, I could pick three to five gallons of blackberries in a morning. That's twenty-five jars of preserves, thirty-five tiny tarts, or fifteen cobblers. I moved my produce stand to a nearby farmers' market and sold all I could make. Of course the money didn't cover a full morning of picking, a full afternoon processing, and another half-day standing around lying to people about where I got the berries—nobody wants to reveal their sources for such things. But picking berries was a habit I had learned on another river. It felt good to find food by my new home . . . and there was more than berries.

My buddy Jimmy, who grew up near the river, was walking the batture one day in December and called me, "Look out your window at the willows. You see what I see?" Overnight one of the batture's most prized crops had emerged seemingly everywhere along the waterfront. In the cool winter fog, oyster mushrooms had formed towering fungal condominiums on the broken and damaged willows. Compared to wading through briars to find blackberries, this was easy picking.

I had lived on the river twenty years when Jimmy called me with a second, more amazing announcement. He had discovered the most unusual and least known "crop" on the batture. It was early spring and the river had risen through the woods under the camps, and was creeping up to the edge of the concrete side of the levee. I was dipping river shrimp in a large pond when my phone rang. "Macon, whatcha doin'?" I told him I was down on the batture shrimping. "Man, I'm on the batture worming," he answered.

Jimmy should be a resident of the batture; he's a forager, a born outsider, and solid crazy. "Worming?" I hopped in my truck, drove to Jimmy's favorite place on the river, climbed the levee and found him on his knees

Worms, the most unusual batture harvest. Photo courtesy of Amelia Graham.

in the wave wash. He was loading earthworms into a five-gallon bucket by the fistful.

The worms had been living happily under fallen leaves in the batture silt until the river began its inexorable spring rise. The water rose slowly, and the worms moved as fast as they could, heading for the hills—the levee. At the very moment the water was just below the concrete, the wrigglers had nowhere to go but up the narrow grassy seams in the revetment.

I started a worm ranch in a pile of straw, threw a couple gallons of wrigglers in my compost pile and used the rest for an afternoon fishing trip. It was a brief harvest. Two days later, the water came over the concrete edge of the levee and the worms were nowhere around. Later I asked Jimmy how he happened to find the incredible worm migration. He proclaimed with all seriousness, "I could hear 'em."

Chapter 5

Ghosts on the Shore

New Orleans is surrounded by water, marsh, and swamp, inaccessible except by bridge, boat, or air. In the late nineteenth century, as the population grew, its batture, back-swamp, bayous, and canals were increasingly subject to informal settlement. Transients, refugees, and other people who couldn't afford to live on the few narrow ridges of high ground found abundant marginal land on these watery fringes.

When I moved to the batture in 1986, there were exactly two close-in urban fringe communities left—the thirteen batture camps and a hundred stilt houses outside the levee on Lake Pontchartrain, on the northern edge of the city. These last watery settlements were my favorite haunts. They captured much of what was special about a city where people enjoyed their own culture and rhythms. Lincoln Beach, one of two closed lakeside amusement parks, was my gateway to the lakefront. It had been built specifically for Blacks during Jim Crow, but was nine miles from the neighborhoods where most African Americans lived and well to the east of whites-only communities inside of lakefront levees. The park opened for swimming in 1939 and closed in 1965 when the more conveniently located Pontchartrain Beach Amusement Park integrated.

Fifteen years later, Lincoln Beach was an urban wilderness. When I first visited in 1982, it was a post-apocalyptic scene of crumbling buildings, deserted rides, and palm trees planted forty years earlier. It looked as if a cluster bomb had been dropped on the midway where artists like Sam Cooke, Little Richard, and Fats Domino had once entertained. I couldn't imagine how so much ruin could be caused by neglect or vandalism.

Families from the nearby Mary Queen of Vietnam community enjoyed the unfenced ruins. Three stagnant swimming pools, filled with cattails and floating plastic, were surrounded by folks barbecuing. The sounds of popular American tunes sung in Vietnamese played on jam-boxes. On the beach itself, the fishing was great. I could toss a cast-net and get a bucket of cocahoe minnows. Other people threw hand lines for trout and sheepshead from a collapsed pier.

As far as one could see in either direction, stilt house camps stood shoulder to shoulder along the lakefront beside the ruins of Lincoln Beach. The camps had long catwalks into the shallow lake. Upstanding residents of the city used many of them as weekend retreats. I heard that Huey Long had visited one and Elvis fans know this is where his character, Danny Fisher, hid out with the actress Carolyn Jones in 1958 when the movie *King Creole* was filmed on location. The lakefront hadn't changed much since Presley and Jones cavorted for the cameras.

On September 14, 1998, Hurricane Georges took aim on New Orleans. The new generation "weather guys" had Doppler radar and computer models. Every last one said, "Get out of town." "Evacuate." "Don't be foolish." There was a lone dissenter, Nash Roberts. New Orleans' first TV meteorologist, Roberts was brought out of retirement with his big paper flip chart. He began drawing the coastline of Louisiana and Mississippi with a magic marker. "No," Nash proclaimed. "The storm will miss us and go east, but we should expect a surge from the back side, over Lake Pontchartrain." Nash Roberts became locally sainted and beatified for this and several previous completely accurate, old-school predictions.

One-third of city residents evacuated. They watched the storm on television as it veered to the northeast and made landfall in Mississippi. Everyone breathed a sigh of relief. However, like Nash said, the back of the storm grazed the north shore of Lake Pontchartrain. Wind-driven waves built momentum and height as they traveled over the thirty-five-mile wide lake toward New Orleans. For thirty hours a violent surf crashed against the camps on the city's shoreline. Nearly all of the historic lake houses were wiped out.

I drove across quiet streets to the lakefront the next day to see the damage and to offer help in salvaging what might be saved. In the arc between the Lakefront Airport and Lincoln Beach in Eastern New Orleans, bare pilings rose out of placid water. The remains of the camps formed a soggy rim of wet splinters dumped along the edge. The air was steamy and still, like it always gets after a tropical storm. A woman, maybe fifty years old and with deeply tanned skin, was working boards loose with her bare hands, pulling them from the tangled wrack line.

Her camp had been a fixture on the shore for seventy years. It was painted blue and red. She asked me, "Please darlin', just get the blue and red boards. That's cypress siding my daddy put up." She had stayed in town during the storm and watched the waves pound the levee. "Them waves went right under our camps," she said. "They hit the Corps of Engineers rock wall and bounced back. The backwash got 'em." We didn't talk while we worked. We silently stacked the cracked one-by-six-inch boards atop the levee. I didn't see how the stuff could be of much use, but she thanked me and assured me, "I'm gonna put it back up."

A week later, a spokesman for then Mayor Marc Morial prophesied, "I don't think they're going to be able to rebuild." The Department of Health and Hospitals wanted residents to install costly sewage lines. Those lines required permission from the Norfolk Southern Railway and the Orleans Levee District; their tracks and levee formed a barrier between the city and the camps. The Corps objected to running utilities through the levee. City permitting agencies weighed in, demanding that rebuilt camps conform to current code requirements. The State Department of Lands, which controls lake bottoms in Louisiana, had their own permitting process.[1]

This wasn't the first threatened eradication of lake camps. In January 1880, City Railway Company petitioned the city to tear down structures at the western end of the lakefront to build a resort.[2] In 1901, a hurricane destroyed the West End camps that remained, but stubborn camp owners rebuilt.[3] Then, in the 1920s, the Orleans Levee Board demolished the West End camps for good as part of a massive "reclamation" project.

In the early fifties, the remaining camp owners, all on the eastern end of the lake, toward Lincoln Beach, thwarted a levee board attempt to "reclaim" their section of lakefront. Many of these same families were fighting for the right to rebuild after Hurricane Georges. The battle simmered for two years until, in early 2001, contractors for the levee board began pulling up pilings.[4] Levee authorities called them a "navigation hazard," although the lakefront hadn't seen significant commercial navigation in almost a century. Even the casino "cruise boat," docked nearby on the lakeshore, never left its moorings. No one had questioned if gamblers should be provided city water and sewage service.

Battered by storms, hemmed in by the railroad, and threatened by local, state, and federal bureaucracies, the lake people fought to save the only thing left of their camps—the pilings. In May 2001, the levee board was in a hurry. The Federal Emergency Management Agency (FEMA) offered to pay 75 percent of the cost of removing the pilings; the offer would expire in September. Camp owners sued to stop the work and lost.[5] They bought time by appealing to the Historic Landmarks Commission for protection. The delay lasted long enough to save most of the pilings from FEMA-funded removal, but owners were never compensated and never allowed to rebuild. This is how a community is erased.

After Hurricane Georges, I looked out from the wrecked pier at Lincoln Beach onto a graveyard of empty pilings stretching along the shore to a distant horizon. My batture colony was suddenly the last fringe settlement in New Orleans. Like the lake people, we had built or added to our houses outside the levees. We too were subject to flooding and relied on accommodations with the levee board and the Corps. A couple of my neighbors had watched the New Orleans Levee Board tear the heart out of my settlement in the 1950s.

There, on the Lincoln Beach pier, I decided to find the story of the last batture settlement on the lower Mississippi before the hand of man scraped us off the levee. Before the levee board or the Corps or industry exercised public servitudes on us. Before we were sued into oblivion by an absentee "owner." Before nature, in the form of an uncontrollable spring rise or a hurricane pushing directly up the river, washed our stilt houses down to the Gulf.

There were ghosts on the batture; some inhabited the thirteen camps. Others roamed the brambles just downriver, where over a hundred stilt-houses had once lined the shore. Homeless souls haunted the place. I picked berries there and saw bearded men splashing river water in their faces and lounging at the water edge. Paths were worn in the weeds where tattered tents, lean-tos, and low tarp structures hid in the brush. There were fire rings and clotheslines and mounds of cans and plastic. At night, from atop the levee, campfires of modern-day travelers winked through the overgrowth below.

A mile further downriver, where Broadway Street intersects the levee, the batture was littered with artifacts from a less visited piece of the old settlement. Along a 200-yard stretch of riverfront, between the Corps headquarters and the dock of Bisso Marine, crushed camp timbers rose from the vines. Hand crank washing machines, chipped enamel kettles, and mangled aluminum coffee drip pots were scattered in the overgrowth.

From atop the levee, campfires winked through the overgrowth.
Illustration courtesy of Elizabeth F. Calabrese.

When my bucket was full of berries and the sun was over the top of the levee, I sat in the shade on the rubble and imagined river-lives spent here.

One day in 1997, a year before Hurricane Georges spurred my search for batture ancestors, I wandered down to the shore. In the woods around the obliterated Broadway camps, tree after tree sported bright red fliers. They urged a different bunch of visitors to "Clean up Our Dog Park! Bring rakes, shovels, trash bags and wheelbarrows," and promised, "A dumpster will be on site." A week later the woods were picked clean of evidence of the camps.

I was happy to see a new constituency fall in love with the batture but was distressed that dog paws were more important than the last remnants of a river story. When I began my search for river ancestors in 1998, I knew the history of batture people would not be found in the archaeology of shifting sediment at the new "dog park."

Search for the word *batture* in any index, file, and database and the first entry is the Batture Case. This legal conflict established our modern understanding—and misunderstanding—of who owns and controls the riverfront. It has affected how citizens relate to the river, both spatially and emotionally, ever since. And it has laid a foundation for who would become the winners and losers on my own bend of the river.[6]

In 1803 Jean Gravier, a wealthy Creole, started building a levee to cordon off the batture, just above the ramparts of the old colony. He claimed the riverfront as a remnant from the estate of his brother, Bertrand Gravier, who had subdivided and sold the adjacent Faubourg St. Mary, a place now occupied by much of New Orleans' Central Business and Lower Garden Districts.

Gravier's batture was on a rapidly growing *building-bank* of the river. When the colony was founded, the wide ribbon of silt didn't even exist. In 1803 it was 400 feet wide. Today the "reclaimed" batture encompasses two-hundred acres, including the entire Warehouse District and valuable riverfront features like the Riverwalk Shopping Center, the foot of the Crescent City Connection bridge, and the Convention Center.[7]

In the opening volley of the batture conflict, incensed citizens complained to the city council that Gravier was excluding them from a public shore where they enjoyed free access and gathered silt to fill their low-lying properties. Residents visited the riverfront for cooling breezes and to watch ships arriving on the shore. The river itself had been the focus of spiritual and civic life since the colony's public square was first laid out, with St. Louis Cathedral and the Cabildo facing the Mississippi. The Council de Ville sided with angered citizens, declared the St. Mary batture a "public" space, and ordered Gravier to stop enclosing it.[8]

The following year, 1804, when the United States acquired the French-speaking city and lower river valley in the Louisiana Purchase, the batture conflict became a cultural battle as well as a legal one. Edward Livingston, a brilliant New York lawyer, arrived in the Creole city just as the Americans took possession. He had resigned his offices as governor and attorney general of New York in debt and under the cloud of an embezzlement scandal. When Jean Gravier hired the American jurist to challenge the Council de Ville for control of the batture, Livingston had a chance to reinvent himself and restore his fortune. His pay would be a portion of the valuable and contested batture at Faubourg St. Mary.

Livingston sued the city in 1805. He argued, based on American property law, that the St. Mary batture, on a building-bank of the river, had accumulated before Bertrand Gravier subdivided and sold the lots in the adjacent faubourg. Because the batture was not explicitly included in those sales, the land must belong to Jean Gravier, who was heir to his brother's estate. American property law, which was just asserting itself in the territory of Louisiana, strongly defended private ownership.

The lawyers for the city were Creoles and made the more complicated argument that public use of the batture was a longstanding custom and protected by public servitude. Servitudes are legal restrictions attached to a property, similar to the American legal term "easement." They are established and enforced by governments to protect public rights and access to property. The Council de Ville claimed that by virtue of customary use, the public had a protected right to access the land along the river.

The Louisiana Territorial Court ruled unanimously in favor of Livingston and Gravier in 1807. The St. Mary batture was declared to be the property of Jean Gravier to develop as he saw fit. Livingston quickly began building a permanent levee around his newly acquired riverfront. This renewed construction inflamed the public. An agitator stood watch on the levee and beat a drum to call a Creole mob to protest when Livingston's workers showed up. Angry citizens surrounded the laborers, hurling insults and impeding progress.

The scene of a Creole rabble, called by a beating drum to defend their riverfront, was a singular moment in New Orleans history that brought together three local icons on the batture—a beating drum, a French-speaking citizenry, and the river itself. The event was one of only a handful of times in the city's 300-year history that common citizens would band together to defend a stake in the riverfront against the powerful economic interests that came to control it. Historian Ari Kelman crystallizes the significance of the moment:

> The mob apparently recognized that if Livingston completed his private port, he would gain control of the riverfront, threatening its public character . . . they made it clear they were unwilling to let Livingston privatize any part of the waterfront.[9]

After the near riot on the riverfront, Territorial Governor Claiborne appealed to President Thomas Jefferson to intervene. Jefferson saw control of commerce on the Mississippi River as a primary benefit of the Louisiana Purchase and had previously expressed a belief that the use of the river and its banks belonged to the public. He also had a long-standing beef with Livingston. Jefferson declared a federal prerogative in keeping riparian land open, labeled Livingston a "squatter," and sent federal forces to secure the property.[10]

The case was far from settled. Livingston sued Jefferson for trespassing and for the loss of tens of thousands of dollars' worth of building materials stored on the batture, which Jefferson's lawyers declared must have been captured by the rising river.[11] Livingston lost, but entered into a prolonged pamphlet war with both the president and attorneys for the city. After a decade of wrangling, Livingston finally compromised with the city, retaining title to the property, but surrendering use of the batture to the "public."

I felt a kinship with Edward Livingston when I learned that no less a person than President Thomas Jefferson had called him a "squatter." I also understood that Jefferson appreciated the riverbank as a place where small farmers of the American West could deliver produce to market. But my heart was with the Creole rabble who beat a drum and rebelled against Gravier and Livingston's attempt to enclose the batture. They didn't see monetary or military advantage in the river's gift of silt. They appreciated the riverfront and batture as a resource that belonged to each and all of them to use.

The Batture Case enshrined the notion that the batture could be privately owned, but could also be controlled by local, state, and federal governments through public servitudes. A levee servitude required riverfront owners to allow for the building of flood control and drainage on their property.[12] Later a commercial servitude established that governments could construct on the batture "all buildings and other works which may be necessary for public utility, for mooring of vessels and the discharging of their cargoes...." These servitudes contained no provision for reimbursing property holders.[13]

Ironically, the so-called "public" servitudes became tools by which capitalists severed the general public from the river. Not only were more formidable levees constructed, but in the name of "public good," the city ceded control of the riverfront to a moneyed elite. Edward Livingston's brother, Robert Livingston and his partner Robert Fulton, were briefly granted a franchise on steamboat trade. Later the city granted space around the river crescent for interconnected wharves, rails, and sheds. Servitudes became the means of dividing the spoils of a batture that citizens had once claimed as theirs.

Chapter 6

American River

When it came to finding who settled my batture and when, history books were a dry well. In the Louisiana Research Collection at Tulane University, however, a librarian produced a thin accordion folder labeled BATTURE. It contained a file of brittle newspaper clippings about the 1954 demolition of over a hundred camps on the Carrollton Batture, just downriver from my home. There were surprises, too. A Works Progress Administration researcher had compiled newspaper accounts of a faith healer treating thousands of citizens from his "tiny yellow houseboat," docked at a "houseboat landing" beside Audubon Park.

An epiphany struck me somewhere in the middle of a full-page newspaper account from the 1930s about a "Bizarre City Along the Riverfront"—a place with "many houseboats used as homes."[1] Suddenly it seemed obvious; just as they don't appear on city maps, batture folks don't appear in *city* histories either—because they were part of a *river* story. For that story, I would have to scour news reports from the wharves and levees of New Orleans and from the countryside with which the river connected. I began to plow through journals written by early river travelers who might have seen people inhabiting the river and its shore.

While the Creole city government and American upstarts fought for control of New Orleans' riverfront, most of the river was still a wild place.[2] American surveyor and diplomat Andrew Ellicott, who traveled from Pennsylvania to Natchez in 1798, described the Mississippi below its confluence with the Ohio River as "an unbroken wilderness."[3] Banks caved in upstream, depositing trees in the current. Myriad sandbars and snags threatened navigation. Sawyers—trees and branches that "sawed" up and

Passengers and produce traveled from upriver hinterlands on flatboats.
Illustration courtesy Historic New Orleans Collection, Acc. No. 1979.325.144.

down and pierced the river's surface—smashed the hulls of unlucky boat-men. Outside two or three bluff settlements above Baton Rouge, the land retreated into a dismal swamp.

The Louisiana Purchase brought unified governance to the Missis-sippi River Valley, and commerce and settlement grew apace. Increasing numbers of American rivermen on keelboats and especially flatboats from the Ohio River Valley joined bands of natives, hunters, fishermen, and trappers. They entered the current, floating west and south. The final stop on many journeys was New Orleans. Once rivermen descended below Baton Rouge, they found the banks tightly lined with the mostly well-groomed landings of plantation country. The riverfront was the high ground, so plantation houses and important dependencies crowded close to the water edge.

Despite the long wild stretches between settlements, rivers were the arterial highways of the day and the Ohio River Valley was part of New Orleans' vast hinterland. The Ohio and Tennessee Rivers and their tribu-taries brought people and produce from farms and merchants on the trans-Appalachian frontier to the Creole port city of New Orleans. As early as 1787, an immigrant to western Pennsylvania noted, "a farm in the neighborhood of these rivers, was nearer the market of any part of the world than a farm within twenty miles of Philadelphia."[4] Another traveler on the frontier recalled, "When pioneers in the territory of Indiana spoke of 'going to town,' they meant New Orleans."[5]

Passengers and produce traveled from upriver hinterlands on flatboats—little more than heavy, rectangular wooden barges, forty to eighty feet long and about fifteen feet wide. The smaller of these could be constructed with rudimentary carpentry skills and good advice. Crewmen steered flatboats with long sweeps and a stern rudder and sheltered along with their perishable produce in ark-like cabins above deck.

Professional merchant boatmen and family farmers used flatboats to transport livestock, pork, tobacco, flour, whiskey, and bulk produce downriver. They were generally manned by three to five rough-hewn young men from Ohio River Valley country. The crews included family members, "teenagers looking for adventure," "discharged soldiers," "frontier vagabonds," "homeless men," and "runaway boys."[6] Some of this cast of characters would find shelter along the flooded shores of the rivers and eventually congregate by the wharves in New Orleans.

Flatboats unloaded at landings along the Ohio River could be sold to immigrants moving to homesteads on the receding frontier.[7] Those pioneers stocked the flats with household possessions and livestock, installed a wood stove and headed west on their "family boats." Others were reloaded with materials destined for another port downstream. When the craft arrived in New Orleans they were usually disassembled and sold for lumber. The crews sold their cargo, enjoyed the sights and vices of their final destination, and began an arduous journey home on foot or horseback on the Natchez Trace. A few made the difficult journey back upstream by keelboat.

The introduction of steamboat travel on the Mississippi in 1812 changed the cultural geography of the western rivers dramatically, allowing goods and passengers to descend and *ascend* the current with speed and relative safety. Cheap passage pushed Anglo and native populations further west and settlements grew at the intersection of streams and on bluffs. These places became new nodes of commerce, served by and dependent on steamboats.

In the 1830s British adventuress and journalist Francis Trollope caught a steamboat upriver and spotted a few pathetic dwellings on the inundated shore of the Mississippi.

But still from time to time there appeared the hut of the wood-cutter, who supplies the steamboats with fuel, at the risk or rather with the assurance of early death in exchange for dollars and whiskey. These sad dwellings are nearly all of them inundated during the winter, and the best of them are constructed on piles, which permit the water to reach its highest level without drowning the wretched inhabitants.[8]

I wasn't convinced that Trollope—who spent an inordinate amount of time critiquing the American habit of spitting and also recorded a preposterous tale of a riverbank family devoured in their beds by "crocodiles"—gave the woodcutters a fair portrait.[9] Nor was I sure that those forlorn settlers, whose main employment was deforesting America's bottomlands in support of the steamboat industry, were antecedents of modern-day batture dwellers. But Trollope's caricature of life on the shore presaged numerous later descriptions of riverbank folk, including a memorable rendering by Mark Twain:

> Behind other islands we found wretched little farms, and wretcheder little log-cabins; there were crazy rail fences sticking a foot or two above the water, with one or two jeans-clad, chills-racked, yellow-faced male miserables roosting on the top-rail, elbows on knees, jaws in hands, grinding tobacco and discharging the result . . .[10]

The woodcutters were part of a growing informal river economy. Mostly without title or permission, they lived on the river and provided the fuel that kept steamboats moving. They eventually joined bottomland loggers and cleared thousands of acres of forest with axes and saws to feed the hungry furnaces of riverboats. They sold some of their wood to men on flatboats, who took the load to the next river port. At busy landings, steamboats attracted "a floating armada of commercial hangers-on, from wood-choppers . . . to a fleet of family owned flatboats looking to siphon off . . . freight and passengers at a competitive price."[11] Flatboats that hovered around landings to negotiate business were described as "lingering."[12]

By the time the flatboat trade peaked around 1855, the rough river outpost of Cairo, Illinois, was comprised almost entirely of floating residents who lived and conducted business on derelict flatboats. There were grog shops, hotels, wood-cutter's boats, occasional showboats, and a variety of

The "sad dwelling" of a woodcutter family, ca. 1830. Credit: Auguste Hervieu.
Illustration courtesy Center for Louisiana Studies, Lafayette. Public domain.

other craft moored at the confluence of the Ohio and Mississippi Rivers.[13]
Crews on flatboats and steamboats could wind up ashore or working afloat
in an informal economy at places like Cincinnati, St. Louis, Memphis, or
New Orleans.

Working boatmen weren't batture dwellers, but they did experience
a river way of life, outside the levees, outside social mores, and outside
the law. As long they remained afloat between the levees, away from city
wharves or in some frontier outpost, the early rivermen were lionized as
hard-driving tamers of the West. Legendary Keelboat captain, Mike Fink,
plied the western rivers from 1800 until his death in 1823. Like Davey
Crockett, who reportedly called him an "Alligator Horse," Fink was my-
thologized during his own lifetime."[14]

When boatmen disembarked on settled shores, disheveled and dirty
from weeks on the river, they were seen through a different prism. This
was especially true in the more urbane environs of New Orleans. In 1836
Edward Henry Durell, who would become the twenty-fifth mayor of the
city, captured the esteem and revulsion with which city people regarded
river folk: "They are a distinct class of beings, livers on the water, known
and designated as 'boatmen of the Mississippi,' an expression that embraces
all that is strong, hardy, rough, and uncouth, with much that is savage, wild
and lawless."[15]

Commercial boats landing in New Orleans were sorted for practical reasons and perhaps by social status. Oceangoing ships were granted space adjacent to the old quarter, while river steamboats gathered at wharves just above Canal Street. Further upriver, beside Livingston's batture, were the large flatboats of professional merchants who contracted with buyers in the city.[16] On the outskirts of town, smaller boats that didn't wish to navigate among massive commercial craft pulled up by the levee. Abraham Lincoln, who famously crewed on two flatboat voyages in 1828 and 1831, probably moored at an upriver landing like the one described by Henry Durell in 1835:[17] "Hundreds of long, narrow, black, dirty-looking, crocodile-like rafts lie sluggishly, without moorings, upon the soft batture, and pour out their contents upon the quay: a heterogenous compound of the products of its tributaries."[18]

Private operators and owners of farm boats who were unable to strike a bargain with large buyers arrayed their merchandise along the "quay" and retailed it on the spot. These lingering flatboats fouled the water and competed with merchants inside the levees who paid rent and taxes. The city council passed ordinances forbidding the sale of produce on the levee near the old quarter and pushed those boats further upstream, where they were relegated to the nuisance wharf—an apt name for a place where the refuse of the city was taken for disposal into the river by barge.[19]

The crews of flatboats were regarded in New Orleans as outsiders, part of a river culture populated by unschooled Americans of the Ohio River Valley. They were treated as hicks and feckless rubes, easily duped by sharps who awaited them in the city. Newspapers repeatedly warned of pickpockets and other predators who greeted incautious arrivals. Reporters covering flatboat landings for New Orleans Recorders Court–Second Municipality provided over fifty years of accounts, relayed in hilarious dialect, of "Buckeyes," "Hoosiers," and "Kaintucks" arrested as "dangerous and suspicious," "drunk and disorderly," and for "sleeping on the levee."[20]

The long-term lingerers among rivermen, those who lost their money through improvidence or theft, and others whose employment was ended by the arrival of the railroad, found refuge on the New Orleans riverfront. They became the vanguard of a counterculture that would later inhabit six miles of riverfront. These denizens of the docks were noticed by a reporter for the *Daily Picayune* on October 11, 1855:

Wharf Rats. Illustration courtesy of Historic New Orleans Collection Acc. No. 1974.25.17.38_o2. Public domain.

> Eventually the … idlers scatter, the day police retire, the wharfingers close their offices, and scarcely anything of life remains except the wharf rats, and such poor devils as have no home to go to. It is hours before the regular thieves and assassins set out in their nocturnal rambles along the wharves.

Flatboatmen referred to unemployed comrades who loitered about the docks as "wharf rats."[21] Steamboat captains employed the term to describe unemployed crewmen who used their contacts aboard ship to raid the vessels' larders.[22] But reporters, police, and wharfingers who decried "depredations of wharf rats," were referring to a broad array of enterprising individuals who found refuge below the bustling waterfront. Idle boatmen, orphans, runaways, hobos, petty thieves, and pickpockets survived on gleanings off the docks and directly from the stores of steamboats.

The wharf rats enjoyed shelter in the "dark and fulsome recesses formed by the extended belt of wharves" that continued to operate throughout the Civil War.[23] In 1861 monetary losses by steamboat and barge operators were estimated at "hundreds of thousands of dollars." Brazen thefts were enumerated in *Daily Picayune* reports: "forty sacks of grain," "100 boxes of sardines," "six sacks of pepper weighing 400 pounds."[24]

Even the outraged local press acknowledged the cleverness of the thieves, "aptly named after that most patient and ingenious animal, the rat."[25] They nailed wooden steps to pilings on the side of the docks and connected to under-deck living quarters by way of a gangplank that could be raised or lowered. The wharf rats removed nails from selected deck-boards and, when rousted from below, escaped through the loose planks.[26]

By the 1870s, the flatboat trade was all but dead, and the nation was in the midst of an economic downturn that became known as the Long Depression. Thousands of laid-off railroad employees contributed to a flow of rootless travelers on the wharves. A *Daily Picayune* reporter explored the riverfront underworld on the hot afternoon of July 29, 1881, and found "nests of wharf rats" at ten places along the flatboat moorage above the old quarter—furnished with beds, benches, and tables. The occupants had caulked or placed tar paper over cracks to prevent rain from spoiling their rest.

The . . . frequenters of these resorts is varied: barefooted urchins scarcely a dozen years old, youths of 16, 18 and 20 years, and bearded men of thirty, can be found at home any evening whiling away the time in playing with a greasy pack of cards, lolling on the rude benches with a fishing line in hand, sleeping in the bunks or throwing dice.

Wharf rats were ingenious in scavenging goods stored on the docks above. When steamboats lined up at the wharves three and four deep, vast amounts of hastily unloaded cargo was often piled upon the docks overnight and covered with a tarp. Thieves sawed entire boards away and snatched material from below. In the morning, the longshoremen might discover a mountain of carefully stacked goods hollowed out from within.[27] Casks and sacks of bulk products such as whiskey, molasses, sugar, coffee, and tea were the most valuable (and easy to fence) items. Wharf rats simply drilled or slashed holes into barrels and sacks from below and emptied the contents into their own bins, buckets, and bags.

Rootless vagabonds encountered organized criminals under the wharves. Professional thieves operated from boats at night and stole entire bales, sacks, and barrels of goods. In the light of day the perpetrators disposed of their bounty "all along the levee" to junk dealers who gladly provided bail and legal help to suppliers who were unlucky enough to get caught.[28]

On the afternoon of June 10, 1900, the notoriously brutal railroad cops organized a sting operation below the fruit and vegetable docks between Calliope and Julia Streets. A sign had been found under the wharf edge identifying the entrance to the "Hobo Social Club." Two officers and two patrolmen of the harbor police, three private agents of the railroad, and "a body of rough riders" descended under the wharf.

> The "Hobo Social Club" was found to possess all the necessary cooking utensils of an up-to-date kitchen. Stoves, pans, pots and skillets were in place and showed that they had been in constant use. The raw materials secured by boring holes up through the wharf and in other ways had been dished up in the club parlors in a style that would make the mouth of an epicure smack with intense delight.

The vegetable wharf posse discovered the "club" inhabited by a handful of young men boiling corn over a fire. A few were roasting coffee beans in a well-appointed kitchen. All but one of these desperados jumped in the water and swam off. The lone arrest was of a ten-year-old boy. The cops seem to have guessed at that point that their prey were mainly homeless people scrounging a living. Even the harbor police sergeant decided the Hobo Social Club was "a rendezvous of boys who went in swimming" and proclaimed, "he was not aware that quantities of vegetables, fruits and grains had disappeared from the wharf."[29] Hardened criminals don't waste energy and risk arrest by pinching stray vegetables.

I chased the story of wharf rats through New Orleans' historic newspapers, and the wharf managers and cops kept chasing their prey. Despite sixty years of police raids on their "dens," "cribs," "nests," and "bunks," the wharf rats frustrated authorities until the early 1900s, when the city clamped down on the riverfront in several ways. The New Orleans Port Authority, in local slang the *Dock Board*, was chartered and charged with providing harbor police and fireboats. By then, the wharf rats had been described as the "pirates" of the riverfront, accused of thievery, setting cotton wharf fires, operating opium dens, stealing the entire cargoes of docked vessels, making off with ships, and murdering citizens and throwing the lifeless bodies into the river.

There was well-documented crime on the wharves, and criminaliza-
tion of the homeless wharf rats was partly in response to pressure from
steamboats and their insurers; but the denigration of the homeless and unemployed on the waterfront came at a time when the city was second only
to New York in immigrant arrivals.[30] The wharf rats were undocumented,
hard to police, and living in a margin increasingly separated from daily city
life by wharves and levees. The river's edge became a place beyond the pale.

In 1914 a panic over wharf rats of the rodent variety gripped the city.
Rats carrying bubonic plague had arrived on the docks as stowaways on
foreign vessels. Thirty people became ill and ten died. A quarantine was
put in place on some ships. At the height of the scare, a city exterminator
placed forty rodent traps on the wharves. Not surprisingly, these caught
the attention of wharf rats and were stolen. A wise riverfront bystander
opined, "When you set a rat trap, you better set a policeman to watch it."[31]

Wretched or romantic, woodcutters, western boatmen, and wharf rats
spent much of their lives outside the levees and on flooded lowlands. They
were part of a lineage of river people I could connect with. They shared the
same geography and social status of generations of "river rats" who would
settle on the shore only to be scorned and pushed aside. But those people
scratching out a living on the river's flanks were not the precise ancestors
of twentieth-century batture dwellers. They were mostly men, mostly on
the river for profit, and they had little recognizable family life.

Then, in a musty corner of Tulane Library, the progenitor of the batture dwellers I would come to know floated into view, drifting into my
search from the pages of an 1875 travelogue that hadn't been checked out
in thirty years.

Chapter 7

Shantyboat People

In December 1875, Nathaniel Bishop crammed his body into a tiny craft called a Barnegat sneak box and shoved off into the headwaters of the Ohio River. Part kayak and part coffin, the sneak box was a favorite among Jersey shore duck hunters. Bishop could stretch out at night in the twelve-foot-long, sixteen-inch-deep hull, secure a lid closely over his head and stay dry and hidden from river ruffians.

In 1869, at age seventeen, the red-haired naturalist and author had hiked a thousand miles across South America. In 1874 he paddled from Hudson Bay, Ontario, to the Georgia coast in a paper canoe. But the first thing that struck the veteran traveler as he began his 2,600-mile sneak box journey down the Ohio and Mississippi Rivers was a new character floating downstream in crafts almost as odd as his own:

> By far the most interesting and peculiar features of a winter's row down the Ohio are the life-studies offered by the occupants of the numerous shanty-boats daily encountered. They are sometimes called, and justly too, family-boats, and serve as winter homes for a singular class of people, carrying their passengers and cargoes from the icy region of Ohio to New Orleans. . . . If the proprietor of the boat has a family, he puts its members on board,—not forgetting pet dogs and cats, with a small stock of salt pork, bacon, flour, potatoes, molasses, salt, and coffee.[1]

With a new search term in hand, I uncovered hundreds of newspaper accounts and over a half-century of books written by river lovers and adventurists like Bishop, describing these floating inhabitants of the river.[2] The more I read, the more convinced I became that shantyboaters were not only kindred spirits, but a missing link to my batture community.

Shantyboat family with goat. Photo courtesy of the US Army Corps of Engineers, New Orleans District. Public domain.

The first shantyboats (sometimes spelled as two words, "shanty-boat") were built on barge-like hulls which traveled with the current; like flatboats, they were steered by a long "sweep" rudder, or oars and push pole. They were always handmade, usually by owners who had little experience building boats. Like the batture camps in Carrollton Bend, their appearance revealed more about the occupant than about prevailing construction codes or conventions.

The materials and habits of shantyboat builders hardly changed over seventy-five years. Nathaniel Bishop described how the construction always started—"first he fishes in the stream for floating lumber." In 1950 Harlan Hubbard, the last of the old-time shantyboaters, floated past houseboats "put together of odd scraps of material and pieces of driftwood and wreckage."[3]

These were my people! I gathered materials to build my own river camp in the same manner—beams from the river, pilings from the telephone company, windows and doors from a demolition site, and countless items from dumpsters. My heart sang in harmony with Ben Burman's account of shantyboat-building during the Depression:

> If he is patient—as all good shantymen are, all the timbers and planks he needs will eventually come drifting down the muddy river. To this he adds some discarded packing crates, a strip of tarpaper obtained

by doing odd jobs in the hardware store, and a few windowpanes collected where a house was being dismantled; his materials now all supplied, with the help of his family or neighbors, the new craft is quickly born.⁴

The "peculiar" shantyboats that Nathaniel Bishop encountered as he paddled down to New Orleans in 1875 were the beginning of an unheralded migration by river of people from farms and towns of the western slopes of the Appalachians to riverbanks along the lower Mississippi. Some were perhaps descendants of pioneers pushed off their holdings in Appalachian coal fields or dislodged from bottomland farms by floods. Other shantyboaters may have been the original "hobos"—homeward bound veterans of the Civil War.

One of the earliest recorded floaters was Ed Smith, who returned from the Civil War to his home in Pittsburgh with nerves too shattered to settle down. Smith was remembered in a posthumous news story about the thriving printing business he started in New Orleans. After the war, Smith built a shantyboat, packed up his stencil-making tools and floated from "place to place . . . carrying on a business in his chosen field" until he arrived in New Orleans.⁵

By 1875 the country had entered its first great depression and the western rivers were awash with economic refugees, migrants, families carrying goods to market, and thousands of "river gypsies" seeking refuge on the current. Tradesmen like Ed Smith hung signs on hastily assembled floating homes, advertising everything from shoe and sewing machine repair to barber and notary service.⁶

Destitute farm families and unemployed factory workers took to shantyboats for shelter and as a conveyance to seek day labor along the stream. They found sustenance and some found profit by catching fish and selling stray logs and lumber corralled from the current. Work was most easily secured near urban centers and "colonies" of shantyboats congregated outside river landings in the same way hobo jungles sprung up on the outskirts of railroad towns.

The shantyboats had no permanent attachment to the shore, but they were river homes. They could tie up along battures and banks throughout the valley. People cooked, slept, and lived in them with their families, pets, and provisions.

Comings and goings of shantyboat drifters were reported by New Orleans newspapers beginning in the 1880s and continuing into the 1930s. A column called "THE RIVER" covered shipping news from cities throughout the valley and often included stories gleaned by telegraph from places as distant as St. Paul and Pittsburgh. By the 1890s, "shantyboat colonies"—numbering in hundreds of boats—were described in Louisville, Cincinnati, and Memphis, where a newspaper man observed "a floating settlement of houseboats . . . made up of representatives of twenty-odd states drained by the Mississippi, and its tributaries."[7]

Shantyboaters were often depicted as carefree drifters. The *Memphis Scimitar* observed that members of the colony there paid no rent; they fished, corded driftwood for sale, and worked as day laborers. The *Evansville Courier* asserted, "The shantyboat people . . . never want for food and other necessities of life."[8] Reporters seldom explored the motivations of the "river-gypsies." But some people just couldn't settle in one place, and prejudice and racism were often a reason.

After the Civil War, African Americans who had served and sought protection at the Union-controlled Camp Parapet, on the river just above Carrollton Bend, found themselves without a federal protector. As freedmen, they migrated to unattended scraps of land on the batture and the wetlands in back of town. They built stilt houses, established small gardens, fished, collected moss, and lived a self-sufficient existence. On May 9, 1866, the *New Orleans Daily Crescent* sounded an alarm:

> What strikes the beholder of these new abodes of the freed folks, is the idea that these people have certainly a notion of leading independent life, of cultivating some little bean or potato patch outside the already cultivated farms or plantations. . . . they build or patch up for themselves some unnamable shanties upon the high roads, in the very bayous, or outside the marshes, on the very shores of the lake, often under the surges, when at high water. . . .
>
> If these people can find means of exempting themselves from the payment of house rent, or room hire, they will . . . lead a life of wretched misery in preference to being subjected to regular labor habits. . . . The proof is patent to our eyes, and when such contrivances are erected in the immediate vicinity of our great metropolis, surrounded by uninhabitable marshes and morasses, how much more

Freedmen found shelter on unattended scraps of land. Photo courtesy of the Frank B. Moore Collection, Earl K. Long Library, University of New Orleans.

reasonable is it to foresee that this will be the mode of life which our emancipated blacks will adopt in the open country, upon vacant public lands, if no prohibition to such a course is interposed.

Beyond racist indignation at the independence of slaves, the *Crescent* editorial showed resentment of people who chose rugged self-sustenance over a life of wage labor and homage to landlords. Attitudes had changed since settlers on the western frontier were celebrated for taming and cultivating previously uninhabitable lands.

Shantyboaters, like the freed slaves, were not simply trying to avoid rent. They built lives of self-sufficiency and a fluid address by choice. There were storms, floods, and maritime accidents and there were river ruffians and cops to dodge—but the river shore offered a life free of many cares that dogged poor people chasing a living wage inside the levees.

One observer of river life, Ben Burman, estimated that there were thirty thousand shantyboats in the Mississippi River Valley as the steamboat era reached full flower in the late nineteenth century.[9] This plethora of preindustrial craft crowded docks and shorelines without paying moorage fees or taxes to local governments. Incidents of gunfire between river people and commercial interests, like this account from the *Daily Picayune* on November 22, 1884, were reported with increasing frequency:

> On last Saturday evening the towboat S.E. Elliot, coming out of the Mississippi with barges, rubbed against a shanty boat, which enraged two men on it, so they fired fifteen or twenty loads of buckshot into the bulkheads of the Elliot. The latter had no arms and could not defend herself.[10]

Steamboats, symbols of imagined mastery over the rivers, represented the rising power of a lucrative industry that dominated public river frontage. Wharf masters, steamboat operators, and insurance agents from Minnesota to Mississippi fought and won ordinances to force shantyboats further from city wharves. A river pilot raged to a reporter in Greenville, Mississippi: "They are an unmitigated nuisance anywhere on the river ... and the government or state laws should rid the river of every shanty-boat that floats."[11]

As communities upstream struggled to drive shantyboats from their shores, the floating homes accumulated around Louisiana towns like Lake Providence, Bayou Sara, Baton Rouge, and Donaldsonville. The last obvious stop for anyone floating downriver was New Orleans and its growing suburbs.

Twenty years after Nathaniel Bishop encountered shantyboats upriver, readers of the New Orleans *Daily Picayune* were surprised on August 4, 1895, by an all-caps headline; "SHANTYTOWN BY THE RIVERSIDE. A Queer Little City Built on the Batture, Where Society is Divided, Where Queer Beings Live." The illustrated story, written in sensational style over two full pages, was the first mention of batture settlement beyond the wharves in New Orleans:

> Everyone has heard of the slums of New Orleans ... But who has heard of the "Riverside Dwellers," a unique class among the large horde of poor and destitute denizens of the Crescent City? ... And

SHANTYTOWN BY
THE RIVERSIDE,

———◆———

A Queer Little City Built on the Batture;

———◆———

Where Society is Divided, Where Queer Beings Live,

———◆———

And Where the Society for the Protection of Children

———◆———

Has Found Considerable Work to Do—

New Orleans Daily Picayune, August 4, 1895.
Public domain.

if these squat, rickety, weather beaten hovels, have evoked the query "what are they," was it followed by an attempt to satisfy the feeling of curiosity? No. Out of sight, out of mind. . . .

Horror, shock. and indignation poured from the city press. The Uptown riverfront had become home to "over a thousand people, white and black, men, women and children . . . ," living in a settlement that stretched six miles, from just above Louisiana Avenue, in the middle of the city's crescent bend, all the way to the site of my community in Southport. "Itinerant artists in every line, photographers, veterinary doctors [and] peddlers of every imaginable kind of goods" had secured their floating homes to the shore. "Fifty or sixty" shantyboats had dropped anchor, grown legs, and become batture camps—so-called "miserable abodes" of "the pariahs of modern society."

Dr. Alfred Clay, founder and president of the Society for Prevention of Cruelty to Children (SPCC), began to accompany journalists on numerous rambles through the fringe communities of New Orleans. Each trip celebrated the doctor's charitable work and expressed abhorrence at the morals and "miserable abodes" of the city's poor:

Whether this flatboat life produces lawlessness and its consequent wretchedness and distress, or whether the outlaw and miserable take to this kind of life because of its freedom from law ... the fact remains that nearly all the offenses that have ever shocked or awakened the sensibilities of the pious ... have had their origin in those places.[12]

Alfred Clay and his minions were the bane of batture residents. In the early days of Jim Crow, "negroes sleeping on the levee" were customarily locked up by the police and charged with being "dangerous and suspicious." The SPCC joined the rout on the riverfront and removed some children of batture families to the Waif Home, their "crimes" racial mixing, poor health, or simply living on a shantyboat. Finally, in 1917, the SPCC categorically declared floating homes to be "unwholesome" for raising children.[13]

However squalid and dangerous life on the river edge was, it was likely better than the cribs, brothels, tenements, and flophouses inside the levees. Shantyboaters and batture folk of New Orleans, looking for refuge in a period of rapid economic change, had more in common with land-side hobos than with criminals in the vice dens of the city. Their life was as unpredictable as the weather and easiest when the authorities did not notice them.

After the first alarming story of a "a queer city," batture folk in shantyboats, shacks, and wharf-rat cribs became the subject of hundreds of newspaper accounts of crime, bootlegging, gambling, brawling, drownings, and arson. But one early account stands out from the rest; it broke my heart and for a time it stopped my writing.

In 1888 a mixed-race couple and their three-year-old son pulled a shantyboat onto the riverbank somewhere near the Orleans-Jefferson parish line, on the east bank of the river—the site of my batture colony. The woman, Charlotte "Lottie" Morris, had been born into slavery in Summit, Mississippi. Taken from the home of her parents and sister, Silvia, as a child she was sold into servitude in Texas. In 1884 Lottie had married Patrick Morris, a white laborer on the cotton wharf in Galveston.[14]

No one knows how Pat and Lottie Morris and their son Pat Jr. wound up on a shantyboat tied to the Southport shore, near my present-day camp.

Patrick worked as a day laborer at the Southport wharf. Lottie ran a "grog shop" and sold homemade sweets from the shantyboat. She served both white and Black customers at a time when Blacks were turned away at nearby whites-only bars. Business must have been good given the explosion of industrial activity in the area. By the early 1890s, two nearby sawmills, ferries, a shingle maker, a brickyard, and the Southport wharf all employed workers on the river. Railroad construction below the levee brought plenty of hungry and thirsty mouths to the Morris' shanty home.

Southport industries attracted unskilled laborers, and a scattering of bars entertained those workers with card games, cockfighting, and dog fighting. Dairy farms and vegetable patches stretched back from the levee to end in the swamp. Barely a mile upriver, Southport's nascent industry collided with Jefferson Parish's old plantation aristocracy. Residents and politicians in the parish proudly proclaimed the territory the "Free State of Jefferson."

The residents of the Free State of Jefferson were offended by the presence of the Morris family and their shantyboat. In those early days of Jim Crow, their feelings were shared by many residents of the adjacent Orleans Parish suburb of Carrollton, which was dotted with truck farms, family-run groceries, feed stores, and businesses serving the riverfront.

In 1891, after two "warnings" from unfriendly neighbors, Pat and Lottie collected their belongings and, with six-year-old Pat Jr., took the nearby Walnut Street Ferry across the river to Westwego. The place was a scruffy village at the intersection of ferry, railroad, and river shipping routes on the west bank of Jefferson Parish, surrounded by rice and sugarcane plantations and swamp—like Southport, but less industrial and less populated. The Company Canal intersected the river at Westwego, connecting New Orleans with the French-speaking coastal fishing towns of Grand Isle and Chenier Caminada. A huge grain elevator was under construction at the intersection of these transit lines.

During their first winter in Westwego, the Morris family lived in a small hut by the river, where Pat collected drift lumber from the water. By summer he had enough material to build a sprawling boarding house on the batture below the grain terminals. The establishment was known among locals as the Catfish Hotel. Like Lottie's grog shop, the hotel operated on what the local newspapers termed a "liberal plan." We can't know whether this referred to the policy of serving customers of any race or to the liaisons consummated in the hotel.

Despite repeated complaints by the railroad company, the construction manager at the grain elevator, and the owner of a nearby bar and
lunchroom, the Morris family stayed put in their Catfish Hotel for over
a year. Lottie managed the business and Pat worked as a day laborer on
the nearby Westwego Wharf. Then, in 1893, their Catfish Hotel caught fire.
Newspapers blamed the fire on Pat Jr. and his cousin who were "playing
with an oil lamp." But the Morris family weren't the only ones forced out
of their homes in the winter of 1893.

Just before the Catfish Hotel met the match, a lynching sent tremors
through the Black community. Roselius Julian, an African American moss-
picker and barber charged with wife-beating, had been on trial at the
Southport courtroom of prominent planter and magistrate Victor Estopinal. Julian had openly supported Judge Estopinal's Republican opponent
in a recent election and the judge had a reputation for dealing harshly
with African Americans. Before the trial could begin, Roselius shot and
killed Judge Estopinal in front of the courthouse located on his plantation
grounds, and fled into the swamps of adjacent Metairie.[15]

A posse rounded up and incarcerated Roselius's three brothers. The
same night, an angry mob removed the young men and hung them from
trees. Vigilantes publicly flogged Roselius's mother and two sisters and
beat to death his friend John Willis.[16] Newspapers fueled the rage of white
people across south Louisiana after the murder, especially in the Free State
of Jefferson and in the riverside plantation country. The *Daily Picayune*
published front page rumors of Roselius sightings. White mobs intimidated
Blacks and ransacked their homes for months, searching for the fugitive.
Terrified Black laborers fled Jefferson Parish, and the crops of the plantation
elite languished in the field. Roselius was never found.[17]

The Morris family abandoned their torched boarding house and briefly
moved to a cabin on the Company Canal. After quarreling with their landlord, they moved to their final home, a shantyboat about a hundred yards
downriver, in the shadow of the new grain elevator. When the river went
down, Pat worked the boat up onto stilts.

From their stilt house on the batture, Lottie made pies and cakes. She
sold homemade lunches and coffee to the workers at the grain elevator.
According to the wharf bosses, she also sold liquor by the drink. Pat continued as a day laborer and Pat Jr. played with his cousin on the riverside,
where the family kept two cows on the levee. As a mixed-race couple living

in Jefferson Parish in 1895, it's hard to believe that Patrick and Lottie didn't know how precarious their affairs were. They had almost certainly had their home searched—and possibly burned down—by vigilantes following the lynchings of 1893.

Between 1892 and 1897, mobs killed at least nine Black people in the Free State of Jefferson. In Westwego, like Southport, unskilled white and Black agricultural workers and laborers rubbed up against the vestiges of planter aristocracy. Lottie's lunch and beverage service competed with Gassenburger's Saloon and lunch house, just over the levee on the main road.

Another population arrived in Westwego in October 1893, when a storm smashed into the Gulf Coast just west of Grand Isle and destroyed the village of Chenier Caminada, killing nearly eight hundred people. Many survivors made their way up through the swamps of Lake Salvador and Bayou Barataria to Westwego. These mostly French-speaking fishermen and trappers settled along the Company Canal and batture, near Lottie and Patrick's stilt house. The Caminada refugees knew how to drink, dance, and fight. They crowded into the social ladder above the freed Blacks.

Maybe Patrick and his wife felt that the batture above New Orleans, where so much life from the river valley was swept up and cast on the bank, was the safest place they could live. Like neighbors on the river who had fled storms and floods and economic hardship, they were seeking refuge. Perhaps they also had an affinity for the river and its providence. If they had stuck with scavenging driftwood and fishing for shrimp in some quieter bend in the river, they might have gone unnoticed. In any case, there was little the couple could do to prevent the events that unfolded.

On the last night the Morris family spent together, they hosted a lively house party at their shantyboat on stilts. "A negro musician was kept busy until after 10, playing on the banjo. There were numerous visitors to the house, and until 10 o'clock there were several negro females present. About 10, however, the carnival ended, and the place closed for the night."[18]

I found the story of Pat and Lottie's life on the batture, and the events that followed their house party, in the New Orleans *Daily Picayune*. The first account appeared on January 13, 1896, under the headline, "Two Lives Taken in Defiance of Law: Another Blot on the Fair Name of Jefferson." The story decried the practice of mob justice but condemned the "character of the woman and the worthlessness of the man." A follow-up the next day explained that a "committee had been formed" by "prominent people of

TWO LIVES TAKEN
IN DEFIANCE OF LAW.

Another Blot Upon the Fair Name of
Jefferson,

Patrick Morris, a White Man, and
His Colored Wife

See Their Flatboat Home Burned Over
Their Heads,

And Are Made Victims by an Armed
Mob—Their Son Recognizes
Several.

PATRICK MORRIS, JR.,
The Boy Who Escaped from the
Flames and Saw His Parents
Perish.

New Orleans Daily Picayune, January
13, 1896. Public domain.

the district" to run the couple off, but things got out of hand. That story featured a first-person account by Patrick Morris Jr., who had escaped and landed in the care of the SPCC:

> Well, about 11 o'clock mamma, papa and I were sitting in the boathouse talking. Someone crawled down the batture and set fire to the bow of the boat, where the front door was. As soon as we saw the flames, papa told us to get out quick as the boat was on fire. Mamma

went out first and I was next to her, with papa right behind me. When my poor mamma got to the door some one of the white men fired at her. Yes, they were white, because I could see them from the light of the fire.

I saw two men I knew; they were Mr. Gassener, who keeps the saloon, and officer Jerome [Jerome LaFrance, a police officer in the district]. Both had guns, and all the white men had guns. I believe there were about twenty-five. Well, the bullet struck mamma in the right side of the neck, and she dropped back dead. Her blood went on my coat. Look, here are the stains near the buttonhole. Don't you see the red?

Just a second later another shot was fired, and the bullet glanced over my right leg, just above the knee, but did not scratch me. This bullet hit papa in the leg, and he was then crippled, he fell by mamma, and they burned up. I grabbed my pants, coat and shoes, because I was in my night clothes, and ran out the back door and got out. I ran along the batture to the Company Canal office, and after putting on my clothes slept under the house.

The *Daily Picayune* said a "silent mob" lynched Pat and Lottie, but the vigilantes left over forty bullet casings at the scene. They desecrated the bodies and threw them back inside the burning house. Patrick did not die from the gunshot to his knee or from the flames. The mob beheaded him to "finish him off." Police found a bloody ax at the scene. They did not, however, find the head. The next day, the bodies were buried in the soft batture silt and within two days the mound disappeared under the footsteps of investigators.

On a still day, giant plumes of smokey grain-dust engulf ships loading at the new Westwego grain elevator. From my riverside deck I sit and look downriver at the towering steel chutes—the only markers for the graves of my fellow batture dwellers Patrick and Lottie Morris.[19]

Chapter 8

Broken Levees, Big Shots, and Bird Men

On the night of March 16, 1891, the river levee blew out at Ames Plantation, a half mile below the Westwego home of Pat and Lottie Morris.
A Black man who lived with his family just inside the break was awakened
by a thunderous noise followed by a shout, "The levee's gone!" He ran
outside and found river water almost up to his knees.[1]

A cry of "crevasse" for a citizen living just inside river levees in the
nineteenth century carried all the terror that a tornado warning does today. Levee breaks during a spring rise created an uncontrolled torrent, a
waterfall of mud and debris that cut channels through fields, floated houses,
drowned livestock, and had the disheartening effect of rapidly eroding the
levee ends adjacent to the breach even further.

The Ames Crevasse occurred after a plantation operator installed iron
irrigation pipe through the base of the levee to flood his rice fields. Such
levee failures were common in the decades after the Civil War. Plantation
owners lacked the funds to repair levees themselves and no local authority
had the power to collect revenue and oversee work. In 1890 alone, over
eight miles of levee were lost to crevasses.[2]

An hour after the plantation worker living beside the Ames Crevasse
evacuated his family, he returned to find water crashing through a ten-foot
gap. At daybreak the next morning the breach was fifty feet wide. Two days
later it was 250 feet wide and growing seventy feet a day. A state engineer
saw little recourse: "The prevailing opinion is that the crevasse cannot be
closed . . . one could easily throw $1,000,000 into the crevasse without
changing the course a ripple."[3]

The Ames Crevasse stayed open until after the high water receded in
June. During the prior three months, every interior settlement west of the

Ames Crevasse on the first day, March 18, 1891. Photo courtesy of William S. Howell. New Orleans Public Library.

river and east of Bayou Lafourche, from Thibodaux to the Gulf of Mexico, went under water. Railroads diverted traffic and the turbid current toppled telegraph poles and inundated the West Bank suburb of Gretna.[4]

Across the river in New Orleans, citizens could hear the roar of water pouring through the crevasse. The din was especially loud in homes around the Exposition Grounds—soon to become Audubon Park—directly across from the break.[5] East Bank residents crowded onto steamboat excursions and ferries to witness the exploding current, the widening breach and the sheet of brown water covering the West Bank as far as the eye could see.

Four months after the crevasse opened, the river had receded far enough for crews to begin closing the 1,500-foot gash. On June 31, 1891, as convicts labored to fill the breach, a 250-foot-long by 40-foot-wide section of batture across the river in Carrollton Bend disappeared into the muddy water.[6] The current had eroded the underwater bank. As the river fell, the accumulated silt on the batture surface collapsed. A further batture cave might undermine the berm.

Unlike the plantation land inside the Ames Crevasse, Carrollton was a busy and populous suburb within the protection levees of the city. A relatively narrow neck of low land sat between Carrollton Bend and the

French Quarter at the lower end of that crescent. In a July meeting of the Orleans Levee Board, city engineer Benjamin Harrod warned that a second cave of the same magnitude would cause "destruction of property and loss of life [that] would extend throughout the entire city and would a thousand times exceed that from any other source."[7]

Harrod had served as chief state engineer with dominion over all the levees in Louisiana before becoming the chief engineer and surveyor in New Orleans. He was a member of the recently founded Mississippi River Commission. What he recommended sent shock waves through the people of Carrollton. The city must retreat from the river to make way for a new levee inside the old one. Engineers called it a "setback," but hundreds of residents whose homes and businesses would be seized understood it was a surrender.

A month after Harrod introduced his plan, the Orleans Levee Board and city engineers met and rejected a series of citizen proposals to save their riverfront, including spur dykes, bank revetments, and a canal to divert the river across from Carrollton on Nine Mile Point. Instead, Harrod's setback was approved. The board resolved to expropriate property and to let contracts for construction of a new levee as quickly as possible.

Carrollton residents gathered in a mass meeting the next day. None of them believed that a new levee was needed but a sense of helplessness pervaded the crowd. City councilmen shared the frustration and promised to seek funds to reimburse people whose property was seized. Speakers voiced a fear that "the repeated moving back of the levee means simply the abandoning of the city by piecemeal."

When the gathering broke up, grieving residents roamed between their houses and the levee, where more than a hundred people gathered. The levee had never been revered but emotions overflowed when homes and businesses were at stake. The levee became an old best friend as neighbors stood on it and cursed the levee board and its commissioners. And they wept.[8]

Work began in October, only three months after Major Benjamin Harrod introduced his plan. A 3,130-foot section of levee, stretching downriver from a point two blocks below the Jefferson Parish line would be set back 200 feet. Laborers demolished the bustling business district on Levee Street. They excised part of the Carrollton Hotel Resort, the elaborate old railroad depot, and a portion of the giant Picayune Fischer Lumber Mill. Over 600 people lost their homes.

Levee Street, surrendered to river, 1891. Photo by C. Milo Williams. Courtesy of C. Milo Williams Photographs, Southeastern Architectural Archive, Special Collections Division, Tulane University. Public domain.

Carrollton Hotel. Surrendered to the river, 1891. Photo by C. Milo Williams. Courtesy of C. Milo Williams Photographs, Southeastern Architectural Archive, Special Collections Division, Tulane University. Public domain.

Carrollton Train Station. Surrendered to river, 1891. Photo by C. Milo Williams. Courtesy of
C. Milo Williams Photographs, Southeastern Architectural Archive, Special Collections Division,
Tulane University. Public domain.

While workers were still tearing down and moving buildings inside the levee, amateur photographer Milo Williams visited the riverfront and captured a scene of bedlam on the batture. A hundred or more Black laborers dug wet clay from the water's edge under the gaze of a white overseer. Other men pushed heavy wooden barrows of dirt across a tall single-plank walkway to the top of a new levee. The city was in retreat, scrambling to protect itself from yet another flood.

Little more than six months after the batture caved, the planning, public debate, destruction, and levee building were accomplished. One hundred and fifty workers had moved 60,000 cubic yards of soil by mule, wheelbarrow, and shovel. In late summer the levee board passed a millage to reimburse property owners for their losses.

Milo Williams's 1891 photographs focused on the lost neighborhood landmarks and the remarkable building process. If there had been shantyboats or camps in Carrollton Bend before the setback, they aren't visible in those images. Shantyboaters who continued to drift into the city skirted the project and settled on undesirable scraps of batture elsewhere. They squeezed between wharves above and below the French Quarter, across the river in Algiers and Westwego, and on a grim shore farther downriver in St. Bernard Parish.

Levee workers dug clay from the water's edge. Photo by C. Milo Williams. Courtesy of C. Milo Williams Photographs, Southeastern Architectural Archive, Special Collections Division, Tulane University. Public domain.

The city was in retreat. Photo by C. Milo Williams. Courtesy of C. Milo Williams Photographs, Southeastern Architectural Archive, Special Collections Division, Tulane University. Public domain.

Just below New Orleans in the community of Arabi, a gaggle of river folk made their homes in tents and stilt houses on a fetid batture by the stockyard dock. They caught and sold fish that fed on offal from the slaughterhouse, while thousands of buzzards formed a sanitation crew. The giant scavengers blanketed the batture and fought over slaughter pen waste that floated ashore.[9]

In 1896, the same year Pat and Lottie were lynched on the Westwego batture, a mysterious hermit appeared across from Carrollton Bend on a tiny mud island formed by the Ames Crevasse, a few hundred yards below where Lottie Morris ran the Catfish Hotel. In classic river rat style, the drifter pulled his shantyboat up on shore and raised it on stilts. He added to the abode with lumber gathered from the river and claimed the clump of silt as his own. According to workers at the Westwego Landing, the old recluse seldom spoke. He corralled logs and seined for catfish and shrimp and sold his harvest silently at the dock, where everyone knew him as Bayou Sara Jack.

Bayou Sara Jack's true identity became known only after he succumbed to a hail of bullets following a squabble with a group of Black men hustling logs—driftwood that Jack claimed to own. News of his murder read as another chapter in the "misery" and "wretchedness" that newspaper men ascribed to batture dwellers, but the river wasn't Jack's last option. A brother who called to claim the body shocked fishermen at the Westwego dock.

The "mysterious hermit" was born John Prather to an established family in Clermont County, Ohio, on the banks of the Ohio River. He stood to inherit a "small fortune" back home, but lost patience with the probate court, where his brother was magistrate, and "took to the river." For years Bayou Sara Jack had made the river his life before dying alone on his mud island in Westwego.[10]

The same amateur photographer who captured the levee setback in 1891 returned to Carrollton Bend six years later to record another flood, one that threatened to overtop the newly built structure. Milo Williams's 1897 photographs reveal a cast of river rats already reinhabiting an unusual shoreline. When the new levee was built, engineers protected it by leaving the old one in place, with cuts that allowed the river to fill the 200-foot

A floating fisherman's hut, Carrollton Bend, 1897. Photo by C. Milo
Williams. Courtesy of C. Milo Williams Photographs, Southeastern
Architectural Archive, Special Collections Division, Tulane University.
Public domain.

gap between them. In the flood of 1897, the gap between the old and new
levees had become a flowing backwater.

In one picture, shantyboats and a floating fisherman's hut dot the outside of a narrow ridge of old levee, stranded far off from shore. In another
photograph, a primitive shack clings to the new levee amidst a raft of
driftwood. Four Black men rest on a bench against the shanty wall, facing
the levee—in the background an oak tree stands 200 feet out in the current. Even before that vestige of the suburban canopy died, batture folk
had returned to the water edge.

Williams took two photographs looking upstream from the heart of
Carrollton Bend toward my colony in Southport. A sturdy stilt house stands
alone, attached to the new levee. On the far horizon, the top of the Oak
Street Ferry and a cluster of rooftops are visible across the parish line. The
photos offer no clue who lived in the tidy stilt house in the foreground,
or who built the distant shacks at the very spot where I found my friend

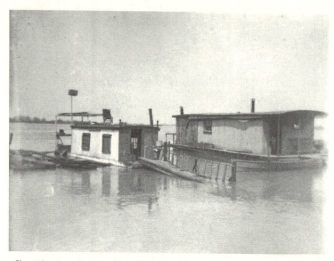

Shantyboats in Carrollton Bend, 1897. Photo by C. Milo Williams. Courtesy of
C. Milo Williams Photographs, Southeastern Architectural Archive, Special
Collections Division, Tulane University. Public domain.

A shack clings to the new Carrollton Levee, 1897. Photo by C. Milo Williams. Courtesy of Historic
New Orleans Collection. HNOC Accession No. 1974.25.31.56_o2.jpg.

A stilt house with ferry in distance, 1897. Photo by C. Milo Williams. Courtesy of C. Milo Williams Photographs, Southeastern Architectural Archive, Special Collections Division, Tulane University. Public domain.

Rob living almost a century later. The images were developed from glass negatives deteriorating in the Southeastern Architectural Archive at Tulane. An archivist had scrawled surmised dates and locations on them. No names. No stories.

I scoured news reports, journals, and photographs from the turn of the twentieth century. But finally, by accident, I found the first clue to a man who must have lived in the camps Milo Williams photographed. When I discovered the river relic, I wasn't even looking for it. I didn't even know what I had.

Two blocks from my colony, on a narrow one-way street that heads away from the river, I pulled over by a big red trash dumpster. I don't remember why; I'll claim it was my river-learned affinity for foraging—not a habit of trash picking. This was 2008, three years after Hurricane Katrina struck New Orleans and plenty of colorful dumpsters filled the city. Nothing was visible over the lip of the container, so I pulled my truck up close and climbed on the tailgate to take a peek.

Someone had torn down a corrugated metal shed, the kind that New Orleanians liked to build behind so many big uptown New Orleans homes during the early 1900s. The contents of the shed lay smashed in the bin, beneath mangled metal sheathing. Under the moldering scraps, I saw a screen-covered wooden box. I jumped in, propped the layers of tin out of the way with a splintered two-by-four and worked it free.

The box was thirty-six inches long and ten inches square, constructed of one-inch rough milled red pine, covered in window screen. Thin strips of molding secured the screen with no gaps or splits or splinters where the wood was joined. Each small nail was set flush to the surface of the molding. The object was functional, not decorative—assembled with obvious care, its purpose obscure. Someone spent a lot of energy on this.

My find was divided into three equal compartments, each with a sliding door made of sheet metal curled at the top to form a handle. A pencil-size perch pierced the chambers and tiny swings hung on soft bent wire. The wood was dry but not rotten, the metal coated with a patina of hardened dust and rust.

I took it directly home. For two years the box floated around my living room and was a subject of much conjecture. Everyone asked, "Who makes a bird cage that has three ten-inch square compartments? Why would the cage have a carrying handle wired to the top?" A few people who didn't know me asked the more obvious question, "Why are you keeping it?" After three years, it migrated to my loft and later I stashed it under the workbench in my shed. I couldn't part with it.

Early one morning, a year after the cage had been banished to the shed, I sat in bed staring deep into the New Orleans *Times-Picayune* historical archives. I had just discovered the online resource. All night, tapped into my neighbor's wireless, I looked for stories of early batture residents. I started in 1820 and had worked up to 1942, although it seemed unlikely that newspapers of that era would have anything about the earliest residents of my batture. Just when my endurance had drained, I found the headline, "Oldest Resident of Batture Finds Himself Hemmed in by Barbed Wire and Soldiers."[11]

Seymour Geisenheimer was born in 1868. His father, George Geisenheimer, was a truck farmer who immigrated to New Orleans from Germany in 1859, just in time to fight for the South in the Civil War. After the war, the family moved to the exurb of Carrollton, where George owned one of the many vegetable gardens in the neighborhood. At age fifteen, Seymour left his parents' home, crossed the levee and built himself a batture house in Jefferson Parish, at the site of my river colony in Southport.

By his own description, Seymour was the first resident of the batture in Southport. He moved there in 1883, but when levee crews began to work on the riverbank revetment in front of his stilt house, the young homesteader simply built another camp perhaps fifty yards downstream and became the first batture resident in the Carrollton Bend of New Orleans. Because the levee work in 1891 began two blocks below the parish line, Seymour's camp would have just dodged demolition.

In an era of industrialization, when many children as young as eleven went to work in factories, Seymour followed his older brothers' footsteps into a most unusual trade. Brothers Emile, Henry, and Simon Geisenheimer are listed in city insurance directories between 1888 and 1898 as "Bird Fanciers" by trade. Seymour, living on the batture, is not listed at all.[12]

New Orleans was a booming market for "cage birds," as avian pets were known. In 1890, cage-builders and bird dealers operated two shops on Chartres Street in the French Quarter; one of them lived in the same Carrollton neighborhood as the older Geisenheimer brothers. Seymour's oldest brother, Emile, became an important broker of "wild animals" and was remembered at his death as "widely known through the North and East" for having "built up a lucrative business selling birds." There is no evidence that Seymour profited much from the enterprise.[13]

As the city surrendered more of its riverfront to industry, Seymour and the other bird trappers went farther and farther afield, securing steamboat passage to woodlands as far as 200 miles upstream. It was a race. As fast as trappers and plume hunters decimated the wild bird population, the lumber industry and fuel-hungry steamboats deforested their bottomland homes. Most songbirds caught in the wild died in transit to out-of-state brokers.

Sitting on the deck of his batture camp in January 1942, Seymour described his expeditions to a *Times-Picayune* reporter:

> Mostly we caught mockingbirds, red birds and blue pops (indigo buntings). The red birds were the most valuable. We got 50 cents apiece for all we caught . . . It was quite a job taking care of them when you were out in the woods tending your traps. We fed them all twice a day. Most of them lived on worms, bugs and grasshoppers. The red birds ate cracked corn, oats and wheat. We'd feed the mockingbirds eggs and potatoes just like humans.

One of Seymour's cages had returned to the batture. Photo by Macon Fry.

Geisenheimer lived a river life I hadn't even imagined. The sun was coming up and I was still hanging on every word in the interview, even though the digitized newspaper was barely legible. I got out of bed and printed it; no luck. I tried twenty-point font; nothing but pixels. Web archive and PDF formats didn't work. I went to twelve-point font with a magnifying glass and the words emerged: "he still has some of his old box-like traps as souvenirs."

I went out to my shed and got the old cage. I placed it on the kitchen table beside the newspaper copy and continued reading. The *Times-Picayune* interview ended abruptly. "He just put on his hat and headed off for a nephew's house a few blocks away, where he eats his suppers."[14]

A house with a corrugated metal shed, down a narrow street a few blocks from the levee?

One of Seymour's cages had returned to the batture.

⚜

The Carrollton levee setback of 1891 remains the greatest voluntary surrender of land to the Mississippi River in New Orleans history. Just five years later, when the river rose to the top of the new levee, residents of Carrollton remembered the dire prediction that the city was succumbing to the river "by piecemeal." In some places water overtopped the new structure. At the head of St. Charles Avenue, where the Carrollton Hotel and rail station once flourished, water seeped through the levee and pooled in the streets.

In response to the renewed flooding, the Orleans Levee Board completed purchase of land along the Carrollton front, and in 1910, began building a monolithic levee atop the one they had setback in 1891. The new levee was wider at the base and four feet taller. It stretched the entire three miles from the Jefferson Parish line down to Audubon Park. The final appropriation of land by the Orleans Levee Board set the stage for the sprawling batture community that soon took root.

People who held positions on or had sway with the levee board were the winners when land was acquired for the levee expansion. In 1909 the Orleans Levee District awarded Cooney Fischer, who had just left the board, $277,500 (the equivalent of nearly $7 million in inflation-adjusted 2017 dollars) for his Fischer sawmill at the head of Carrollton Avenue. At one time the mill sold 10,000,000 feet of lumber a year and advertised "the largest and best cypress logs ever brought to this or any other market."[15] By the time Cooney sold to the levee board, the family had cut the most profitable virgin timber from holdings in the swamps of Louisiana and Mississippi. He left behind a batture that appeared huge on levee maps but was composed almost entirely of sawdust that had to be removed at great cost.

Joseph Bisso, the other big winner in the Carrollton levee setback, immigrated to New Orleans in 1852 when he was eleven years old and worked for the Fischer lumber business from 1886 until 1890. Bisso then opened his own lumber dock nearby on property his wife owned at the edge of Audubon Park. The Bisso family used the space between the old levee (left in place in 1891) and the new levee to start a batture-based marine empire. They sold sand from the property, developed a ferry business, a coal tippler, and a marine towing and salvage business that survives to this day. They became the biggest provider of coal to steamships in New Orleans.[16]

Industrialists shared a vision with New Orleans civic leaders of a more efficient and profitable riverfront. The recently instituted boards of the Orleans and Pontchartrain Levee Districts (levee boards), the Commissioners

of the Port of New Orleans (Dock Board), and the just instituted Public
Belt Railroad worked in concert to commodify and control the river.

By law, two of the members of the levee board were representatives
of railroads operating in the city. Hunter C. Leake, general manager of
the Illinois Central Railroad in New Orleans, as well as president of the
Pontchartrain Levee District, appeared before a congressional committee
in 1916 to appeal for federal funds:

> We all know that if that great river were a continuous line of railway
> it would not only be the duty of the states to take care of it . . . and if
> the water that annually goes through Louisiana and Mississippi, com-
> ing from the 23 or 24 other states of this Union, were a commodity
> instead of water it would be a matter of interstate commerce . . . and
> we ask you to treat it in the same manner that you treat any other
> line of communication or any other commodity that goes from one
> state to another.[17]

Power brokers in the city saw the Mississippi just as they viewed their
network of steel rails. The river was an engine of commerce, its waters a
commodity. They wanted the stream regulated, reliable, and safe for the
exchange of goods for money. They served a public that banked in the
business districts of New Orleans and New York and Chicago. The homes
of river people wouldn't figure into their plans.

River historian Ari Kelman offers a succinct appraisal of New Orleans'
changing relationship with the Mississippi at the turn of the twentieth
century:

> The city reclaimed the waterfront in the name of the public by build-
> ing a system of municipally owned docks, enormous warehouses,
> and miles of rails along the city's border with the Mississippi. . . . And
> as New Orleans overhauled the riverbanks, the number of people
> who could access that space shrank, recasting one measure of the
> waterfront's public status.[18]

"Reclamation," founded in a faith that engineers could control nature, blos-
somed as a philosophy and public policy in the early twentieth century. The
federal government had established the Mississippi River Commission in

1879 to design and implement plans to improve navigation and commerce on the river. In 1902 the US Reclamation Service was founded to manage the diversion, delivery, and storage of water in western states. Reclamation, a word that described "the process of claiming something back or asserting a right" was used by engineers and planners to describe "The cultivation of waste land or land formerly under water."[19] The determination of what was "waste land" turned the process of reclamation into a political and economic tool to displace undesirable people.

While New Orleans had "reclaimed" most of the city's batture with a four-mile-long barrier of contiguous sheds and rails in the 1890s, within the levees, philanthropists and landowners founded Audubon Park and City Park. Places where folks had harvested moss, fished, hunted, and occasionally staged duels became parks where better citizens could enjoy "nature" safely, away from pestilential back swamps, dangerous currents, and odd squatters.

In 1913 Sewage and Water Board engineer A. Baldwin Wood invented a revolutionary pump, a technological advancement that drained New Orleans' back swamp and launched a century of reclamation that increased the dry footprint of the city sevenfold.[20] Wetlands that were once home to refugees and outcasts, be they freed slaves, urban poor, or restless river-folk, were "reclaimed" for industrial or residential development. Lots on higher ground, on Metairie and Esplanade Ridges, were eventually advertised "for whites only."

New Orleans' newspapers, which regularly scorned the indolence of shantyboaters, celebrated the appearance on the riverfront of Gilded age houseboats and their wealthy inhabitants. In 1902 "The Finest Houseboat on the Mississippi" arrived at the head of Canal Street, carrying an "esteemed party" of "three lumbermen and a capitalist money lender." There was no mistaking their houseboat, *The Idler*, for a shantyboat. The floating mansion was built by a lumber baron from Indiana who had made a fortune deforesting the headwaters of the river. It had steam heat and hot water for bathing.[21]

As steam-powered floating palaces lined the riverfront at Canal Street, batture dwellers enjoyed a life that had more in common with the western boatmen of the 1820s than their wealthy houseboat neighbors. Whatever work they found in the city, most denizens of the river caught logs, split firewood for fuel, fished, or gardened on the fertile batture.

On June 19, 1904, a *Times-Picayune* reporter described shantyboaters
and stilt house people dotted along the entire riverfront "from Southport
to Canal Street":

> They are not oppressed by poverty . . . They are not stifled by conven-
> tion, for such as they have is of home manufacture; they are a law
> unto themselves, and chiefest of all, they are not unhappy, for their life
> is utterly without responsibility and the wanderlust is in their blood.

Chapter 9

Miracles

Dead From Drink—A Shanty-Boat Man Expires in Prison Cell—Police Think Crime Committed by Shanty-Boatmen—Shanty Men Fight And Scissor Grinder Chapman Is Shot To Death—A Shanty Fire—Failure Afloat—Shanty-boat Brute—Shanty-boatmen Rob a Stranger From Georgia—Shanty-boat Burns—Waif Rescued From Houseboat Colony

Observations by a few wandering romantics aside, the news from New Orleans' batture in the early twentieth century beat a grim refrain. Stories of fistfights, fires, and feuds made for sensational headlines in city newspapers; they also traced an unmistakable migration—batture folks were moving upriver, pushed by a nearly continuous rim of rails, sheds, and wharves along the crescent riverfront. On October 19, 1914, the *Times-Picayune* reported on a "houseboat community at the head of Henry Clay Avenue," on the very edge of Carrollton Bend at Audubon Park.

No single face emerged in any detail from the sordid accounts of life on the batture until March 11, 1920. A front-page headline, "Strange Faith Cures Laid at Door of Tiny Houseboat," appeared on page one of the New Orleans *Times-Picayune* above a photograph of a white-robed man with long snowy hair and beard. The man's face was gaunt, his eyes sunk deep into dark sockets. Within weeks the story of the aged shantyboater became national news.

John Cudney, his seventy-seven-year-old sister, and elderly mother had eluded mention in the lurid crime reports about river people. For four years the family lived in obscurity on a "little yellow houseboat" at Henry Clay Avenue, where Cudney practiced the common trades of a shantyboater. He collected drift to sell as firewood and worked as a watchman on the government dredge *Tonty*, docked alongside his houseboat.

Brother Isaiah greets crowd in front of his shantyboat. Photo by John Tibule Mendes. Gift of Waldemar S. Nelson. Courtesy of Historic New Orleans Collection. Acc. No. 2003.0182.254.

At age seventy-four, John Cudney became Brother Isaiah, "the miracle-man" of the batture. It was reported that for weeks, Cudney, "who prefers to be known as 'Brother Isaiah,'" had been curing the sick and lame on the deck of his shantyboat and refused to take money. Word spread. He restored sight to a blind girl. He cured a four-year-old "paralytic."[1] After the morning news, supplicants crowded the wooden planks connecting shantyboat to shore. The evening newspaper, the *New Orleans States*, displayed a banner headline: "Thousands Rush to Miracle Man."

The following morning, March 12, headlines in the *Times-Picayune* cascaded from page one to page two, capturing the birth of an unprecedented phenomenon in the city:

Blind Hope, Aroused to Passion, Forces Army of Lame, Weak, and Sick to Healing of New 'Isaiah'—Alleged 'Cures' Carried on for Months Culminate in Wild Stampede for Little Houseboat on River— Car Line Service Taxed to Capacity—John Cudney Refuses Gifts and Payment and Makes Weird Figure Exhorting Crowd to 'Have Faith.'

Cure seekers swamp the shantyboat landing. Photo by John Tibule Mendes. Gift of Waldemar S. Nelson. Courtesy of Historic New Orleans Collection. Acc No. 2003.0182.255.

Cure-seekers swamped the shantyboat landing. Policemen worked to control the crowd of thousands who pressed against the side of the levee and stood in the mud by the river for hours. A boy on crutches leaned against the gangplank to Brother Isaiah's shanty. Armless and legless war veterans were passed bodily over a wooden breakwater at the bottom of the levee, where they joined the throngs awaiting cures.

Folks arrived on foot, ferry, train, automobile, and streetcar. They came to be healed, to accompany infirm friends and relatives, and to witness miracles on the riverfront.

> The crowd that gathered on the levee Thursday and swarmed down on the other side, ankle deep in the gray, putty-like mud, was one to inspire the imagination. . . . White, black, old, young, rich, poor pressed shoulder to shoulder with intense eagerness.[2]

Among the early visitors to the shantyboat landing were a host of pastors, police, and politicians. A couple of psychologists and scientists were the primary doubters; they pointed to the likely effects of "suggestibility" in Isaiah's cures. Some clergy questioned the ability of mere men to perform miracles. But skeptics were drowned out by the many who *wanted* to believe that cures were taking place. The crowd quickly grew to an unprecedented mob, and newspaper accounts fanned the flames of hope with new testimonials.

City authorities embraced the work of Brother Isaiah. District Attorney Luzenberg "found no law that could be invoked to interfere with his present method of treatment." Dr. W. H. Robin of the City Board of Health noted that jurisdiction for medical matters fell upon the State Board of Medical Examiners. Superintendent of Police Mooney declared "hands off." District Police Captain Capo, who brought a friend of the superintendent's to be cured, offered a stunning testimony; "He knew it to be a fact that while he was on the scene Brother Isaiah had restored the sight of a person completely blind."[3]

The throng by the shantyboat landing grew to tens of thousands over the first weekend, breaking attendance records for Audubon Park and packing ferries, roads, streetcars, and inbound trains. More than once on Friday and again on Sunday, the tiny houseboat nearly sank, and men were kept busy bailing water from its listing deck.

The sun set and the crowd stayed. "Watch fires were built all along the levee and down on the river beach late Saturday night by those who were determined to obtain close-up positions when Brother Isaiah resumed his practice."[4] Firelight reflected between bobbing shantyboats and stilt houses and out across the dark river as supplicants sat on logs and gathered around the flames to stay warm and await the healer.

After the weekend onslaught, Dr. E. Mahler of the State Board of Medical Examiners appealed to the police to charge Brother Isaiah with practicing medicine illegally—after all, Mahler reasoned, he couldn't be a faith healer because he didn't belong to a recognized denomination. But Brother Isaiah had cultivated the authorities. The amiable superintendent of police demurred that it would be unwise to "invoke the law for fear it would be interpreted as an act of persecution."[5] Isaiah took the next day off from the river to visit the home of City Commissioner Alex Pujol and treat his wife for rheumatism. He was back on the batture Wednesday when Mayor Behrman proclaimed, "It is not my duty to stop Brother Isaiah . . . for there are other authorities to pass upon his work."[6]

In less than a week, news of the "Miracle-Man" spread to newspapers as far off as Seattle, Washington. Pilgrims poured in from everywhere, and Brother Isaiah's work was quietly institutionalized. With permission from the head of the Audubon Park Commission and support from the mayor and city commissioner, the American Red Cross erected sixteen tents in the park beside the shantyboat landing. The city constructed a stage, strung lights, and appointed a police security detail for the healer. Brother Isaiah took up residence at night on the adjacent government dredge boat *Tonty*, safe from entreating multitudes in the clay below.

On weekends, a carnival atmosphere prevailed by the river. Opportunistic evangelists like "Brother Euclid" and "Brother John" showed up on the verdant levee to sermonize. Preachers, politicians, pickpockets, and pop vendors joined the throng by the park. On Henry Clay Avenue, fruit wagons abounded and photographs of the healer at work were offered for sale. In response to increasingly frustrated crowds, some of whom waited for many days to be treated, Brother Isaiah began blessing handkerchiefs, accepting many by mail to be anointed and returned.

The strangeness of a healer treating the multitude in such a humble setting inspired reporters. Their stories transformed river and muddy bank into the "Sea of Galilee" and the shantyboater "garbed in the roughest of garments" was described as a modern day "apostle."[7]

Overtaxed hospitals and charitable organizations struggled to absorb the flood of desperately ill arrivals and maintain a virtual city of indigent sick people on the riverbank. Some folks arrived in New Orleans by train, alone, penniless. Some lacked even the ability to rise from their seats. Six hundred "crippled and diseased" people camped on the levee at what the newspaper began calling "Brother Isaiah's island of misery."[8] An Easter plea went out from the Traveler's Aid Society in New Orleans. "We must do all we can to stop the pilgrimage of the sick, helpless and afflicted who continue to come from all over the country."[9]

Word of depressing conditions and failed cures spread as charitable groups began paying return fares for disappointed pilgrims, some of whom had waited a month in tents packed with 165 people. Newspaper headlines dwindled and public interest flagged as the spectacle became stale news and summer temperatures rose on the shadeless levee. Three months after capturing the public imagination, Brother Isaiah moved from his berth on a government boat back to his little yellow shantyboat.

In late July only a handful of supplicants gathered on the muddy and trampled riverbank.

The bearded healer didn't float off down the river. As quietly and mysteriously as Cudney washed up on the shore, Brother Isaiah vanished from local newspapers in late July. The epilogue to his six months on the batture provides a clue to how New Orleans' riparian fringe became home to a vast settlement.

The *Los Angeles Herald* of April 1921 announced: "Brother Isaiah, titled 'The Miracle Man,' will arrive in Los Angeles in a few weeks for a prolonged visit with friends ... he will receive sufferers of various ailments during his stay here and continue his work." Over the next six months, the healer moved from practicing at a private home to entertaining audiences of 15,000 at a city park—dubbed "Miracle Hill"—to a stage on Venice Beach and finally to the Vasquero Ranch on Santa Monica Boulevard.

Things went badly for Brother Isaiah in the City of Angels. A woman who had been treated but not cured sued Brother Isaiah $25,000 for using her photograph on a souvenir postcard. District Attorney Thomas L. Woolwine dogged the healer, whom he quickly labeled a "fakir" and a "dangerous fraud." Woolwine saved his choicest words for Isaiah's followers, observing, "Suckers, morons and simpletons, it seems are born by the hundreds, every fraction of a second."[10]

While the district attorney mulled charges of mail fraud over Brother Isaiah's anointed handkerchiefs and investigated the skimming of vendor profits at Miracle Hill, local newspapers advertised the screening of newsreels showing the healer working miracles. After he advocated bathing with less clothing, the sponsors of the Venice Beach swimsuit competition tried to recruit Isaiah as a judge.

When a sixty-year-old woman died after a treatment, District Attorney Woolwine brought manslaughter charges against the healer. Isaiah made bail and promised to return for a court date in the spring, then he quietly returned to New Orleans by limousine on Christmas Day 1922 to await trial. His driver parked the car at Henry Clay Avenue and Isaiah moved back onto his floating home. After a dozen long-haired and bearded followers joined Isaiah on the batture, the local press began referring to the humble shantyboat landing as "Camp of the Saints."[11]

City officials, aware of Brother Isaiah's trouble in Los Angeles, forbid him from healing by laying on hands. By this time however, he was content to spend his days responding to bulging bags of mail that had accumulated. He anointed handkerchiefs and occasionally traveled to seek a new home for his growing colony of followers. When the healer returned to Los Angeles on March 1, 1922, a throng of faithful supporters outside the courthouse cast rose petals in his path. Isaiah was acquitted before a courtroom full of adoring followers.[12]

A month after his acquittal, the healer announced plans to open a farming, faith community of vegetarians on the Back Bay in Biloxi, Mississippi. He returned to New Orleans, hired a motor launch to tow his shantyboat to Biloxi, and in June left for good in his limousine.

After two years in Biloxi, Isaiah moved his followers to the Estero River below Fort Myers, Florida, but the colony there dissolved in acrimony over land ownership.[13] Brother Isaiah's last stand was in Oroville, California, where it was unclear whether the healer or his followers had less contact with reality. When a member of his cult died on November 6, 1931, Brother Isaiah proclaimed the death to be a result of her "disobedience of god"—a cause disputed by the local coroner. Isaiah convinced his forty or fifty Oroville followers that he was immortal, yet the old man failed to awaken one morning. Delusions of his immortality evaporated after the body sat in one hundred degree-plus heat for several days.[14]

Brother Isaiah had something in common with hundreds of batture dwellers before and after him. The "real" John Cudney remains unknown, another ghost inhabiting the seasonally flooded silt along the river. A couple in Phoenix claimed him as a long-lost brother. Others were convinced that he was a Seventh-day Adventist minister born in Ontario, who had disappeared in a shipwreck in the Pitcairn Islands. Cudney cultivated his own origin myths. He told followers in Mississippi that he was born on a steamboat on the Mississippi River. A reporter in California described him as a veterinarian from New Orleans, and the faithful in his "City of New Jerusalem" in Oroville were convinced he was the eighty-eighth reincarnation of the prophet Isaiah.

The most grounded account of the healer came from a fellow river rat at the Henry Clay shantyboat landing. On December 18, 1922, after Isaiah had left for Mississippi, a powerful northeaster swept through the city. Two-and-a-half inches of rain fell, and the temperature dropped to thirty-nine degrees. The wind blew through the flimsy batture shacks and the following morning, eighty-seven-year-old Edward Hinkle was found in his shantyboat nearly dead from exposure.

Hinkle had landed his boat at what would become known as Camp of the Saints while the nation was embroiled in the Civil War. He operated a rowboat ferry to the West Bank for most of the sixty years that followed. To Hinkle, Brother Isaiah wasn't a healer, a curiosity, or a fraud; he was just another shantyboater, and a bad neighbor:

> Brother Isaiah came and sat down in my back yard. I'd tramped that land for over 60 years going to and from my ferry. I tried to talk to him. No use. It wasn't his land, and Brother Isaiah had a powerful liking for what wasn't his. I run him out though when it come time to plant. He kept off my garden after that . . .

From his bed in Charity Hospital, Edward Hinkle told a reporter his last wish—to be back on the batture: "That's been my home since I came down the river as a kid. I started shantying there and I'd like to stop shantying there." Two days later the ferryman died in a hospital bed.[15]

Brother Isaiah wasn't persecuted, prosecuted, or run off in New Orleans. On the batture, he stayed outside the reach of authorities, but in plain view of tens of thousands of people who crossed the railroad tracks, climbed the levee, and looked toward the river. His indisputable miracle was bringing the public back for a few months to their forgotten riverfront and the wave-washed land beside it.

The colony of houseboats and shacks at the Henry Clay landing was doomed even before Brother Isaiah pulled up stakes and headed for the Golden State. Within a few weeks of his emergence in 1920, an ad appeared in the classified section of the newspaper, lost behind headlines celebrating "miracles" on the batture. A new owner, the J. S. Otis Mahogany Company, asserted rights to the riverfront below Audubon Park:

> It will interest you to know that 'Brother Isaiah, the Miracle Man,' His Houseboat and Platform are on part of the land where we will build the world's most modern mahogany sawmill to cut genuine Honduras Mahogany lumber which is used in all homes of refinement . . .[16]

Otis Mahogany was one of the biggest companies on the New Orleans waterfront at a time when the city was about to become the nation's biggest
producer of hardwood lumber. Mahogany logs required perpetual submer-
sion to be ready for milling, and the protected bend below Audubon Park
was a place in which hardwood looted from the Caribbean could be stored
and processed.

The mahogany and banana importers in New Orleans owned land in
Honduras and Nicarágua. They relied on US troops or mercenaries to subdue
local populations and install tyrants willing to forfeit their nations' resources
for a pittance and the promise of continued power. This is how the "banana
republics" of the day were created and one reason New Orleans became
known as the northernmost banana republic.[17]

None of the river rats at the Henry Clay landing was scared off by Otis
Mahogany's plans—they had no nation-wealth to plunder and no real land to
claim—but in 1922, an even bigger lumber company purchased the Otis mill.
Mengel Mahogany expanded operations on the riverfront, and in 1925 called
on the US Marines to suppress an indigenous uprising that threatened their
holdings in Nicarágua. Most of the shantyboaters and shack dwellers beside
the sprawling Mengel mill drifted off to find more hospitable batture land.
A mile upstream, just above Audubon Park, their migration collided with a
homegrown banana republic, the Bisso Company collier, wharf, and ferry.

William Bisso Sr. was a hard-nosed businessman and a tough politician
who used his political influence to defend the riverfront empire founded by
his father. He was elected to the New Orleans City Council in 1904 and still
held a council seat a few years later when his company won a lucrative city
garbage barge contract. The following year, when the Dock Board asserted
control over the city's wharves, the powerful and connected Bissos claimed
ownership of their batture and retained the valuable privilege of operating
their dock privately.[18]

Bisso became a boss in the Old Regular political machine and he used
his role as a Democrat leader in the city's Fourteenth Ward to win a seat
in the state legislature from 1912 to 1920. The Old Regulars were known as
bare-knuckle political operatives and Bisso landed in court on several oc-
casions. He was accused in 1913 of settling a contract dispute "with his fists,"
and in 1917, of stoning a Black man he believed to be a labor organizer at
his Carrollton Bend wharf.[19]

The Old Regulars dominated politics in southeast Louisiana through
patronage and brute force. They anointed judges, sheriffs, and mayors in New

Orleans for half a century. In his businesses and through the rich patronage
of the Old Regulars, William Bisso controlled thousands of jobs, including many on his own private batture. One of his employees, a stevedore
named Johnny Jackson, had a daughter who would become a heroine in
the neighborhood, revered in the city, and famous around the world.

In 1916, the same year John Cudney landed on the Henry Clay batture,
Johnny Jackson's daughter, a five-year-old girl living upriver by the Bisso
Ferry, joined the youth choir at Plymouth Rock Baptist Church. Cudney
was white and had floated down the river, while that little girl, Mahalia
Jackson, was Black and was born by its side. They had a green half-mile
of Audubon Park between them, but both had a river at their back and a
faithful following in their future.

Mahalia was born in 1911 on a bit of Water Street, truncated by the
new levee, and a short distance above the Bisso wharf. Her birthplace,
documented in a photograph by her friend, the music historian William
Russell, sat just a few feet on the city side of the public belt railroad. In the
background of his photograph, the rooftops of batture camps peek over
a towering levee.

Mahalia described the place this way: "When I was a little girl down
in New Orleans we lived out by the levee. The levee wasn't far from the
railroad track and then the levee banked the Mississippi River. There used
to be people that used to live back there, and they used to catch fish back
there."[20]

Mahalia's recorded memories are the clearest account of her neighborhood, now known as the Black Pearl, and the adjacent "Black batture" community in the early 1900s. The batture houses occupied about two hundred
yards of shore, bordered on the downriver end by the Bisso industries and
cut off from the upriver Carrollton Bend by the headquarters of the US
Army Corps of Engineers. Those enterprises and the adjacent railroad and
government fleet provided excellent employment opportunities for Blacks
in that part of New Orleans.

Mahalia's grandfather, Johnny Jackson, worked as a straw boss for Bisso,
selecting crews of day laborers from the crowd that milled about the Walnut Street ferry landing each weekday morning. Her father, Johnny Jackson

Mahalia Jackson birthplace by levee. Rooftops of batture camps in background. Photo courtesy of the William Russell Collection, Historic New Orleans Collection. Acquisition made possible by the Clarisse Claiborne Grime Fund. Acc. No. 92-48-L331.787.

Jr., worked on the Bisso dock, and women in her family were reportedly domestics in the Bisso household.[21] Most of the people on the Black batture shopped and got their mail and water at the Bisso store, beside the levee at 123 Walnut Street.

Life in the Black Pearl, according to Mahalia, was not that different from life on the batture. Dirt streets ran down toward the river where the curving levee had been set back and formed triangles instead of square blocks. The houses were "pretty shabby" and the rent was "no more than six or eight dollars a month."[22] Although the neighborhood was racially mixed, most families were working poor. Mahalia recalled that many residents depended on the river and their industrial neighbors for food and fuel:

> The only way that we could get coal, we had to go a mile down where Bisso was and pick up coal on the tracks, and we would bring that coal back home sometimes across our backs or up on our head, that we might have enough coal for the winter to keep the house warm.... Some of the families would raise their own vegetables and so many times we would go out to the riverfront and catch our own fish.[23]

Mahalia sang on Sundays in the youth choir at Mount Moriah Baptist Church, a half-block from the levee, where her maternal grandfather was

Mahalia's church, a half-block from the levee. Illustration courtesy of Elizabeth F. Calabrese.

minister. Sometimes on Saturdays she paid a dime to watch movies in the church meeting hall (local theaters were segregated).

As a teenager, Mahalia was baptized in the Mississippi. Stewards in white robes and deacons dressed in black led the Mount Moriah congregation out the doors of the church. The procession stretched for over a block, and down at the end of Magazine Street it met the congregation of the Broadway Baptist Church. The combined multitude crossed over the levee and marched slowly down to the batture, singing "Let's Go Down to Jordan."

Mahalia handed her shoes to the baptism stewards, and the pastor reached out and blessed the water as Mahalia waded in. The ministers lowered her, immersed her fully into the Mississippi, and she emerged "reborn in Christ." A month later, Mahalia caught a northbound train and left New Orleans to escape the overbearing supervision of Aunt Duke and to live with her Aunt Hannah in Chicago.[24]

Biographers can't agree on several details of Mahalia's life. Was she born in 1911 or 1912? Did she leave for Chicago in 1927 or 1930? But everyone was moved by her story. Her grandparents were born into slavery in Louisiana. Mahalia herself was raised under the harsh constricts of the Jim Crow South, where Blacks worked for white people at half-wages. She lived blocks from the segregated carousel and swimming pool at Audubon Park but found her joy singing with friends on the grassy levee and wading in the river.

Brought up in poverty, Mahalia launched a singing career in Chicago that led to audiences of presidents and royalty. By the 1950s she was called the Queen of Gospel, and in the words of Sonari Glinton of NPR, her voice was the "soundtrack of the Civil Rights movement."[25] People who stood with her on the steps of the Lincoln Memorial at the 1963 March on Washington recalled that she inspired her friend Martin Luther King Jr. to deliver his most famous oratory by shouting out, "Tell them about the dream, Martin! Tell them about the dream!"[26] And Mahalia had a voice, honed on the levee and in her southern church, that could make a nonbeliever weep.

I discovered her music while collecting phonograph records in the 1980s. At the time I had no idea she was from New Orleans, that she grew up by the river, or that she walked the batture where I picked berries. But I found her records everywhere, from the estate sales of wealthy white families, to stacks of brittle and worn 78 RPM records sold at yard sales in "back-of-town" neighborhoods.

Her music was uncompromisingly spiritual yet expressive of the everyday struggles of growing up in the Jim Crow South. The two songs she sang at the 1963 March on Washington, "How I Got Over" and "I've Been 'Buked," were about a spiritual journey but also spoke to the miles of travel and hardships endured by many in the crowd. Those songs reflected Mahalia's own journey from a shack by the riverside to the steps of the Lincoln Memorial.

In black-and-white news footage of Mahalia's 1963 performance, a sea of white shirts stretch from the Lincoln Memorial and around the reflecting pool on the National Mall.[27] Mahalia sings: "I been fallin' and risin' all these years. But you know my soul look back and wonder, how did I make it over." She begins clapping. "I had to cry in the midnight hour comin' over." Her wide shoulders and chest swell. "I rose this morning and I feel like shouting.—I feel like shouting.—I feel like shouting!"

Mahalia's journey to the March on Washington began on the banks of a river that historian Ari Kelman describes as "too dynamic, too dirty, too hard to appreciate, too commercial for too long . . . ," a river that by the 1920s "did not seem to have healing or spiritual qualities."[28] But to Mahalia and to a host of batture dwellers I would get to know, the river was a place with meaning that couldn't be quantified. Mahalia describes her own dream in a soft and thoughtful audio interview on the Smithsonian Folkways record label:

I used to dream I could live better. I used to find myself wandering down around on the other side of the levee near the Mississippi, picking up wood. And I'd find myself wandering out around this riverfront all the time because, I don't know, it seemed like I would be able to think. I've always been a child that thought way and beyond the future. . . . I didn't know what it would hold for me, but I would find that out on that Mississippi.[29]

The many journalists and biographers who described Mahalia's youth wanted to put her as close to the river as they could. One claims: "She started life six feet below sea level in New Orleans" and that her birthplace had once been a stilt house. A writer for *New Orleans* magazine asserted that she "grew up on the batture."[30] Still others claimed she was born between the railroad tracks and the levee.[31] None of these accounts are borne out by the simple, reliable photograph taken by her friend William Russell.

The legends surrounding Mahalia's birth on the Mississippi, however, serve a particular truth. Mahalia was "reborn" in the river, and the Mississippi remained a touchstone throughout her life. In 1971, a year before her death, she performed at the emperor's palace in Japan. Shortly after the show, Mahalia volunteered how she pulled herself together in the royal presence:

After I began to sing, I said to myself, lord, lord, get your glory . . . And my mind drifted off back down to Louisiana . . . I forgot the people was there for a moment. And I saw myself as a child, coming down the tracks with a sack, picking coal, from Greenville up to where I stayed. And I saw myself out on the Mississippi River bringing in wood that was drifting down the stream and putting it on the banks and letting it dry . . . and then later on, bringing it home and putting it in the bin. Then I saw myself setting on the levee . . . a big bunch of us around the fire . . . look like some was eating sugar cane and some was baking sweet potatoes, and we was singing, and the train was passing. Oh, we were having a glorious time. And then I came out of that and realized . . . I was in the palace of the king, and emperor of Japan.[32]

Mahalia died in Chicago on January 27, 1972. After a memorial service in the Windy City, she returned by air to New Orleans where, over the course of a day and a night, 60,000 visitors lined up in a cold wind outside the Rivergate Auditorium for a chance to pay respects. The next morning a slow procession of twenty-four limousines carried Mahalia uptown to the Black Pearl section of Carrollton Bend.[33] Black families from the neighborhood, including a few who still occupied a dozen dilapidated batture shacks, lined the toe of the levee along the railroad tracks. One last time, the Queen of Gospel passed by Mount Moriah Church and the river that had been her muse.

Chapter 10

Floods

In the late winter of 1922, Seymour Geisenheimer watched the river surge high beneath his stilt house at the Jefferson Parish line and anticipated a bountiful spring harvest. He had abandoned trapping songbirds after Congress passed legislation in 1916 and 1918 forbidding the practice. Instead, he made enough money for sundries and food by fishing for shrimp and collecting and cording driftwood for sale. A rapidly rising river is the best time to harvest drift from the stream.

Levee officials and city engineers noted the swelling river and kept a wary eye on endless rain upstream, but on March 3, they pronounced levees around the city to be "in fine shape."[1] For Geisenheimer, who had seen a dozen high water events and two record floods in his thirty-five years on the batture, the high water would be a wood gatherer's bonanza if he could keep his neatly corded lengths above the rising river.

I found no reports of other stilt houses in the heart of Carrollton Bend between the levee heightening that began in 1910 and the spring rise of 1922. As the surging river floated shantyboats on the batture in March 1922, Brother Isaiah was on trial in Los Angeles. Mahalia Jackson and her friends would have watched the rising water with excitement from atop the levee. In early April, levee authorities posted guards and placed sandbags on low spots. Finally, on April 25, the river reached an unprecedented height of 21.27 feet in New Orleans—high enough to put a foot of water above the kitchen floor of my present batture home. That record has never been surpassed.

The river would have gone higher, but on Thursday, April 27 at 3 a.m., a levee collapsed at the small town of Poydras, twelve miles downstream. Tugboat captains saw 200 feet of levee slide into the Mississippi and sounded their whistles to alert slumbering residents. Seven hours later the crevasse had widened to 400 feet, and in the afternoon, water was halfway up the windows of houses near the river.

As water poured through the Poydras Crevasse, flooding the homes of thousands of wetlands residents in St. Bernard Parish, the level fell in New Orleans, dropping two-tenths of a foot in twenty-four hours. While engineers and work crews struggled to close the levee, civic leaders in New Orleans and Jefferson noted the efficiency with which a levee break elsewhere could lessen the threat to the city.

Spring turned to summer and the river fell rapidly. One morning in July when the threat of flood seemed long past, a wide semi-circle of the Southport batture collapsed into the river. Engineers from the Orleans and Pontchartrain Levee Districts determined that a hundred-foot-deep bite of batture had disappeared into the current, undercut by the powerful flood of the previous spring. Seventy-five feet of shore remained. A second similar event would undermine the levee by twenty-five feet and could cause a major crevasse.

Government officials from New Orleans and Jefferson, two levee boards, and the Safe River Committee argued over the necessity of setting back the levee and who should pay for it.[2] Although the Southport batture cave was on the Jefferson Parish end of Carrollton Bend, it was more of a threat to New Orleans. A crevasse in Jefferson seventy-three years earlier had brought floodwater up to the edge of the French Quarter, and it had taken months to drain the floundering city. The recent levee failure at Poydras was fresh in everyone's minds.

As a result of political bickering and the need to reroute roads, the levee setback in Southport wasn't completed for three years. Levee maps from the time show the biggest levee retreat occurred about fifty yards above the parish line.[3] The project maps don't show any batture structures on my side of the parish line, and it is unlikely anyone would have built a home there until after the work was finished.

Some of the delay in getting action from authorities at Southport was probably a result of the political sway of the entrenched and well-connected illegal casinos that dominated the neighborhood just inside the levee.[4] While riverside businesses made their fortunes by transporting raw materials extracted from America's heartland and the jungles of the Caribbean, casino operators were amassing a fortune by extracting cash directly from patrons' pockets. O'Dwyer's Southport Club rested right at the base of a levee that would have to be moved.

Southport was a gambling mecca long before Las Vegas's glitter gulch bloomed in the desert. In the 1890s, wagering on cock fights and dog fights had been popular in the rough-and-tumble bars of the "Free State of Jefferson." By the early 1900s, the Hyland family ran a horse racing track and operated an eponymous gambling club facing the levee. Another local family opened Palmisano's game room nearby.

Gambling in suburban parishes enjoyed a blind eye from law enforcement, whose leaders could claim a cut of the illegal profits. Jefferson Parish Sheriff Louis Herman Marrero was the leader of the Old Regular political machine in Jefferson and enjoyed extensive power and patronage. From 1896 to 1920, under Marrero's un-watchful eye, gambling exploded along the New Orleans line and across the river in Gretna, in the neighborhood surrounding the Jefferson Courthouse.[5] An industry was born whose legacy would haunt those of us living on the Southport batture into the twenty-first century.

On Sunday afternoons after Marrero took office, a Southport Cockpit a block from the levee attracted competitors nationwide and featured fights with purses of $10,000 and more.[6] Nearby gaming houses attracted hundreds of customers nightly. Sheriff's deputies reportedly patronized and worked security details at the gambling dens.[7]

Sheriff Marrero had no reason to fear for his office. His son, L. H. Marrero Jr., was district attorney, and the police jury and grand jury were staffed with insiders and allies. One juror, Edward O'Dwyer, sat on the Jefferson Parish Democratic Committee and reportedly ran a keno parlor near the courthouse.[8] O'Dwyer's children, Rudolph and George, apprenticed at Hyland's Club. Emile Geisenheimer, brother of the birdman of the batture, lived next door to O'Dwyer in Southport. Emile sat on the grand jury, the school board, and the Pontchartrain Levee Board. Geisenheimer also operated a ferry that delivered gamblers directly to the doors of casino operators.[9]

In 1920, "good government" candidates defeated the Old Regulars in New Orleans and Jefferson. These inept newcomers made little effort or progress in curbing entrenched graft. The Old Regulars resumed control in Jefferson in 1928, and an even more powerful head cop, Sheriff Frank "King" Clancy, would serve in Jefferson for nearly thirty years while organized crime infiltrated the Southport casinos.

From the O'Dwyer and Geisenheimer interests at Southport to William Bisso's dock beside Audubon Park, the industries and families who would shape the fate of the sprawling Carrollton Bend batture settlement were all in place as the flood of 1922 subsided. In the middle of the mile-and-a-half-long bend, the imposing compound of the US Army Corps of Engineers gazed down on an empty batture that would soon be home to a vibrant river village.

No announcement in the newspaper proclaimed a new batture development in Carrollton. There was no advertisement of "Free Lots with Fresh Air and River Views." But the levee builders of 1910, abetted by the record flood of 1922, had created a perfect palette for settlement—a sturdy levee and vacant batture. Even better for homesteaders, the Carrollton batture had an unobservant, institutional landlord. The Orleans Levee Board had purchased the mile of riverfront between Bisso and Southport before the levee heightening of 1910.

When the water receded in 1922, Adam Rowbatham pulled a shabby one-room houseboat onto the batture at Carrollton and St. Charles Avenues. The sheet metal mechanic was looking for a new start after losing his job at the Standard Oil Company in Baton Rouge. He raised his boat on stilts and moved his wife and two children from a cramped apartment onto the river. Adam rigged a jigsaw out of a discarded sewing machine, then built a skiff with the jigsaw. He earned a living rowing workers and supplies from the Carrollton Wharf to a derelict World War I fleet moored across the river.

Rowbatham's home became Camp #1. Bernadotte Rowbatham, who was pregnant, stayed home, spruced up the ramshackle stilt house, and cared for three-year-old Henry and five-year-old Doris. Doris spent hours paddling around the camp in a "canoe" that her father made by cutting a barrel in half and covering it with painted cloth. The Rowbatham kids loved the batture and were thrilled when the Evans family pulled up a houseboat next door. Jimmy Evans was a lifelong river rat and a deep-water diver. He kept his diving gear ready in the doorway of an immaculate floating home and delighted the batture children by accumulating a personal zoo of caged chickens, rabbits, guinea pigs, parrots, a possum, and an alligator on his deck.

Shortly after the Evans family arrived, George Gebhardt built a camp upriver beside his old friend, Seymour Geisenheimer, with whom he had trapped birds as a child. Gebhardt was a master carpenter, but after falling five stories on a construction site, he retreated to the batture.[10]

Adam Rowbatham with children, Lillian and Harold. Originally published in Kent and Margaret
Lighty, Shanty-boat (New York: Century [now Hawthorne Publishing], 1930).

Between those first homesteaders, a retired mariner constructed an eight-foot-by-five-foot tin shack. A fisherman named Uncle Will moved in and set his lines, and in June 1925, a groom carried his bride down the levee and over a plank onto their floating first home.

Itinerant folks in tents and boats came and went, but the settlement became a community, a place where people moved for personal reasons. Many stayed through three decades of shared challenges. On May 5, 1925, a New Orleans *Item-Tribune* writer christened the settlement "River Village," a "humble little suburb" where a "kindly, helpful group of struggling folk live 'twixt water and shore at the edge of New Orleans."

New Orleans roared into the 1920s and River Village grew in plain sight on one of the city's busiest shores, a place temporarily denuded of trees by recent levee work. It would be thirteen years before a bridge would span the river two miles above the village, but a confluence of ferries, roads, and rails made Carrollton Bend New Orleans' gateway to the west. Bisso's Walnut Street Ferry crossed to the industrial suburb of Westwego and

Emile Geisenheimer's ferry connected Southport to all points west via the Old Spanish Trail. As automobile traffic and suburban development grew, these connections brought countless commuters and long-distance travelers past the settlement.

Card rooms and casinos were open all night and a wild-west aura pervaded Southport, Westwego, and the downriver suburb of Arabi. Depending on political winds, and whose payments were current, officials staged raids at the gambling houses. Somehow, they always managed to reopen. On the lakefront and in the red-light districts of the city, jazz clubs and brothels entertained patrons, and with the advent of Prohibition, New Orleans became the "wettest city in the country."[11] Ferry landings bustled with legal and illicit traffic, hauling workers and goods between the east and west banks of the river.

A few people got very rich. William Bisso Sr. recaptured some of the wages paid to his dockworkers by operating a "beer parlor" just over the levee from the family wharf. He had taken to wearing a diamond horseshoe in his necktie and built a second home on his private batture.[12] According to testimony in his 1924 tax fraud trial, Bisso owed $1.5 million in back taxes and was spending up to $80,000 annually at the racetrack.[13] The owner of the Mengel Mahogany Mill, which at the time covered most of Brother Isaiah's old shantyboat landing, built a palatial home on "Millionaires Row" in Louisville, Kentucky.

In Southport, the property transactions of Emile Geisenheimer were noted on the front of the newspaper's real estate sections. The sons of Edward O'Dwyer, who had apprenticed at Hyland's Game Room, took over the casino and renamed it the Southport Club. They hired sheriff's deputies to watch their door and paid drivers to pick up folks at streetcar stops and hotels and deliver them to their lair.[14]

Nationwide, stock market averages, income, and consumer buying soared. By mid-decade, the "average American" could afford a Model T automobile, but the law of averages hid another truth. While incomes among factory workers rose 9 percent, income of the top 1 percent of earners nearly doubled. Presidents Coolidge and Hoover declared an era of "Republican prosperity," but those were empty words for the women in Mahalia Jackson's family, some of whom labored as domestics in the homes of wealthy white people and barely made enough to pay rent and buy groceries at the Bisso store.

The lakefront community of Milneburg would be razed. Photo courtesy of the Frank B. Moore
Collection, Earl K. Long Library, University of New Orleans.

While real estate speculators like Emile sold land in the suburbs, authorities in New Orleans turned their eyes toward the lakefront. In 1921
the Louisiana legislature passed an act empowering the Orleans Levee
District to construct beaches, parks, an airport, and other improvements
on lands under its purview. The following year the board announced a plan
to reclaim 1,700 acres of marsh and open water along the city's lakefront
to create new neighborhoods and parks.[15] Their first step was to initiate
the eviction of thousands of "squatters," including the vibrant lakefront
community of Milneburg.

Since its founding in the eighteenth century, Milneburg had been a place
where trappers, fishermen, and bootleggers lived beside the gambling dens,
nightclubs, and weekend retreats of doctors, lawyers, and merchants. City
people rode to the lakefront on Smokey Mary, the oldest continuously
operating train in America. Hundreds of homes and small businesses as
well as schools and a church were slated for demolition.

The levee board litigated and negotiated with titled landholders on the
lakefront, but they dismissed the 1,600 occupants of Milneburg as "squatters"

The "reclaimed" lakefront. Only the yacht and rowing clubs remained. Photo courtesy of the Frank B. Moore Collection, Earl K. Long Library, University of New Orleans.

who "mar the landscape with their unsightly camps." Only the Southern Yacht Club and St. John Rowing Club were to be allowed to remain.[16]

The rout of "squatters" spread to other parts of the city. On Bayou St. John, a sluggish waterway which cut from the lake to the back of town, a flotilla of artists, bohemians, and poor people battled with wealthy neighbors on Esplanade Ridge. The taxpaying residents of the ridge convinced the city to pass ordinances pushing houseboat people further out the bayou toward the lakefront.[17] In 1925 a group of "400 business leaders" toured New Orleans' urban fringe by rail, traveling past Carrollton Bend, the Bisso wharf, and the leveeside birthplace of Mahalia Jackson. From clubcar windows they observed ". . . three ramshackle and improperly kept shacks for every good residence there is in the city."

The elite who ran the city and their allies in the press championed slum eradication to convert "substandard" housing on the urban outskirts into neighborhoods for a better class of citizenry. Their expressed desire was "to protect the slums against themselves" and enact laws "to make possible the keeping of a healthy and decent citizenship."[18] Developers bought raw land from speculators like Emile Geisenheimer and lured the "right kind" of homebuyers to new suburbs in Jefferson, Old Metairie, and Gentilly. Their real estate ads assured: "We do not sell to any other than a desirable white person. We do not permit the erection of shacks, or sheds on any lot, for dwelling purposes—but make the restriction that—No Residence Can Be Built on This Property For Less Than $4000."[19]

People living outside the mainstream of city life, whether subsisting on canal banks, city dumps, or on the ephemeral river batture were caught in a pincer. While developers worked with city boards to enclose, drain, fill, and sell land that had been previously neglected, city officials and the press engaged in a campaign of disparagement and harassment. Police arrested folks living in informal settlements for gambling, intoxication, dangerous and suspicious behavior, and bootlegging, even as speakeasies and illegal gambling houses in their districts flourished. A representative of the Society for the Protection of Children reported a "difficult" batture case to the State Conference of Social Betterment. She explained, "the mother belonged to the shantyboat community, and . . . her idea of morality was not that of the ordinary city dweller."[20]

Neighborhoods for whites grew in drained backwaters. The lakefront was mostly cleared, and in 1926, the levee board began pumping the first 36 million cubic yards of lake-bottom muck to create an expanded shoreline. They promised neighborhoods of fine homes and parks to rival Chicago's famed waterfront. The power of engineers, planners, and capitalists to command the landscape seemed ascendant until 1927.

During the winter of 1926–27, heavy rains saturated the Mississippi River Valley. By March 1927 levees failed upstream, and by late May the Mississippi coursed through a dozen or more major crevasses. Convicts, plantation workers and thousands of Corps flood fighters struggled to contain the raging water.

The Great Flood covered 27,000 square miles of the nation's heartland, left 627,000 people homeless, and remains one of the nation's worst natural disasters. The story of the catastrophe is one of greed and hubris, race and class, faulty engineering and governmental failure, and immense human suffering and loss. The brief account here is inspired by *Rising Tide*, Jonathan Barry's remarkable history of the flood.[21]

The rains of 1926 and 1927 fell on a landscape where private companies and agribusiness had converted huge prairies to farmland and had clear-cut forests throughout the river watershed. River engineers exacerbated flooding by adopting a levees-only policy. Their strategy was to contain excess water within the riverbanks, and to build a wall of continuous and higher levees. Proponents of levees-only believed that the outflow, increased by closing off distributaries, would scour a commensurately deeper channel. They got it catastrophically wrong.

The flood of 1927 was a clear case of engineers unable to reclaim something they never had control of in the first place. The Great Flood showed what natural reclamation looks like, as the river renewed a millennia-old habit of spilling floodwater over its banks and into its valley. The energy of water stored within the wall of manmade levees exploded with disastrous effect.

Because of numerous levee failures elsewhere, and a cynical decision to dynamite a levee downstream at Poydras—where a natural crevasse had saved New Orleans five years earlier—the river crested in the city a foot lower than the record set in 1922. Thousands of fishermen and trappers living in wetlands downstream were, however, less fortunate. Flood historian Jonathan Barry describes the decision to dynamite the levee as a "dollars and cents" calculation by the same city power brokers who had been displacing poor people for decades:

> New Orleans was run entirely by bankers who did not even bother to consult local officials; they simply decided they were going to dynamite the levee to reassure the correspondent banks in New York, London and Boston that they would never allow the Mississippi to threaten the city.[22]

Like the record flood in 1922, the Great Flood washed out itinerant batture folks in Carrollton Bend, but Adam and Bernadotte Rowbatham, George Gebhardt, and the old fisherman Uncle Will were among many who stayed put. Jimmy and Anna Evans loosened the mooring on their houseboat and let it float by the shore. Seymour Geisenheimer had been through worse; he wasn't going anywhere.

With over 1 percent of the nation's population displaced, a raft of flood victims floated downstream in shantyboats and landed on the batture in St. Louis, Vicksburg, Baton Rouge, Donaldsonville, and dozens of smaller towns in the Atchafalaya Basin. The 1930 US Census reflects this influx

A raft of flood victims floated downstream. Photo courtesy of Center for Louisiana Studies, Lafayette. Public domain.

on the Carrollton Bend, where transplants from upriver states like Ohio, Indiana, Kentucky, and Missouri outnumbered earlier residents whose parents had immigrated from Europe.

For people who didn't live in the flood-stricken river valleys, attention quickly turned from the disaster in the heartland to a frenzy of speculation. In the autumn of 1928, Wall Street stock market averages smashed all previous records. Even on the normally arid high plains of Texas and Oklahoma and across the Midwest, a wave of homesteaders got easy credit, bought equipment, reclaimed hundreds of square miles of tall prairie grass, and planted wheat.

A year later, the stock market crash that ushered in the Great Depression dominated the news. By 1930 the western prairie reclamation fueled by greed, cheap land, easy credit and fortuitous rainfall was buried in dust.

The resounding economic crash of 1929 and 1930 and the Dust Bowl created not a ripple in the shantyboat colonies and batture settlements along the Mississippi. Folks in River Village hadn't moved there for profit, hadn't been living on easy credit, and didn't own cars or even radios. Their lives still more closely resembled those of nineteenth-century river folk than their urban contemporaries.

A local newspaper pointed out that the "Orleans Colony pays no rent or taxes, no fuel or light bills either."[23] Of course, they paid no bills because they had no utilities. They were free of burdensome rent because they dwelled in self-built homes on the city's most vulnerable fringe.

Although homesteaders on the batture hadn't amassed fortunes, between the floods the folks in River Village had grown roots and branches. George Gebhardt took in Dixie Trueblood, a high-spirited Native American woman from Missouri who had developed a rap sheet for gambling and prohibition offenses. The Rowbathams added four rooms to the family shantyboat. Their two-year-old daughter pestered her mother to take her next door to visit the Evans family and their homemade zoo.

Jimmy and Anna Evans waited out the flood to raise their boat onto pilings. Their two tykes scrambled over their father's diving gear and played at the water edge. Anna pronounced the batture "a fine place to bring up children," and proudly noted that three-year-old Arthur and four-year old JJ were already swimming, having proven themselves in falls from the deck of the pitching houseboat during the flood of 1927.[24]

I had never considered how the river and its floods connected my batture with people and places far upriver until the river rose around my shack in 1991. A four-by-four-inch weathered wooden block bobbed past my shack and caught against a willow tree. It was about sixteen inches long with an eyehook affixed to a tapered end. I paddled out and plucked it from the current. Nailed to the side, a stamped metal tag read KANSAS FISH AND GAME COMMISSION. Floodwaters had snatched the buoy from a fisherman's trap on the Missouri River and carried it over a thousand miles downstream to my batture.

The float was a message in a bottle, a connection to neighbors far upstream, an invitation to seek its origin and trace its path. I called an old college buddy and we began to plan. David is a moviemaker and, more important, a skilled canoeist. Two other friends, Mike and Steve, had won a grant from the National Science Foundation to paddle the entire river and take water samples. We would start at the Mississippi's headwaters in Northern Minnesota and travel in tandem. I wanted nothing more than to meet my upstream "neighbors."

It was raining in mid-June as Dave and I drove out to pick up our expedition canoe in Winona, Minnesota. It was still raining on June 23 when a friend dropped us off at Lake Itasca, the "true head" of the Mississippi. It continued to rain for four cold days as we paddled through spruce forests, tamarack bogs, and glacial wetlands above the twin cities of Minneapolis and St. Paul. Like my first river, the Rappahannock, there were places where people had camps scattered along the shore, but no one else was afloat. Even hardy northerners knew this was no time to be on the water.

When we arrived at the town of Bemidji, mid-morning on June 27, our gear, food, and firewood were soaked. The northernmost city on the Mississippi is stranded between the small Lake Irving and ten-mile-long Lake Bemidji. It is at the convergence of three native Indian nations and proudly calls itself "Home of Paul Bunyan and Babe the Blue Ox." Bemidji is often identified on national weather reports as the coldest city in the lower forty-eight states.

We surveyed the wide gray lake before us, tied up, and walked across an empty street into a cafe on the shore. Dave and I agreed we did not want to spend a night there. We flipped a coin whether to paddle twenty miles along the shallow shoreline or dart directly across its ten-mile channel. The short route won, but we decided to hurry. We downed our coffee and ate a wretched midwestern version of a pot pie, known as a "pastie."

Mike and Steve hustled into the cafe just as we were leaving. We agreed to meet them on the far shore and headed out. The clock on the Bank of Bemidji read 1:30 and the temperature was forty-seven degrees. The sky was slate, rimmed in black.

By the time we reached mid-lake the water stood up in two-foot tall whitecaps and the black rim of clouds was a fortress of storm before us. We couldn't see our friends behind us but hoped they hadn't left Bemidji in their donated whitewater canoe. Their craft had a low curved bow made for deflecting rocks, not cutting through waves. It had no flotation.

Our canoe was made for wide, "flat" water and bad weather, but waves still cascaded over the bow. I sunk to my knees. Dave merely laughed and began to chant, "Paddle like hell . . . paddle like hell . . . paddle like hell." We did. We kept paddling and didn't slow down until the tops of wild rice appeared above the waves.

From the deck of a dam on the eastern shore, David fitted a telephoto lens onto his camera and scanned the horizon. We spotted Steve and Mike's canoe mid-lake, sunk gunnel-deep in the frigid water. Waves broke over the blue tarp that covered their scientific gear and guitar. Our friends clung to the outside of the canoe—their heads bobbed in the frigid water. In the distance a lone motorboat churned to the rescue.

A rainy week later, on July 10, we pulled ashore in Minneapolis. The same friend who dropped us off at the headwaters offered us showers, laundry service, and a chance to forget the weather. We found Mike and Steve, who had hitched a ride around lake country, in a bar, watching baseball on TV. Unsettling news crawled along the screen. A flood was gathering around us. The Corps had closed the river between Minneapolis and St. Louis.

David was sure that "closed to all navigation" couldn't possibly include hapless travelers in canoes. The weather had beaten us up in the headwaters and we reasoned that better days, maybe even some sunny days, lay ahead. No one in our two-team expedition was ready to quit. We had no idea what this flood would become.

The flood drowned our dreams of leisurely conversations with river folks. It submerged the islands we hoped to camp on and the rain never stopped. Our two canoes, separated by about twenty miles, rode a river jammed with floating school buses, refrigerators, and uprooted trees. All twenty-nine locks and dams were thrown open. Bridges closed. Idled barges plunged through levee breaks and into farm fields. Sewage and water plants went under, chemicals spilled, and oil tanks erupted in flames. Convicts, volunteers and National Guard troops worked shoulder-to-shoulder sandbagging levees.

The river was a lonely place, as empty of traffic as it had been in a hundred years. Three days below the Twin Cities, a crewman on an idled tugboat hollered out, "You better get off the river, there's a Coast Guard boat five minutes in front of you. They picked up a couple guys in a canoe this morning." Authorities, who feared that saboteurs would dynamite or damage a levee upstream to save property below, had forced Mike and Steve from the river. Our friends parked their canoe, got tetanus shots, and helped sandbag the levees.

David and I never got a chance to join people reinforcing the levees. We clung to the channel and paddled into the evening to avoid detection. On July 23, above Quincy, Illinois, a sound emerged over the pounding rain—it grew to a roar from the left bank. David buried his paddle in the current and I bow-ruddered hard to the right. Around a bend, an avalanche of river poured through a gash in the levee. We passed the crevasse, the rain stopped, and for a moment we rested in midstream. Then, a Coast

An avalanche of river pours through the levee. Photo courtesy of David Ellsworth.

Guard helicopter swept in and spoiled our quiet float. The chopper hovered overhead, broadcasting a warning, "Get off the river now." We flipped the bird, but our nerves were frayed.

There was no place to get off the river if we wanted to. There was no land in sight. The Mississippi was a moving lake, nine miles across. As night fell, we entered a line of flooded treetops, found a lone roof above the water, and tied to a gutter. We didn't know if there were bodies in the house, or flooded cars below. We pitched our tent at an angle. Dave smoked a cigarillo to keep the mosquitos out while I studied the treeline and wondered if the house itself would float downstream.

The following day, July 24, we arrived outside Hannibal, Missouri, our mid-journey mail drop. The river had risen to the level of the railroad bridge. A mass of trees, vehicles, and debris stretched across the river—smashed against the span—no paddling under that one. We checked into a motel and enjoyed bathing in something other than cold river water. We washed laundry and walked over to the post office where we found packages of cookies and worried letters sent from home. Then David and I climbed 244 steps from Main Street to the Mark Twain Memorial bluff. The fifty-mile-long Sny Levee across the river had failed that morning, and we watched the water spread over miles and miles of rich farmland.

The flood of 1993 was the biggest flood ever to strike the Upper Mississippi. Cities and farms had grown in that heartland since the Great Flood of 1927 on soil enriched by millennia of river inundation. Residents felt protected by their higher levees and dams. In 1993, however, those dams were thrown open, levees broken. When the river went down, the levees had to be cut to allow fields to drain. At St. Louis, Missouri, near where my "Kansas Department of Fisheries" float had entered the Mississippi, the river crested at forty-nine feet, a full twenty feet above flood stage.

Dave and I never met the fisherman who lost his buoy. Mike and Steve lost their water-testing gear that first week on Lake Bemidji. But the flood of '93 swept the four of us, along with a load of sediment, flotsam, and stories, downstream without injury. On the lower river, the channel became deep and easily absorbed the floodwaters of the Midwest. The southern sun beat down, and below Baton Rouge we joined tankers and container ships heading toward the Gulf of Mexico. Like generations of river rats, and refugees from earlier floods, we pulled up in Carrollton Bend. I was glad to be home.

The Other Side of the Other Side of the Tracks

I t was easy to find the stories of outsiders and displaced people living on New Orleans fringe—they lurked behind every account of the expanding and prosperous city. But those narratives were mostly written by crime reporters or starry-eyed travel journalists. I felt like I had read a book and learned little about the characters.

A newspaper story published in the depths of the Great Depression finally brought me face to face with my predecessors on the batture. The *Times-Picayune* reported on May 27, 1935, that a strong current had swept a rowboat with four female passengers under the long sloping bow of a barge moored in Carrollton Bend. Louis Dumser, a fisherman in a nearby skiff, with two friends, Garfield Beattie and Adam Rowbatham, sprang to the rescue. The three batture folk "improvised a sling with a life preserver and a rope" and hoisted the ladies to the deck of the barge.

When I found that story about batture bravery, I realized that the rescuers, people who once lived in my bend of the river, might still be alive. I opened the 1998 Bell South phonebook and found Garfield Beattie—five blocks from the river, less than a mile from my camp. I picked up the receiver on my old black rotary phone, dialed the number and got a crisp, "*Garfield Beattie.*" Just a name, but at last a connection.

Two days later, a handsome eighty-six-year-old with close cut hair the color of galvanized steel strode down the catwalk to my camp. He wrung my hand and looked straight into my eyes. As he began to speak, Garfield's voice crackled as if it were coming out of an old vacuum tube radio.

I was hooked. Just as the river pulled me to its shore, I was now gripped by its voices. After I met Garfield, I sat down at the Formica table in my kitchen with a list of names gleaned from newspapers, a fat telephone directory, and the old phone. For three years at the end of the twentieth century, I collected dozens of interviews from people who hadn't even earned a footnote in the histories and geographies of New Orleans. They were people who occupied my shore between 1927 and 1954, people who dropped houses on themselves, who fished in the river, and salvaged from the river. Their stories overlapped with each other's and with mine.

Garfield Beattie's father, Bert, was a boilermaker, but in 1916 a stroke left him paralyzed in his left arm and jobless. In 1921, when Garfield was seven years old and his sister Libby only five, Bert and Ida moved the family from the leafy suburb of Carrollton to a cheap rooming house owned by a friend, Alfred Stenson.

The place was on Poydras, between Baronne and Dryades. My mother paid twenty dollars for three rooms and worked in the flophouse. She cleaned up anything you can think about, where the rooms had twenty men in twenty beds at twenty-five cents a night. Mr. Stenson paid her a dollar a day and my father got a job as a watchman for the public market merchants in the neutral ground.

Like thousands of other children in New Orleans during the "Age of Prosperity," Garfield never finished grammar school, but found work to support himself, his sister and struggling parents.

I had my first job with Orkin Pest Control when I was ten. At twelve I carried bananas on the Thalia Street Wharf. The United Fruit Company would bring in ships from Latin America and they didn't all have refrigerators. Sometimes you just peeled bananas to eat them right there. I carried bananas for a year and that's where I learned to play dice. Instead of going to school I was playing dice on the wharf. I shipped out as a deckboy at thirteen and had my fourteenth birthday aboard a ship. I knew my mother had to have money, so when I signed onboard the ship, I left her my twenty-dollar allotment and got five dollars when I got over to Europe. I washed clothes onboard for the men. I charged ten cents for a pair of pants and a nickel a shirt and had all the money I needed. I played dice and must have been lucky 'cause I came out on top all the time.

Shortly after Garfield shipped out in 1926, Mr. Stenson sold the flophouse and invited the Beatties to move with him to Carrollton Bend. They

At age twelve Garfield found work on the banana wharf. Photo courtesy of the Frank B. Moore Collection, Earl K. Long Library, University of New Orleans.

left their squalid rooms for the batture the same year Mahalia Jackson left the city for a better life in Chicago. When the flood of 1927 receded, they used the money Garfield gave them to add a room to their stilt house.

Fourteen-year-old Garfield Beattie returned from the sea in the late fall of 1928. He hoisted his duffle bag and disembarked from the ship at the Poydras wharf.

I had been gone a year. I came in on the ship and worked until five o'clock. It was getting dark by the time I got off the ship at Poydras and caught the streetcar. Here I was coming home to a place I had never been . . .

Garfield hopped off the streetcar at Carrollton Avenue and walked up onto the levee in darkness, just as my old friend Rob and I had done the night I discovered the batture settlement back in 1986. Immediately below him lay the camps of the Rowbatham and Evans families. He traversed the grassy levee crown, walking upstream, and counted the hodgepodge of camps and boats along the river until he found the catwalk leading to #4. Garfield walked down the narrow ramp to his parents' stilt house.

Garfield Beattie's seaman license photo, age fifteen. Photo courtesy of National Archives and Records Administration; *Application for Seaman's Protection Certificates.* Public record/public domain.

The Beatties' home had fewer amenities then Garfield enjoyed in his cramped cabin at sea. He watched fishermen, firewood merchants, and laborers pulling oars on the muddy river and decided he wasn't ready to put down roots on the batture. At age fifteen he already knew he could make money at sea. After a few months at home, Garfield persuaded his father to sign papers for his seaman's license, falsely declaring him to be eighteen years old. He caught the next ship out, working below decks as a "wiper," just as the so-called "Age of Prosperity" was about to crash.

Garfield returned in the fall of 1932 to a batture filling up with hard-pressed city folks. He found employment on one of New Orleans' great public works projects. Construction had just begun on the first bridge over the Mississippi River below Vicksburg, two miles upriver from his parent's camp in Carrollton Bend. He may have seen William Bisso Sr., the boss of the local political machine, to get the job. Mayor Walmsley assigned Bisso the task of creating a list of applicants for federal work projects and extracting patronage from them.[1]

I was seventeen years old and living with my parents on the river when I went to work on the Huey P. Long Bridge. I worked thirty hours a week, three ten-hour days. We were building mats of willow trees, working in the water off barges. We laced the willows together and tied them in a mat which we sunk along the bank with rick rack, cement stones. This gave stability in building the bridge.

The Huey P. Long Bridge revolutionized travel in the state, but Garfield's crew employed a nineteenth-century technology to solve a big problem. When test pipes were bored for five of the bridge piers, the current had immediately eroded a deep scour behind them. Garfield worked with a crew building and laying 250-by-400-foot willow mattresses around the site of each pier.

I started out and worked three days in the water pulling cables, wrapping them around, and securing four-inch or five-inch willows to make the mat. You would reach down and wrap this heavy wire and pull it with a block and tackle, and then nail it so it would stay. I was wrapping the rope around my arm and pulling, and somebody else would hammer a nail and bend it over. That evening when we knocked off, I had already pulled all the skin off my hands. When we came in somebody said, "The boss wants to see you." I thought, "Here I am and by God I pulled the skin off my hands and I'll be fired 'cause the last hour I couldn't hold the rope." The boss asked my name and said, "You had a rough time, but it'll get better. You're a foreman now. Instead of making thirty-five cents an hour you're making forty-five cents. Instead of working three ten-hour days you're working seven ten-hour days. The first day you stay home you're fired." I said, "Thank you, mister," and walked off.

It was hard to keep Garfield's mind between the levees when he was talking about work; before I could stop him, he pushed back his chair, looked me in the eye and resumed.

It took most of a year and when the job was done, I found work with the phone company. I went in as a temporary employee doing anything that had to be done and became a lineman. I worked thirteen years before I had my first absentee day and I was always on time.

Up until this point, there was little to distinguish twenty-year-old Garfield's life from those of ambitious young men living in poverty around the city—except perhaps his years as a child mariner and a love affair with dice. He was no shantyboater, fisherman, or drift collector. He showed little affinity for the muddy river. Garfield's river bounty was a freedom of self-determination during an era of grinding poverty. In 1934, when homeless encampments were growing around the country, Garfield erected a batture home for himself and his fiancée, Dorothy Trapagnier.

The second time I met Garfield was at the small brick house he rented not far from me in Old Jefferson. I hoped he would explain how he met Dorothy and brought her to the river, but he had a different story to tell. Garfield folded into a straight back chair at the dining room table and leaned forward.

Dorothy and I needed to find a place of our own, and about thirty feet upriver from my parents, Robert Campbell had a refurbished barge. Mr. Campbell was a watchman for the Marine Department fleet across the river on Nine Mile Point, and he was getting too old to be crossing the river at night. He sold me the barge for $300. The bottom of the barge was the floor. I knew that if the river came up, it would have water on it, so I decided to jack the thing up to get it where it was level with the levee. I was working for the telephone company and my foreman gave me poles for stilts. I had one automobile jack and found railroad ties by the tracks to hold the barge up as I raised it.

From my own experience raising a camp, I had a bad feeling about where this "jacking up" story was heading, but Garfield had a head of steam and his brown eyes radiated pride as he described in detail how the place that he and Dorothy would call home grew legs.

The barge was forty-two feet long and the sides were four-inch by twelve-inch cypress boards, stacked six high. My father suggested using side timbers as cross pieces to hold up the barge once it was raised. I would go to work each morning and my father, who was paralyzed on one side, would saw a twenty-foot board down the center the long way. One day he cut two of them. I jacked a corner up, put a railroad tie under, then went around to the next corner. I was doing that when all of a sudden it fell and landed on the cross ties underneath. I said, "That's it, we're gonna' start tying it down." I borrowed a block and tackle from the telephone company and pulled the telephone poles over the levee. I had worked at Orkin and knew about termites, so I put a four- or five-gallon can of old motor oil in the holes first. I got the center pole at a slant, bear-hugged the thing, and dropped it in. The others went in easier. This was at five a.m. before I went to work, and I had my khaki work clothes on. I ruined them. There was a shower of oil down the line as we dropped the pilings into those oil-filled holes.

There was nothing my wife and I didn't do. When we got utilities on the batture I did my own plumbing and my own electric work. I hated carpentry but I did what I had to and got a neighbor to do the doors, windows, and screen porch. I put on the new roof and my wife got up there with tarpaper just like a man would. She hung monk's cloth between the kitchen and the bedroom to keep the heat and odors from coming in. We fixed the place up and put white asbestos shingles on the outside until it didn't have any more barge affect. When my wife saw it done, she was just ecstatic. She told me, "I didn't think you could ever do anything like this!"

Garfield sat back in his chair. His fists rested on the table before him. He spread his hands wide open with the palms up and gave a rare tight-lipped smile. I knew what Garfield felt at that moment. He hadn't taken to the river or the batture as a way of life, but on that shore, he had done something he needed to, something he never knew he could do. Dorothy and Garfield married in 1935. Her sixty-eight-year-old father moved with them into the house they built on the river.

Garfield's life remained anchored in the city, where he worked as a line-man installing telephone service and where his sister Libbie was a dancer at the Crescent Theater. Dorothy Beattie loved to go out and dance and she joined Libbie on late evenings out on the town. Garfield recalled that on Saturday afternoons his sister would bring her bohemian friends up to the river to slum.

In the beginning of the day I'd turn the ice cream tank. I had a swing under the house. Those entertainers and jazz musicians left their smoke and liquor and everything else in the French Quarter. I enjoyed seeing them out there with their feet in the sand and a bottle of beer from a tub of ice, watching the kids eat ice cream out of a cup.

Of his river neighbors, Garfield recalled: *It was a group of people, you might not even know the name of everyone . . . but it wouldn't surprise you at all that somebody knocked on the door and asked, "Hey, they tell me you've got some boards left over, you need them?" Another time it might be, "Hey, we had a nice catch of fish, can I clean you one?"*

Garfield's one close friend on the river was a fisherman, Louis Dumser. When the two batture dwellers had rescued occupants of a dinghy crashed beneath a barge in Carrollton Bend, the New Orleans *Item* honored twenty-eight-year-old Louis with the headline, "Hero of Waterfront Saves Woman for His Fifth Rescue."

Louis's father, Charles Dumser, had moved his family to the river in the 1920s, about the same time that the Beatties arrived. Charles was a machinist at Delgado Trade School and he constructed his home beside the ramshackle dwelling of Adam Rowbatham with a machinist's precision.

Garfield Beattie had double-dated with Louis Dumser and his sister Joy when he first came back from the sea. Louis's date was another batture girl, Georgie Benovich. Garfield remained friends with Louis but the relationship with Joy Dumser tanked one evening when the four young people walked from the Poplar Theater into the Double Dip Ice Cream Parlor and encountered Louis's and Joy's parents. Mr. Dumser loudly informed his daughter, "I don't want you associating with him—he's a river rat!" Sixty years later Garfield still seemed puzzled: *The only difference between her and me is that she was a female river rat and I was a male river rat!*

Garfield described his final years on the batture with detachment, as if he suspected all along that he would cross back over the levee to yet another life.

I enlisted in the army in April 1942, and they called me in November. Dorothy and I had been married eight years and she got pregnant before I left. I went overseas in 1943 and my son was eighteen months old before I saw him. I came back and lived on the river for three years, but I had a difference of opinion with Dorothy and moved off the levee. My son moved in with me in the city when he was six, about 1950. It was that week I heard the Army Engineers had orders that all the batture houses would be dismantled. It was just a new way of life. That was yesterday and it's gone, so you just stay with what you have.

I never saw Garfield after his last visit to the batture in 2000. Before he left, we walked down the levee and stopped at the point where he and Dorothy made their home. He turned his back on the unbroken wall of tallow and willow trees along the shore and looked out across the railroad tracks and over the city. Garfield said something that revealed more about his experience on the batture than anything he told me in our hours of conversation.

There was a saying about being "from the other side of the tracks." My father explained it to me. He said "Poor folks live on the other side of the tracks. But over here, we live on the other side of the other side of the tracks."

A new job, a hurricane, and a disastrous citywide flood intervened before I looked for Garfield again. I found an obituary for "Garfield Beattie, 'The Telephone Man.'" The death notice reported he had lived a hundred years. "He told anyone who would listen that he shipped out as a cabin boy when he was thirteen and had his fourteenth birthday at sea." One person signed the funeral home's online guestbook, an employee of Boomtown Casino. There was no mention of his life on the river.

Social workers who visited Carrollton Bend settlement in 1933 called it "Depressionville," and in 1937 the New Orleans City Guide described it as a "ramshackle shanty-town sometimes called 'Depression Colony.'"[2] Shanty-towns grew on urban fringes across the country during the Depression—on public lands and on disused industrial space. Some had self-appointed names like Hardlucksville and Depression Valley. They became known generically as "Hoovervilles," mocking the failed economic policies of President Herbert Hoover.

It would never have occurred to Garfield Beattie or the other river folk I met to call their batture homeplace any of those names. They found refuge and opportunity outside the levee, and some of them bonded with the river in a way that was impossible for people inside the levee to understand. Those residents became known among city folks and sometimes among themselves as "river rats."

Charles Dumser got it all wrong when he called Garfield Beattie a river rat. Garfield escaped poverty and built a home on the batture, but his life was never part of the river. The real river rats were Charles's own son Louis, and his very young sweetheart Georgie Dumser.

Louis Dumser was long deceased when I met Garfield for the last time in the late summer of 2000, but Garfield mused that his friend's widow, Georgie, might still be alive. Within weeks I had one of the great spirits of the batture at my doorstep. At age eighty-two, Georgie had been away from the place for nearly fifty years and she could barely control her excitement. *Oh my! Being here, I have the most beautiful memories. You best believe it.*

Georgie hung her giant handbag on my doorknob and set her copper-tinted Hollywood sunglasses on the Formica table. Her eyes were the color of the river in flood and sparkled like ripples in the sun as she described her family's circuitous route to Carrollton Bend and how she and Louis found a calling on the shore.

The family all lived in the city until our house burned down in the twenties, then I moved in with my grandmother and went to school. That's when my uncle talked my daddy into moving down to Venice. My uncle had a quick skiff they called the "Little Launch," which they took up to Bootheville, where they snarfed out a houseboat, I think for $250.

Georgie's father, George Benovich, and his brother-in-law beached their floating home near Venice, Louisiana, where the only southbound road ended in miles of swaying marsh grass. They may have worked as fishermen, as they told federal census takers. According to Georgie, they may have also hunted alligators. But before moving to the batture at the end of Prohibition, they also earned a living by transporting illegal booze, a common endeavor at that time for small boat operators of the Croatian, Cajun French, and Isleno communities in Louisiana's crow's-foot delta.[3]

Georgie didn't know the details of her father's enterprise but smiled and said, *My father and uncle hunted alligators until they got scarce, and then they took up rum-running.* She laughed and claimed that her father gave her some of the contraband to put on a bad poison sumac rash, but she drank it instead "and never got poison sumac again."

In the mid-twenties the Coast Guard sent high-speed patrol boats to intercept rum runners near the mouth of the river, and by the end of the decade most illicit shipments arrived further west through Bayou Lafourche and the Atchafalaya Basin. George Benovich abandoned Venice in 1931, tied the Little Launch to his shantyboat and pulled it a hundred miles upriver to Carrollton Bend. The middle of the bend, where the Evans, Dumser, and Beattie boats had been propped on stilts, was filling up and was considered the more high-tone section of the settlement. Benovich landed a short distance upriver. The men of the batture pulled the houseboat up a ramp and onto short pilings. Georgie and her mother moved in and their new home became Camp 19.

Unlike Garfield Beattie, who worked hard and grew up fast, Georgie's memories were of socializing with neighbors on the green levee that was her front yard. Here, she found love and enjoyed a river that provided food even when times were hard. If her father made money running illegal hooch, the profits didn't lift the family's lifestyle much.

I was twelve years old in 1931 when my mother and I moved to the river. The houseboat had a kitchen and a little room that was the toilet. It had

Camps in Carrollton Bend in 1930, from Jefferson Parish to Audubon Park.
Photo courtesy of US Army Corps of Engineers, New Orleans District.

*mantle beds, which you could fold up and put under the floor. There was
a deck all around and a hatch where you stored things. Kitchen, bathroom,
bunkroom. I wouldn't trade it for anything in the world. My father found work
as a contract painter. When he didn't have a job, he didn't have a job. When
we had to, we ate beans without seasoning. The* Willow *paddlewheeler used
to anchor at the government wharf, about two doors down from us. That's
the steamboat that used to fix lights on the river. Whenever the* Willow *was
there, we ate like kings. The cook would give us all the leftovers.*

    *I met my husband, Louis Dumser, on the river when I was fourteen; we
married when I was a little past seventeen, and in-between I am not talking!
The thing was, we were just friends. Him and my girlfriend and I used to sit
on the levee and smoke his pipe. It was the best pipe you ever tasted. I decided
he was the man for me, and when a woman gets her mind set, what chance
does a man have? After living with mom and dad, Louis and I moved into
Camp 2½. It was one room. My husband was 6' 7" and it was too short for
him to get into. So, we took a saw and cut the roof off and raised it. We lived
in that one-room camp for a year until my first child was born. All we had
was a bed, a cedarobe, and a little kitchen.*

Georgie described sawing the roof off her house as if it was as simple as opening a window. It was a classic batture solution, not unlike people drilling holes in the floor of flooded camps to let the water drain out, building a house on a tree stump for support, or jamming a carpenter's level under the sagging corner of a camp to shim it up. But reengineering a house and meeting her husband weren't the things Georgie wanted to talk about. She wouldn't leave that first day until she told me what was most important to her.

I was the fish lady . . .

When I met Louis, he was the fisherman. He'd carry fish on strings to sell around Carrollton for ten cents a bunch, fifteen cents a bunch, whatever. One day someone came up the levee and asked if I knew where the fisherman lived. I said "Sure, right here!" Then they said, "Well, we want some fish; when will he be home?" I didn't want to wait on Louis and lose a sale, so I rowed out to the live box, got the fish out, brought 'em back and sold them for ten cents a pound. They found out I was the fish lady, and people all around Carrollton came to buy fish from me. There was a screen door in the kitchen, and I kept three coffee cans over the door. I'd put the big bills in one can, little bills in another can, and in another I'd put the silver. When the money started to fall out, I'd buy something.

Georgie and Louis eventually saved enough to build a house in the suburbs, but for Georgie, life on the batture wasn't about the money that fell out of her tin cans. Her voice burbled like the current rushing through willows. She spoke of fishing with Louis in almost mystic terms.

We'd go out there and he would dip the bailing can. He'd taste the water and say, "time to use shrimp," "time to use potato," or "time to use dough balls." He could taste the water and tell you what kind of bait to use. And he knew. He was a fisherman from the word go. One time we put out some hoop nets. It must have been four or five in the morning; my husband shook me. He said, "I'm going out 'cause I had a dream—we had a thousand pounds of fish in the hoop nets." When he came back, he didn't stop at the live box. He rowed the skiff in to show me. There in the bottom was a snow-white catfish. His mouth was six inches wide and he was as long as this table.

Georgie left the river in 1948, the year that the Orleans Levee Board first publicly discussed plans for destroying the batture community. I asked her to tell me about how she left but she demurred and asked if she could come back with her son-in-law Dyton and talk about it next time.

Georgie and Louis bought a house in the suburbs. Photo courtesy of Louis Dumser III.

Dyton held Georgie's hand on that last visit. She wanted to tell this part, but after half a century away from the river, she still didn't want it to end the way it did.

Everybody got along. We was all poor. I mean people stood in soup lines. My mama stood in the soup line sometimes, and I never ate so many red beans. We needed every penny we got. Well, we didn't need it; we wanted every penny we got. I bought the property where I live in Metairie with cash. You know how I did it? I never paid a nickel rent.

We finally moved off the river in February 1948. There was one old—Can I say this?—bitch!—at McDonough 23 School that constantly downed my child because he lived on the river. He went to school dressed like a little prince at all times, but everything that would happen, she would blame it on my kid. They didn't think he was good enough to go to their school because we were on the river. And I had more than they did, I really did! In many ways I had a lot more than they did. That's why I decided to take my children off the levee. I always regretted moving off the river. That was the best years of my life.

⚜

Cotton Blossom showboat, beached in Carrollton Bend. Sketch.
Illustration courtesy of Elizabeth Calabrese.

Long before Georgie decided to leave the levee, even before she married
Louis, the slow art of drifting that brought so many batture dwellers to
New Orleans was nearly over. The steamboats that had made floating ob-
solete were themselves succumbing to a transportation revolution. Diesel-
powered towboats easily pushed rafts of steel barges upriver. On the distant
horizon, the Huey P. Long Bridge could be seen from the shantyboats and
camps of Carrollton Bend, carrying automobiles across the river. Ferry
landings crumbled in rust.

The *Willow* steamboat that fed Georgie's family spent ever longer winter
layovers at the Carrollton Wharf. She was the last side-wheel steamboat
to tend navigation lights between New Orleans and Memphis. However,
engineers from the Corps had increased the river flow since the boat was
commissioned in 1927, and thus the *Willow* struggled to fight the early
spring current.

A more famous steamboat spent her last days docked near the *Willow*.
The *Cotton Blossom* had been an inspiration for the Broadway hit *Show
Boat*, but in the 1920s and '30s floating vaudeville theaters succumbed to
the popularity of motion pictures. Steamboats and the river itself no longer
captured the public imagination. The *Blossom* was pushed from her home
on the busy Canal Street waterfront to cheaper moorage at Carrollton,
where a final curtain call came after a 1932 performance of *Uncle Tom's
Cabin*.

The *Blossom* sold at auction the following year for twenty dollars, and in September 1934 was still moldering on the Carrollton batture beside the camp of Seymour Geisenheimer. A reporter lamented that "nothing is left hardly, beyond a few barnacled keel planks. Soon, even that will be gone. River squatters will of necessity or laziness try such out as firewood this winter."[4]

Even illustrious captains of the steam age washed up in the bend. The same month the *Cotton Blossom* closed for good, Captain Sam Cotton, master of the steamboat *Ouachita*, died in his self-built houseboat, tied up on the Carrollton batture. A year later, the distraught family of William E. Prather, captain of the abandoned *Cotton Blossom*, notified newspapers that the veteran riverman had disappeared. A *Times-Picayune* reporter located the old mariner in Carrollton Bend, living on a three-sided platform built from driftwood and pieces he pried from the rotting showboat. Captain Prather was "living on his earnings as a collector of firewood and shrimp."[5]

Downriver, beside Mahalia Jackson's Black batture, and past the reach of Dock Board anchorage fees, derelict and disused steamboats and ferries floated and occasionally sank in rough water. Across the river, towering hulks of forty-six rusting World War I ships awaited disposal.

On the modern river, batture dwellers became an anachronism—"river rats," living a pre-industrial life, surrounded by the relics of river industry.

Chapter 12

River Gypsies

Georgie Dumser helped me put together a list of her batture neighbors. She called out names camp by camp and explained how the families cropped up along the shore. "People built their own houses piecemeal. Half of the time, like with the Judds and Aunt Rose Martoni and Uncle Sil, they built a platform and put a tent over it until they could get a house built."

Then Georgie said something that startled me. *Aunt Rose and the Judds were "Rummychilds"—that's what they called themselves. They were gypsies.*

More than once I had seen shantyboaters described as "river gypsies." But that was intended as a colorful, and probably pejorative way to slur river people. Georgie's meaning was different. She noticed my wide-eyed surprise and explained.

Aunt Rose and Uncle Sil lived next to our camp. Rose was a fortune-teller. She had a funny kind of root she got out of the river, called St. John the Conqueror root. Her customers would pay extra to make a wish on it. They had a big family, the Judds and the Milliets. They all lived up here and they spoke a different language among themselves. Everybody knew Willie Judd.

After Georgie left, I found a William Judd in the phone book. I called and left a message. A few weeks later I tried again. Still no answer, but clues were piling up. I called Garfield Beattie and he remembered people who "might have been gypsies, living in tents." He had seen their truck "go over the levee once a month, loaded with furniture."

Meanwhile, I met another batture dweller who had a much more distinct memory. It was clear there was a bigger story. Harvey Menne had lived on the river as a child in the late 1930s and he had no doubt:

Sure there was gypsies! They walked their goats along the levee. If you wanted milk, you could buy it from them. They were always there, but I don't think they lived there. There were too many of them to live in any one house.

They wore long gowns, bright necklaces, bracelets, and colored prints. I never heard the women speak, only the men.

I had to find Willie Judd. On my third try, a woman answered the phone. "He got your message. He won't talk to you and he doesn't want me to talk to you." But she kept talking: "I will tell you this, Willie was beautiful. He always wore bright clothes and scarves. The girls were crazy about him . . . he was something to look at! . . . Listen, I can't talk. Why don't you call his brother? Joe lives in Oklahoma now."

I hadn't been off the phone ten minutes when it rang, and a belligerent voice rasped out.

"This is Willie Judd. You see that towboat and barge on the river in front of your house? I'm on it. I been on the river going past these camps my whole life. I got nothin' to tell you. We never caused no trouble up there. It was a bunch of us: Rose and Sil and Red and my brothers and sisters. But none of 'em will talk to you!"

A big pushboat churned upstream, slowly maneuvering a stack of twelve barges toward Nine Mile Point. I didn't know if Willie was really on board but if he was I was glad there were seventy yards of open water between us.

Gypsies, or Romani as they call themselves, likely originated in Northern India and migrated to Europe in the eleventh century. One interpretation of the name Romani traces back to the Sanskrit word for "people who roam about." After centuries of persecution in Europe for their migrant ways, dark skin, and inscrutable origins, many arrived in the United States. Those who settled on the batture in the 1920s and '30s found a place that fit their cultural traditions of mobility and insularity; a place where people were left alone and where the neighboring river and train tracks could swiftly lead to another riverbank or town.

Each voice from my batture connected me to a forgotten riverlife, but when Joseph Judd picked up the phone in Oklahoma City, I felt like an archaeologist unearthing the bones of an undocumented species. His southern-slow voice, warm and husky, couldn't have been more different from Willie's. He was planning to visit with his family in New Orleans for Thanksgiving, and we hatched a plan to meet at my camp after their gathering.

Joe Judd visited me in November 2000. He was stocky with deep-tan skin and black eyes. His broad hands were strong from years working as a sheet metal mechanic. Joe chucked the chin of Sweet Pea, my baby goat, and laughed when the bearded lady tried to butt him.

Joe was born on the river in 1930 and left the settlement when he was only fifteen, but his was the voice of the quintessential river rat. His family were outsiders by choice, outsiders among outsiders. The Judds were stubbornly tight-lipped—a reticence that had worn on Joe. He put a hand on my shoulder and began talking as we walked through my house and found a bench on the deck overlooking the water.

This river is in my blood. I was born on the batture in Baton Rouge, where we lived in a tent by the levee. All our people were gypsy, but if you asked mamma and daddy about our kinfolks, they wouldn't tell you nothin'. Us gypsies have always stuck together. There wasn't many of us, so if you wanted to talk Gypsy, you had to talk to each other. I was six months old when we moved to New Orleans. My big-grammy Moriah and aunt Rose moved up before us. Rose was the fortune-teller and folks from all over the city came to see her. We lived in a tent until daddy built a big one-room house beside them.

A towboat passed us on the river, and I couldn't help but wonder how much trouble Joe would be in if older brother Willie was to pull up on shore and find him talking to me. Joe was about the most relaxed guy I ever met. He smiled and unselfconsciously addressed a delicate subject.

There were seven or eight of us and we all lived in one room. We didn't have heat or water. We didn't even have no bathroom. We had cardboard around the pilings under the house. That's where we used the bathroom, on a piece of paper and threw it in the river. For the first twelve years of my life we drank out of the Mississippi River. We'd go out and dip a bucket of water and let it settle, didn't boil it or anything. When I was ten years old, we had to go to Charity Hospital. Me and my brothers all had yellow jaundice from drinking Mississippi River water. After the jaundice, we got our water from the icehouse over the levee.

Countless visitors have chewed around the subject before finally asking me, "What do you do about the toilet?" Joe just put his story right out there. I'm not sure he even connected the lack of a sewage system or running water with the "yellow jaundice." Most batture "septic systems" of the time were similar to the one Shoe Gaudet had installed under my camp in the 1970s. Shoe knocked holes in a salvaged fifty-five-gallon drum, dropped

Joe Judd and Shirley Benedict at St. Elizabeth's, the batture community center.
Photo courtesy of Joe Judd.

it in a hole under the camp and filled it part way with shells. Sewage ran from the house through a pipe that was jammed into the top of the drum.

Sanitary conditions on the batture would become a rallying cry for authorities seeking destruction of the camps, but into the 1940s, many houses in New Orleans still had outhouses. Well into the twentieth century, Bisso towboats pushed garbage barges downstream and dumped the city's waste into the channel. A buried drum with holes wouldn't pass modern health codes, but it wasn't cardboard on the beach either. Joe described the arrival of utilities on his batture.

Nobody up here had water until the forties. Then we got five or six people on one meter in my mamma's name. I remember one lady didn't have no water and my mamma gave her a bucketful. Mr. Skinner, who lived a few camps down, heard about it. He came over and told mama, "You can't give that away 'cause I paid for it." He had a shovel to dig up our water line. My mamma went in the house and got her shotgun. She said, "Listen, you stick that shovel in the ground, you better dig a hole deep enough for you, 'cause I'm gonna put you in it!"

Joe's tales had been simmering under a lid of family secrecy for decades. I sat back and laughed out loud as he described the Judd brothers' hustles. If there was a nickel to be made, it wound up in their pocket.

Aunt Rose, the fortune teller.
Photo courtesy of of Joe Judd.

As a kid I'd go to town and get magnolias off a tree and sell them for five cents. I'd pick up pecans and go from house to house selling them, too. I'd cut the fronds from those little palm trees by the streetcar tracks and sell them at the Catholic church for a nickel. We would make the rounds every evening and shine shoes at the bars on Oak and Willow Street.

Everyone who lived on Carrollton Bend noticed people selling baskets and wicker chairs along the levee. Even the famous WPA *City Guide to New Orleans* mentioned people selling bentwood furniture by the river—but no one could say for certain who crafted these items. I had reached the source. The Judds, no less than the fishermen, bird trappers, and driftwood collectors of the batture, had a gift for gleaning income along the shore. They were the willow artisans of Carrollton Bend.

Joe modestly credited his cousin Red and Uncle Charles as the masterminds behind the woven-willow enterprise.

My cousin Red Mullen lived up here and he taught me about willow furniture. Red's uncle, Charles Askins, would drive in from his batture camp in Yazoo, Mississippi, for three months at a time and park his truck down by the river. He was the one that knew how to make the chairs. Uncle Charles came in and we'd get started. Red would go right out there and cut willows and bring 'em home. When people make willow chairs now, they just leave the bark on, but us kids had to sit around and peel them willows. I wore my teeth out just biting them to get ahold of them. We'd load the truck and take everything out and sell. Baskets were a dollar and you could buy a whole set for ten dollars. Anything you could make out of willow, we made it.

Joe mentioned that his cousin Red was living across the lake from New Orleans in Slidell and could tell me more about the furniture. But he warned that Red's family "wasn't too proud" of their grandfather's river rat past and gypsy heritage. Joe said not to call him but promised to let him know about me. To my surprise a pale and freckled Red Mullen showed up at my door a week later.

Red Mullen looked weary. He was in poor health and on his way to a nearby hospital. He had only a moment. He placed a tattered shoe box he had been carrying under his arm onto the table and sat down.

My Aunt Rose and my Aunt Irene Judd had camps up here and they had some room between those camps, so my daddy went to the levee board and got permission to build. We built Camp 15½. I never went to school a day in my life. I stayed on the batture until I was fourteen and my daddy and I started having trouble. I left home in 1938—crawled on a freight train right where the tracks run by the levee. The first place the train stopped was Cairo, Illinois. I settled there and worked for the Federal Barge Line until I had to come home and get my birth certificate for the draft. My Uncle Charles was a real gypsy. He spoke the language. We went to his brother's funeral and Jesus! You wouldn't believe all the chanting and carrying on. Anyway, he taught me how to make the furniture and it's something I've done my whole life.

Red pushed himself up and said, "I'll have to tell you about all this when I come back." He lifted the lid of the shoebox that had been sitting between us. The box was stuffed with old square photographs with serrated edges. A visitor had captured dozens of images of the family. There was a truck full of willow chairs by the river edge. In another Red and Joe sat on the tailgate peeling willow branches. A tent rested on a platform and an iron pot smoked over an open fire.

I hated to let Red go, but he was late for the doctor. He shook his head and confessed, "I think about the river all the time. About us living up here and playing up here when we was kids. What a rough life we had."

I couldn't call him, and I couldn't hold onto the photos. He held the box closely and promised to bring it back. I never heard from Red again. I found a number, but no one in his family would speak to me. Later the line was dead. In 2014 an obituary appeared for a "housepainter," Elmer Mullen. There was no mention of swimming in the river, or making willow furniture, or hopping trains. Our short conversation and those square black-and-white images haunt me as much as any batture ghost ever has.

The hard life of Red Mullen's childhood was softened by Joe Judd's memories of those black-and-white river scenes.

There was a dredge boat captain friend of my daddy's who would come to our house almost every Sunday and have dinner with us. Mr. Stone would buy pig tails and cabbage and mama would cook it. Uncle Sil played the guitar and we'd sit on the front porch and eat pig tails and cabbage and the whole family would sing.

Joe and his cousin Red lived just across the parish line from my camp, near Seymour Geisenheimer. It was the rougher end of the village, where tough kids from big families tangled with each other and anyone else that passed by. Joe recalled staking out his turf.

To tell you the truth, we were ornery; we really was. We probably got blamed for a lot of stuff that we were guilty of! There weren't too many people came down to this end of the levee. When they got in this district, they went down to the railroad track. We was mean, just like little dogs fighting over our territory.

The cousins grew up fearless and were matter of fact about things that would have been traumatic for a city-dweller. Without a trace of the emotion that wracked city survivors of Hurricanes Katrina and Betsy, Joe recounted how the river claimed all three of the camps he lived in.

The first year on the batture, our house fell down and we built another one. In the flood of '44, the water was high and got real rough; you know sometimes it'll do that. The river washed that house right off the pilings. We rented the last place we lived in. That one fell down, too.

The floods that claimed the Judds' homes told a story in themselves. After the Great Flood of 1927, the Corps had sprung into action creating spillways to divert floodwaters from settled areas. They built dams to sequester water upriver, raised levees, and laid concrete revetments.

The engineers' spillways prevented a replay of earlier catastrophic floods, but their other work came with unintended consequences. The higher

People began to notice the shore eroding under their camps.
Photo from the *Times-Picayune*.

levees upstream and closed distributaries prevented the river from spread-
ing across its floodplain and sent even more water downstream. Revetments
narrowed the channel and pushed levels higher. Minor flooding upstream
that wouldn't have caused concern before translated into towering crests
in Louisiana.[1] The new Bonnet Carré Spillway was opened three times as
spring floods rolled downstream in 1932, 1937, 1944, 1945, and 1950.

While spillways prevented flooding in New Orleans, the Corps cut off
fourteen bends in the lower river and shortened its journey to the coast
by 120 miles. The current rushed through its straightened course and over
the smooth asphalt and concrete revetments. People in the colony of self-
built homes in Carrollton Bend began to notice the shore eroding beneath
their camps.

Joe couldn't remember exactly when their first house fell but it was
probably in late winter of 1937. That year the crest would have been the
highest on record if the Bonnet Carré Spillway had not been opened. On
the night of Monday, April 3, 1937, a storm raged across the cresting river.
Fifty-mile-per-hour winds delivered hail, ripped the roofs off houses, and
pushed water against the Carrollton shore.

At the height of the storm, the Judds' next door neighbor, Mrs. Brookshire, was nursing a sick child when she felt the camp shudder and heard
her husband yell, "We're going down." Mr. Brookshire and his son John had

the presence of mind to douse two flaming oil lamps and all ten occupants fled safely. The house was blown eleven feet from its pilings and landed at the river's edge.[2]

Floods and storms brought reporters and other curious city folks to the top of the levee, and they always noted how batture dwellers had "learned to fight the river," but they missed the point. The Corps were the ones who were *fighting* the Mississippi, and with very mixed results. Batture people learned to adapt and rebuild.

Two camps downriver from the Brookshires' fallen house, sixty-seven-year-old fisherman "Uncle Will" Olsen watched the water begin to squirt between the floorboards of his camp. He gathered blocks of wood from the stream and built a false floor over the flooded one. His standard response to a flood was the same as during the high water three years earlier: "I don't think it will be any worse than it has been before. But it makes things mighty unhandy for us."[3]

On May 19, 1944, things became "mighty unhandy" again for the Judds and the Brookshires when the river rose against their floor. As night fell, a forty-eight-mile-per-hour gale backed the river up nearly a foot and forced the evacuation of ten to fifteen households on the Southport end of the settlement. Joe Judd's second batture camp was about to float away.

The collapse of another home was unremarkable to Joe Judd, who demurred to me that his brother Leonard "was quite a hero that day." Joe and Leonard's mother was less sanguine; she described a harrowing scene to a reporter from the *Times-Picayune*: "The older ones held to the house from the walk outside, attempting to keep it from floating away. All the children were out but the baby, Carol Ann. Leonard darted into the drifting house and returned almost immediately with the baby." With Carol Ann in his arms, nine-year-old Leonard jumped back across a widening gap of storm-driven waves between the floating house and the shore.

The following day, Leonard was fishing boards from the water edge when the reporters visited. He complained that he had to interrupt his swimming "to pull out nails from the wreckage of the old home to use in a new house."[4]

Barely ten months after the Judds' second home flooded, Easter Day 1945 brought an April Fools' surprise. Families left their stilt houses in the morning for holiday outings and returned in the evening to find water on their floors. People rushed to place items beyond reach of a gathering

crest. Chests of drawers, toys, kiddy cars, rocking chairs, and other fur-
nishings lined the crown of the levee. Eight batture houses were washed
away, including the homes rebuilt by the Judds and Skinners the previous
spring. Several other camps had crumbled from their pilings and rested
on the river edge.

The Red Cross offered housing, but most batture dwellers moved in with
neighbors. The Judd and Skinner children were spied by a *Times-Picayune*
photographer fishing from Red Mullen's porch. Victor Strong, who had a
foot of water in his house, bored holes in the floor so that water would
drain out when the flood receded. He placed wooden blocks under his
bed, stacked his possessions atop the coverlet and was discovered by the
reporter, stretched out among the boxes, reading pulp magazines.

For teenagers on the batture, a flood-crippled house was an adventure.
They paddled about on rafts made of the scraps of smashed piers to salvage
treasures from the wave tossed wreckage. Leonard Judd sailed on the roof
of his "floating" home while his brother and two neighbors dove from the
roof of the sunken Skinner house until it was finally "swept away" by the
swollen river.[5]

The Judd family maintained their sangfroid. Joe recalled: *We didn't worry
about it when the houses fell. Whatever daddy said, that's what happened,
and the women had no say whatsoever. If daddy said we were going swimming, everybody got in the river.* With wartime rationing, nails had to be
saved. The family waded out to work.

Fallen houses weren't enough to chase the Judds off the river, but by the
end of the war Joe's father had saved enough money to move the family
across the lake, away from levee boards, industry, and curious neighbors.

*Daddy bought a five-acre place and moved us to Covington. The levee
board was already making noise about tearing all the camps down. I was
fifteen and I hated it. Taking a boy from the river and putting him on a five-
acre farm was like taking this dog of mine and tying him to a tree out there.*

Joe and I walked with his hound dog out to the end of my pier, high
above the silt beach. He tried to recognize landmarks across the river—the
grain elevators, the Huey P. Long Bridge in the distance. He concluded
that it didn't look much the same and theorized: "We must have cut all the
trees down for firewood." As he was leaving, Joe promised to come back
and suggested that I not try to call Willie again. I told him I hadn't ever
considered that, and he laughed and recalled:

Kids in the city would tease us and some of the girls didn't want to go out with us. Because we lived up here, we wasn't good enough for them. I'm sure their folks felt that way. They called us "river rats" and, of course that's what we was. But really, we would brag about living up here. It's funny. I was telling you how poor I was. It wasn't until I got grown, I realized how rich I was, having the Mississippi River as a back yard.

Chapter 13

Batture Row

Marie Meliet was known among her neighbors on the levee as "the angel of the batture."[1] During the Depression, the thirty-five-year-old mother fed transients and kept an eye on everyone's children. In January 1940, she was struggling to provide for her own eight children, ages four to seventeen. Her husband, Henry Meliet, had lost his job as a steel construction worker and Marie was let go from her part-time job in a box factory.

Marie knew it wasn't right that people had to go to a ward boss to find work, but the political machine of Governor Huey Long had joined forces with the Old Regulars in New Orleans. Those organizations thrived on patronage and there were few families in Louisiana, even among those living along the batture, that did not have a relative working in a job controlled by corrupt politicians.

After Governor Huey Long was assassinated in 1935, his brother Earl took control of the family political machine. Earl ascended to the governor's mansion in 1939—when the equally corrupt Richard Leche resigned in scandal—but in the election of 1940, Earl was challenged by a "good government" candidate. Sam Jones promised to roll back the graft of machine politics.

Earl Long's forces in New Orleans were marshaled by the Old Regular ward boss, William Bisso Sr. Bisso's own voting district included part of the Carrollton batture, where he ran a marine industrial empire and maintained an office and home. On February 14, 1940, a week before election day, Marie Meliet complained to the *New Orleans Item* that a Long precinct official threatened to "move her off the batture" if she didn't "shut up this Jones talk." He cautioned, "The batture is Governor Long's land, and you people ought to at least have the decency to give him your vote since he's been kind enough to let you all live out here like this."

Marie campaigned hard and, despite intimidation and alleged death threats from ward politicians, she got her neighbors to go vote. When Sam Jones defeated Earl Long in the district by sixty-nine votes, Marie proudly claimed that all she had done was convince her neighbors they had "nothing to be afraid of."[2] Eight years later, when Earl Long was finally elected governor, batture people would have reason to question the encouragement Meliet had offered so fearlessly in 1940.

After the election of Sam Jones, Marie Meliet disappeared from the news and batture people returned to their habitual political disengagement, but powerful agencies pushed to eradicate the settlement. In a letter addressed to the board of the Orleans Levee District, the Corps asked the levee board to evict batture dwellers who were driving stakes into the levee revetment. The *Times-Picayune* suggested that "the city or state must seek a solution to the problem of the settlement that has grown up on the Carrollton Batture."[3] In 1945, the New Orleans chapter of the Red Cross of America joined the chorus of complaint, petitioning the levee board to address "deplorable" conditions "to prevent epidemic and loss of life on the batture."[4]

Despite these political threats, the batture folks had a surprising ally in the early 1940s. Levee board posts were among the patronage jobs controlled by Governor Sam Jones. Jones's board granted batture dwellers permits to build camps and allowed telephone and electric lines to cross the levee. Chief counsel for the board, Severn T. Darden, responded to complaints from the Red Cross and recommended against evicting batture dwellers. He suggested that complaints of unsanitary conditions should be "referred to the proper health authorities."[5]

Orleans Levee District chief engineer Armand L. Willoz offered a clarion endorsement of the batture community:

Insofar as the safety of the levee system is concerned, the presence of the camps may be considered beneficial, because in the past when the Mississippi River water was extremely high, the occupants of the camps jealously guarded the levees in the vicinity and would not let strangers near the levee.[6]

The Carrollton settlement seemed immune to national campaigns of "shack removal" and "slum clearance" that marked the end of the Great Depression, but residents in blighted neighborhoods throughout the city felt the muscle of federal planners. New Orleans was one of the first cities in the South to replace dilapidated homes with federally funded housing projects. The earliest projects were well-built and provided housing to many of those they displaced.

A second wave of apartments were built in the low-lying "back of town." Some were situated on former city dumps where hundreds of people, Black and white, still lived in settlements of self-built shacks. People in the dump villages had raised families there, planted gardens and fished in the filthy canals that drained the city. A shacktown known as "Silver City" (for the mounds of shiny tin cans and scraps of glass that glinted in the sun) would later become the Calliope housing project. A "dump-village" on Melpomene Street, once dubbed "Melpomenia, A Unique Burg within City Limits," was later covered by the Melpomene housing project.

Back-of-town housing projects were planned mainly for Black residents, but their needs quickly collided with those of war workers and then returning soldiers. Two weeks after newspapers announced the groundbreaking of a housing project for Blacks on the Agriculture Street dump, state social workers informed the seventy-five families living on the site that they would have to find housing elsewhere—the new apartments would house war workers.[7]

The levee board completed its lakefront land grab with the help of WPA labor. A tangled suburban street grid appeared where the stilt house village of Milneburg once stood and in 1939, lots went up for sale in Lakeside West, the first of four sprawling developments on the shore. The lots were unaffordable to working poor and were redlined to keep Blacks out.[8]

The housing crisis deepened. People sheltered wherever they could find or throw up a roof: a cabin near the Desire Housing Project, a railroad car in Central City, a disabled tugboat beside the New Basin Canal, converted boathouses on the lake, in the remnant houseboat colony on Bayou St. John, and around dozens of small dumps that dotted the city fringe.

The Bayou St. John houseboats were a canary in the coal mine for the batture community in Carrollton Bend. They had been threatened in the 1920s, when the city began reclaiming its lakefront, but won a reprieve during the Depression. Then in the 1940s, nearby landholders complained

Gambling houses by the levee were a less obvious threat. Photo courtesy of the Charles L. Franck Studio Collection at the Historic New Orleans Collection. HNOC Acc. No. 1979.325.144_o2.

about unsanitary conditions. Some neighbors lobbied to have the bayou incorporated into City Park. By the end of the decade the city had cleared Bayou St. John of its colorful community.

Batture people, nestled outside the river levee and for a time protected by a benevolent levee board, dodged threats of slum clearance, gentrification, and political retribution. A less obvious threat, however, festered just inside the levee in the booming gambling houses of Southport. Huey Long had cultivated a relationship with the mom-and-pop casino operators in the neighborhood. They were raided, but always seemed to be warned in advance. When Earl Long assumed control of the Long political machine, he met with national crime figures Meyer Lansky and Frank Costello. These bosses and reputed local crime kingpin Carlos Marcello moved in and took over the gaming rooms one by one.[9]

Local operators Rudolph and George O'Dwyer retreated with enough cash to open gaming establishments further from the river. I visited an old O'Dwyer family home close by the site of their Southport Club when it went up for sale in the 1990s. Through a covered carport, a doorway led to a wide basement with plenty of space for tables and two restrooms labeled "gentlemen" and "ladies."

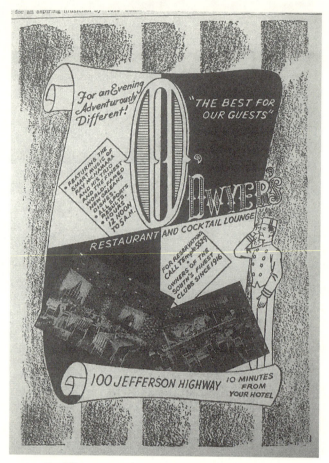

The O'Dwyers opened gaming places farther from the river.
Illustration courtesy of New Orleans Public Library.

After Rudolph O'Dwyer died in 1940, his brother used their casino profits to purchase a large tract of land stretching back from the Southport levee—land once owned by Emile Geisenheimer, the brother of the aging river rat Seymour. There was nothing other than that land sale to directly connect the O'Dwyers with the Geisenheimers. But they had been next-door neighbors. None of the old batture folks I spoke with heard about that land sale, but thirty years later another generation of O'Dwyers would show up and claim my flooded sliver of Southport silt.

Seymour Geisenheimer had no interest in gambling. In a 1942 interview with the *Times-Picayune* he insisted, "I like to get some benefit out of my money." For fifty-five years he had made a home on the Carrollton batture. At age seventy-two he still fished for river shrimp and sold his catch to local bars and fishermen. He rowed out and corralled logs from the current, dried the wood, cut it to stove-length and sold it atop the levee for $6 a half-cord.

After the Japanese bombed Pearl Harbor, life got complicated for Seymour. Fearing that the enemy might poison the city water supply, authorities erected a chain-link fence topped with barb wire that surrounded both the Orleans Parish water intake and Geisenheimer's adjacent camp. Seymour needed an identification card to get past an armed guard to reach his home. To sell his firewood, he tossed cut lengths over the ten-foot barricade, walked around the guard, and stacked it outside the fence.[10]

Seymour didn't live to see the fence around his batture home come down. In 1943 the bird man was buried in a family plot in Carrollton. He had never married and never moved from the levee. He lived there longer than anyone else—from the end of Reconstruction to Jim Crow, World War I, the Great Depression, and finally, the start of World War II. He witnessed it all from his self-built river camp, a few blocks from the fine homes of his brother Emile and Emile's neighbors, the O'Dwyers.

I wondered why Seymour Geisenheimer chose to live in a "squatter" community on the batture while his brother, Emile Adam August Geisenheimer, achieved economic, social, and political prominence a few blocks over the levee in Jefferson. No present-day Geisenheimer would admit to me ever hearing of Seymour. Like Bayou Sara Jack, who floated away from an inheritance to camp on a mud island in Westwego, Seymour repudiated a life of city comforts to live the life of a river rat. But perhaps Emile owned the bit of batture where the bird man built his camp.

In the Jefferson Parish Office of Mortgage and Conveyance, an aged clerk asked me if I needed help finding anything. When I told him I was looking for purchases and sales by Emile Geisenheimer he replied, "I'm sorry, we close in four hours. What decade do you want to start with?" Emile's transactions dated back to the late nineteenth century, when savvy investors snapped up former plantation land along the river. I spent an afternoon staring at hundreds of entries without finding a clue to Emile and Seymour's divergent fortunes.

Even as the first generation of Carrollton river rats like Seymour, Adam Rowbatham, and the fisherman Uncle Will Olsen died and departed, the Carrollton settlement grew. Census records demonstrably undercounted batture folks, who fled from authority and often lived at the end of precarious walkways guarded by dogs and livestock. Federal recorders found three "fishermen" living "on the river" in 1910; one of them was Seymour's brother, Simon Geisenheimer. In 1930 they recorded thirty-four people in thirteen households. A decade later the 1940 US Census counted 215 people in 110 homes. Aerial photographs and Sanborn Insurance maps from 1945 show one stilt house after another jammed along the shore between Southport and Audubon Park.

Batture dwellers joined the war effort with the same enthusiasm as their counterparts inside the levee. Fathers and sons served in the military and built PT boats and landing craft at local shipyards. Gold stars appeared in windows along the levee and flags flew from posts fished out of the river.

The centers of batture social life in the 1940s were two stilt house churches. Black families attended the appropriately named Noah's Ark Baptist Church on Mahalia's batture. White kids gathered at St. Elizabeth's, a community center and sanctuary on stilts funded by the Catholic Church. The kids from my end of the settlement threw parties and concerts at St. Elizabeth's and charged "a piece of rubber" or a penny for admission, which they donated to the local USO office to support the war effort.

Quiet reigned among old-timers on the "highbrow" end of the settlement near St. Charles Avenue. C. H. Dumser left each morning to teach at Delgado Trade School. Sixty-four-year-old Bert Beattie and his wife Ida sat on their levee-side deck every afternoon with a seventy-three-year-old neighbor, Florence Shaw. They faced the floods of 1944 and 1945 without the company of their sons fighting in Europe.

Further up the levee toward the Southport camps where I live now, quiet was hard to find. There were more than fifty young children living in a couple dozen small camps on both sides of the Jefferson Parish line.

Carrollton Bend in 1940. There were at least 215 people in 110 homes.
Photo courtesy of US Army Corps of Engineers, New Orleans District.

The Judds, Brookshires, Meliets, and Skinners had six or seven children per household; the Benedicts had eight. With fathers gone to war or working long hours in the shipyards, batture life among this vast crop of river children was like an unsupervised field trip. My window into the Southport end of the settlement came through the eyes of two of those children of the Depression and war: John "Hot Pepper" Benedict and Harvey Menne.

I don't know how John Benedict found me, but I do remember the day I met him. I was building a shrimp trap on my deck one breezy morning in September 2000, when I noticed a gaunt man with a snarl of long gray hair walking atop the levee. A wisp of a guy in a green hospital shirt worn over sagging khakis, he leaned hard against the wind. He appeared to be either singing or talking to himself, but the sound was lost. I waved and turned back to tacking screen onto my shrimp trap.

It wasn't unusual for recently released patients from the psychiatric ward at nearby Ochsner Hospital to ramble past on the levee. But to my surprise, I felt footsteps descending the catwalk, and when I looked back,

John Benedict shows how to build a shrimp trap.
Photo by Macon Fry.

the scarecrow was hanging on my gate, peering through the chain link with wild blue eyes. "I hear you been looking for people that lived up here." I gave an affirmative if tentative nod, and he introduced himself.

I'm John Benedict, but you can call me "Hot Pepper." I'll tell you what I remember. I'm not ashamed of anything. I've been to jail. I've been in the penitentiary. I've been in the crazy house.

This was going to be a unique conversation. Hot Pepper's rant lacked an arc, and he refused to stay on one subject except when it came to the building of shrimp traps. He looked at my handiwork, turned the hardware-cloth cage in his wiry hands and pronounced, "That'll never work—let me show you." Hot Pepper and I eventually developed a friendship around the pursuit of river shrimp, but from that moment I wanted his story.

My daddy had a barbershop over the levee on Oak Street until 1931 when somebody set a fire. I was only three at the time and don't remember it, but we lived in the back. It was midnight and he got what furniture he could out by himself, 'cause mother was watching us kids. It was bad smoke, and he took sick from it and had to let the shop go. Daddy borrowed about $400 from his younger brother and built a one-room camp. The eight of us lived there and *we added onto it a little at a time. A lot of big planks and sills came down the river when they built the Huey P. Long Bridge. We used to row up there to look for pilings that had been discarded to add onto the place. There were pilings under the camp I couldn't get my arms around. When the bulldozers came to knock it down, they had a hell of a time.*

John remembered getting more grief for being an Italian than being a river rat. The Carrollton neighborhood was full of Germans and Anglos who had been there almost since its founding, but few Italians. Quick fists (and older brothers) were a big asset for batture kids.

They called us "river rats," but if we played the city kids in marbles or whatever and won, it would be "Stinkin' Dagos cheat!" Al Capone was having his fun at the time and we got all kinds of crap. We'd get in fights with 'em. If a guy would be too big for me, my older brother would fight him. If he was too big for him, my other older brother would fight him.

With four older brothers, John had plenty of muscle to back him up. The Benedict brothers fought, chipped creosote wood from the levee revetment to burn in their wood stove, and when the river was high they fished for shrimp and dove into the water from the roofs of flooded camps. John remembered sitting on the levee with the other batture families and watching flames tower over O'Dwyer's Original Southport Club "after the mob muscled in." No one publicly proclaimed arson to be the cause, but John was sure. He recalled it clearly, *Fire trucks came from everywhere, but in the end, there was nothing left except a big safe.*

One cool October evening, two Benedict boys and a group of free-range kids found a body floating in the driftwood over the river at Nine Mile Point. They notified a sheriff, who identified the corpse as the first person to jump from the new Huey P. Long Bridge. John didn't disclose to me what the boys were doing in the gathering darkness, across the river on the heavily wooded shore.

John's brother, Joe, moved to a dairy across the river and rowed home to bring his earnings, seven dollars each week, to his parents. His older brother, Salvador Benedict, shipped out in the merchant marine. James Benedict enlisted in the army at eighteen and died on a battlefield within weeks of deploying to Europe.

Conveniently forgetting some chapters in his own history, John slyly remarked of his neighbors, *The people on the river were happy people. There were no murderers, no thieves, no lawyers, no doctors that ever came from up there.* Then he reeled off dozens of disconnected tales of batture dweller exploits.

Frank Brule lived next door in Camp 37. He dated my sister Shirley, but he got shot shining rabbits down by the railroad tracks, and the train hit him in the back of the head. Frank's brother, Agnes Brule, was a longshoreman, and he used to make beer with rainwater. It was so strong, when you belched it came out your nose. I lay awake at night and could sometimes hear the bottles blow up. POW!

John never mentioned why he had "been in jail," as he confessed when we first met. Much later I found the story in a copy of the *New Orleans States* dated July 3, 1947. Below the fold on the front page was a picture of two remorseful-looking teenagers and the headline, "Two Youths Seized in Audubon Burglary." Hot Pepper and a friend had used a screwdriver to pry open a park concession stand. They made off with $25 in nickels and pennies and three boxes of gum. The two might have escaped if they hadn't been pulled over for driving a motorbike against traffic on Carrollton Avenue at 3 a.m. Police recovered the loot and a year later John shipped out in the merchant marine.

Newspapers painted batture dwellers as the forward edge of an urban crime wave, in the same way they had peered over the levees to tell sordid tales of flatboat men and wharf rats. Most riverfront mischief was the same petty theft, domestic violence, and drunkenness found throughout the city. John Benedict's heist was pretty typical. During the lean years of the Depression and wartime rationing, the riverfront was a resource-rich environment, and everyone had a hustle.

Mahalia Jackson scaled parked train cars to kick lumps of coal off to her friends waiting below.[11] Georgie Dumser's husband "found a sack of flour floating in the river," and John Benedict's neighbor, Charles Menne, sometimes discovered an "abandoned sack" of grain in an unlocked boxcar below the levee. Batture dwellers who owned skiffs salvaged lumber that "fell" from upstream wharves and sometimes they earned a lucrative bounty by returning logs branded with a company logo to the hardwood mills along the river.

After the war, kids who had ratted around and pilfered on the riverfront often graduated to working on the water. John's two older brothers went to sea first. When he saw his neighbors Willie Judd, Harold Rowbatham, and Sam Cotton Jr. take to the waves, he was hot to go.

Willie Judd went first to France. When he got back, he'd been gone about six weeks and had money. He told me what a good time he had. Shit, that's what I wanted. I went to the union hall and boy, they had jobs all over the board. It was about four months after the war. I was gone eight months and twenty-two days and made about $2,500. I stayed with it 'til I retired.

John's father, "Papa" Joseph Benedict, never recovered his health after fire destroyed his barbershop. He found peace on the river and a good way to escape his brood of eight lively children by rowing off in his skiff. In the flood of 1945, Papa told a reporter he had seen higher water and didn't worry anyway, because his skiff was "his real home." Each morning Joseph Benedict disappeared with shrimp traps and a fishing line.

He would stay out there all day long shrimping, fishing. He'd be rowing and singing and whistling; I mean the world was his! The word "squatter" wasn't in his vocabulary. People didn't come out here just to dodge rent. Some just wanted to be by the river. It wasn't all poor people that lived out here. In my father's case it was cheaper ... but he loved that river.

John's father, who could build an entire river camp by hand, was lost in the right angles and straight lines of city life. Leaving the river hit him hardest. There, a proud and independent man could pull in a fish or catch some shrimp to feed his family. But as the younger generation moved out and found wives and work elsewhere, no one remained on the river to care for their father.

We found a house on Bellecastle Street for $4,000. It needed a lot of work and daddy wasn't much of a city carpenter. He didn't want to move, and he told everybody, "I'll just stay up here by myself." But we didn't have a choice.

A wide-eyed six-year-old named Harvey Menne arrived on the levee in 1938, about seven years after John Benedict. His family moved from an inner-city rental into a flimsy stilt house a few doors up from Benedict and right beside the shack that would become my first home on the batture fifty years later.

Benedict and Menne remembered the same place and time—a batture emerging from the Depression—through very different eyes. Benedict's earliest memories were of wilding on the river with a fleet of older brothers. An only child, Menne spent his first six years in the sweltering inner

Harvey wrote his story on a page titled "Things to Do."
Photo courtesy of Harvey Menne.

city, under the protective watch of a worried mother. Even after he arrived on the rough-and-tumble Southport batture, Harvey Menne never left his childhood innocence behind.

I wasn't home when Harvey came by my house the first time. Like John Benedict, he didn't call first. I got home from work one day and discovered a sheet of paper sandwiched between the screen door and the jamb; it was torn from a pad with a colorful, factory-printed header, THINGS TO DO. The lines were numbered 1–10, and scrawled over those lines, front and back, Menne had sketched the story of an enchanted batture childhood.

Harvey returned to meet me on a clear fall morning in 2001. A cool front had blasted the humidity from the sky and the river's muddy water hid beneath a shimmering surface. I didn't hear him approach but spotted a short, lumpy-looking man standing quietly by my gate. He wore khakis and a suede jacket the color of camel hair, scuffed at the elbows. He squinted and smiled with disarmingly warm brown eyes. I had to lean forward to hear him: *I'm Harvey Menne. That's "Menne" like MINI-skirt. I lived just four camps from where you are now.*

Harvey and I walked down the batture to where his father built a house for the family and we sat in the shade of a sycamore tree. With our backs against the trunk, Harvey filled in the details from his "to-do" script in order, without ever consulting it.

We were living in the 300 block of Galvez Street, right off Poydras, between a Black church and grocery store. My mom was scared to death the people there were gonna do me something. When they decided to move, I took all the belongings I had and put them in a little shoe box, and we came up on the batture. It was so spacious! I fell in love with the place right away. We had a phone, but no electric, no bath, and no running water. We bathed in a washtub, had a wood stove for heat, and boiled Mississippi River water to drink. The house had holes in the floor and rats as big as a small poodle dog would come in at night and walk around. If you tried to scare them off, they just looked at you like you were crazy. We could set a large rat trap and it would be gone the next day, so my dad used to shoot them with a .38.

Harvey unspooled a reverie of life apart from the city. While the sycamore leaves rustled overhead, he spoke gently of a world of dodged threats, glancing blows, and a verdant levee on which to unpack his shoebox of homemade toys.

For a child it was just ideal. There were many, many snakes: blue runners, tree snakes, water moccasins, and I caught frogs and lizards. When the river was low you could walk out a block. We used to wade out and play "cow-belly." You'd stomp on the ground and keep going down. We'd get down to our knees and stop 'cause we couldn't get out. We had to get a friend to pull us out. Somebody would shout "go further" but I don't know—you might go down to your neck. It was a beautiful place to play until you ran into that cow-belly.

Mary Bennet was two doors up in Camp 4. We used to walk over to the Roxy Theater at Eagle and Willow street together. It was a nickel to get in on Wednesday and you got popcorn to go with it. Next door in Camp 3 was the

Brookshires. Me and Rudy Brookshire heard about drowned men that had washed up; we walked down and threw rocks at them and they bounced off like a trampoline. The shrimp had eaten their eyes out.

Harvey's paradise was tested every day as he passed the tough kids who lived over the parish line into John Benedict and Joe Judd's territory.

I wasn't allowed to mingle much with the kids around here. They were all bad. Every one of 'em went to prison. When I passed them walking to school at McDonough 23, I'd walk down on the railroad tracks. They treated me fine at school, but I'd get beat up on the way there and on the way back, 'cause I was a little sissy. I didn't like no fighting. I'd come home all bloodied up and my daddy would kick my ass again for letting 'em do that.

Harvey's father, Charles Menne, made a living the same way Joe Judd's father did. He labored on the stadium and bridges in City Park as a WPA employee, until he found war work at Higgins Shipyard. Harvey smiled broadly: *Daddy worked the night shift building PT boats. He would come home at three in the morning and bring Jim's Fried Chicken. I'd wake up with the smell of that chicken.*

In his spare time, Charles Menne began building a better house for his family, using donated and found materials.

Daddy knew the house we were living in was falling apart, so he started building one behind it. I'm still so proud of that second camp. I swear, my daddy built it with his own hands. No help. No miter saw. Somebody gave him some wood and he found the rest. He would take one of those big railroad spikes with a hook on the end, pound it into a floating log and tie a rope on. He had a nice skiff he made of plywood, and he would row out, drag the logs in, and tie them up to the house. Sometimes they'd be dog-eared, and he could sell them back to the lumber mill.

Like his neighbors Rudy Brookshire, and Joe Judd, who also lost houses in the flood of 1944, Harvey recalled the event without a trace of trauma.

The river came up real high once, I think it was 1943. We were all diving off the roof because the water was ten feet deep. My mama couldn't hardly swim but she wanted to get up there and do it too. So she jumped and never did come back up. Junior Breaud dove in and picked her out or she would have drowned. Daddy was just finishing the second house and the first one fell in the water and floated away. I mean we watched that sucker float away.

To make ends meet, Harvey's parents fished, gleaned, and bartered with neighbors.

We lived on shrimp and fish. Mamma and daddy fished every day, right under the Oak Street Ferry Landing, which came down beside your old shack. They used cane poles and worms for bait. The only day I remember that they didn't fish, the ferry landing collapsed. If they'd been under there, they'd be dead. They would set out shrimp boxes that had a screen funnel on each side so the shrimp could go in, but they couldn't come out. We'd put them out over the weekend and come back and they would be packed with shrimp. We sold them because we couldn't eat them all and there was no such thing as refrigeration. My daddy and Mr. Bongard used to break into boxcars and steal what little grain was left in them. If they got a whole sack, you're looking at a week's pay. We had chickens and sold eggs, and Mrs. Robo kept two cows tied to a stake. We'd get that milk hot, right out of the tit, and go home and boil it. It was rich, with the cream on top and mom used to make cream cheese.

When the Menne family moved to a small house in the suburbs in 1946, the batture was showing signs of postwar prosperity. WPA work and war industry had provided an influx of cash and young men sent military pay deducts home from overseas. Despite back-to-back floods in '44 and '45, many houses were freshly painted, connected to phone lines, and sprouting radio antennas. Children ran as wild and free as the goats, cows, dogs, and cats that prowled the levee, and old-time river folks supported themselves in the ways they always had.

It was a halcyon time on the batture when a reporter visited in 1946 and gave the place a new name:

> The good neighbors of Batture Row . . . can practically feed themselves there along the bank. If they want to repair or enlarge their houses, they can hook onto timber that floats by with the Mississippi's current past their doors. Their clothing requirements are few, not just for children but for adults, since the social competition in Batture Row is not what you might call keen.

For the last time in a long time, an observer was able to look out over the long settlement and remark, "The city seldom thinks about this community, and apparently this community seldom thinks about the city. . . . They don't bother anybody, and they don't want to be bothered."[12]

The days of being left alone were numbered.

Chapter 14

Batture Apocalypse

O n May 11, 1948, a storm more destructive than batture folks had ever seen gathered on the horizon over Carrollton Bend. Earl K. Long was elected governor. The election wasn't close, but Captain William Bisso Sr., industrial titan of the Carrollton batture and caucus chairman for Long's forces in New Orleans, remembered his comeuppance eight years before. He wasn't taking any chances. It was later reported that seventeen people claimed Bisso's padlocked store and former office on the Carrollton batture as their residence when they registered to vote.[1]

Governor Earl Long rewarded William Bisso Sr. for his loyalty by appointing his son, William Bisso Jr., to the board of the New Orleans Levee District. The son understood levee politics and river business and ran the daily operations of the family's towboats and coal tippler, but the *New Orleans Item* pointed out that all of Long's appointees to the board shared one characteristic, "a close and thoroughly disciplined allegiance to Earl Long."[2]

William Bisso Jr. became the levee board's fiercest critic of the batture settlement. At his first board meeting, Bisso suggested "undesirable dwellers might be evicted under health regulations" and complained that camps near his family-owned batture were "health and fire menaces."[3] While he mounted this offensive, a waste oil dump on his batture caught fire. It was the fifth time in two years that the toxic pit ignited. Flames soared a hundred feet in the air and automobile and train traffic was halted by the billowing smoke.

Orleans Levee District lawyers speculated that some residents in Carrollton Bend might soon claim thirty-year squatter's rights to their homes, but old-time batture folks who knew a little about local government put no stock in that possibility. Seventy-six-year-old Louis Letamendi scoffed: "People on the lakefront out at Milneburg had lived there all their lives but the government put them out. So this ownership don't mean anything to me."[4]

Carrollton Bend residents ignored levee board machinations and kept their eyes on the ever-higher spring floods. In 1949 and 1950, for the fourth and fifth time in a decade, the Mississippi reached crests that still rank in the top twenty. On February 8, 1949, C. H. Dumser and his wife sat at their kitchen table, listening to the radio. Suddenly, in a resounding crash, the front of their home crumbled into the river.

> We thought it was a bomb. My wife and I were waiting for a radio program at 7 p.m. The lights went out and she grabbed my arm . . . I pulled [her] to the window, broke it out and we climbed through into the yard. Gas was escaping from the broken pipes, but I took a hammer and bent the outlet closed.[5]

The pilot of the towboat *Lafourche* had become disoriented in fog on the swollen river. The oil barge she was pushing smashed into two batture homes. Former river pilot James Kelly, who lived a few camps below the Dumsers, prevented further destruction of batture houses. He shouted directions to the *Lafourche* crew, threw them a rope, and secured the fog-bound boat to a stout willow tree. The Dumsers settled in court with the Oil Transport Company and moved to the city just before all hell broke loose.

The high-water season of 1949–50 began a year of heartbreak for one of the biggest families in the settlement. Alan Mitchell, whose descendants still live on the batture today, had moved onto the river during the late 1930s with his brother Leon and their extended families. They occupied camps on both sides of the Orleans-Jefferson parish line. The Leon Mitchells and their six children lived in Southport, next door to Leon's sister and brother-in-law, Theresa and Sam Selman.

In early February the Mitchells and Selmans listened to waves kiss their floorboards, small spouts of water appeared between cracks when ships went by, and their friend Dennis Bertrand narrowly escaped when his own camp sank into the river. The wind blew hard against the east bank, and by February 18 batture families found themselves wading from room to room. The Red Cross brought tents, and that night the Mitchells and their six children sheltered atop the levee with Theresa, Sam, and fifteen-month-old Sam Jr. Early the next morning Jesse Jones, chairman of the

Ms. Leon Mitchell with three of her six kids, flood of 1950.
Photo courtesy of the *New Orleans Times-Picayune*.

Dennis Bertrand leaves his fallen house in flood of 1950.
Photo courtesy of *New Orleans Times-Picayune*.

Pontchartrain Levee Board, woke them up and ordered them to leave. He told them, improbably, that their tent pegs had damaged the levee.

The refugees camping atop the levee ignored orders from Chairman Jones to break camp. They stacked household possessions outside their tents and waited for the flood to recede. A week later they returned to sodden homes, washed the mud off of the floors, hung bedding out to dry and life returned to normal. Sam Selman Jr. received a puppy for his second birthday in October; at Christmas, Santa visited the batture by boat to distribute toys.

On January 29, 1950, Theresa Selman walked next door to speak with her mother and returned moments later to find her camp afire. She could hear Sam Jr. inside in his crib and fought to get through a curtain of flames sprouting from the door. Firemen arrived quickly, but there was no water on that section of the batture. Sam Jr. and his puppy died in the blaze.

Little more than a month after the tragic fire, Sam and Theresa Selman were sheltering with the Mitchells when a wave caved in the back wall of the house. The Red Cross provided a room in the city, and the women and children moved out. The men stayed with their flooded home on the batture.

Floods and fires couldn't dislodge families like the Mitchells and Selmans. The wrecking ball, however, began a slow descent on Carrollton Bend on November 17, 1952. The date was just shy of the thirty-year anniversary of the settlement, a moment when some folks might have hoped to accrue squatter's rights.

The Corps announced a plan to raise parts of the levee in Carrollton Bend and place concrete on the riverfront slope. They wrote to the Orleans Levee Board to request access to the batture, and they wanted it cleared. I discovered the details of how the plan was approved after a visit to the office of the Orleans Levee District in 2001.

The levee board command center was then shoehorned into the old and seldom-used Lakefront Airport, where a public relations officer led me upstairs and apologized. "I'm sorry this is such a mess but take your time, baby—and let me know if I can copy anything for you." She left me in a closet that was knee deep in unfiled, unsorted, and unstacked papers. The tiny room looked like a burglar had tossed it.

I sat on an overturned file cabinet and winnowed the clutter until I had a stack of minutes from levee board meetings dated between 1918 and 1955. Four years after that visit, Hurricane Katrina damaged the roof at Lakefront Airport and sent water cascading into the tiny room full of documents.

On a yellowed page from November 1952, I found the following entry:

> It was moved by Commissioner William A. Bisso, Jr. . . . and carried unanimously that the following two resolutions be adopted: grant- ing the requested "right of entry to the U.S. Corps of Engineers" and also "authorizing the Legal and Engineering Departments to take the necessary steps to effect the removal of all squatters' dwellings from the affected area."[6]

When the board met a month later, Bisso read aloud a letter of complaint submitted to the board seven years earlier by the New Orleans chapter of the Red Cross of America. Citing the "menace to health" suffered by occupants, he proposed and the board approved "total removal of dwell- ings" from "battures and levees of the Mississippi River in the Parish of Orleans." This edict included the camps by Bisso's own batture compound as well as clusters of homes downriver in the city's Ninth Ward and across the river in Algiers.[7]

The levee board didn't take up the human or cultural cost of destroying a community and sending residents into the overtaxed housing market. Nor did they consider the possibility of saving the homes in Carrollton while the Corps completed levee repairs. They had bigger projects on their agenda. People were buying lots in the board's reclaimed west end Lake- front subdivision, so they moved forward plans to reclaim more land and destroy the remaining stilt houses on the eastern lakefront near Lincoln Beach.[8]

Just before Christmas in 1952, the levee board announced that residents of the 140 camps in Carrollton Bend would have six months to vacate their homes. The river folk hatched plans to fight. A hundred residents of the Carrollton batture banded together to form the Batture Dwellers Associa- tion (BDA). One of their leaders was James Kelly, a World War I veteran and hero of the Dumser barge accident. Kelly set about the seemingly impossible task of organizing the intractable and stubbornly independent river rabble, a community that had always preferred non-engagement.[9]

Batture dwellers had no money, no visibility, and in a state where patronage was the key to the courts, they had no political allies. They were fighting two of the most powerful institutions in the city, the levee board and the Corps. These agencies were entrusted to protect a "public" that batture folks were not part of.

James Kelly addressed the first official meeting of the nascent BDA outdoors on the levee. It was a sunny spring day. Old women sat in rocking chairs on the levee crown, children chased dogs down the slope, and men in hats clutched eviction letters from the levee board. Some leaned forward, listening closely to a state representative who promised to voice their concerns.

The BDA employed a grassroots strategy to raise money and court public opinion. Many residents held union cards, and there were dozens of veterans of both world wars among them. They turned to the men who had worked and fought with them and secured donations, free office space, and volunteer services. Then they hired a lawyer. They weren't claiming land title—they just wanted to be left alone.[10]

A handful of residents gave up and sought other places to live, but affordable housing options were scarce. The city had espoused an urban renewal plan that required landlords to repair and renovate existing homes. The policy may have helped preserve New Orleans' cityscape of beautiful old houses, but it sent rents spiraling beyond the means of common people. Returning soldiers and their growing families depleted the number of available rental units and further inflated rents.

Just before the batture case went to court, *Life* magazine ran a photo spread on the controversy, titled "Waitin' on a Levee for the Dispossess." It was an odd title, but "dispossess" captured the river people's plight perfectly—they weren't just being evicted. The government was taking their homes, their means of survival, and their way of life. Pictured were Dennis Bertrand, the seventy-one-year-old "poet laureate of the batture"; Otis Domas, a shell-shocked veteran who spent "his days sketching and making paper cutouts"; and a smiling Katherine Motta, a piano teacher who offered "lessons in the shack she shares with a dozen cats." James Kelly, the leader of the BDA, is seen harvesting a piling from the river.[11]

The Orleans Levee Board may have underestimated this ragtag cast of characters. When the suit for eviction was heard in civil court on July 16, 1953, the board was woefully unprepared. To avoid arguing the *necessity* of taking the homes, they claimed the right to evict batture dwellers under a state statute known as the Sharecropper Act. This statute had allowed plantation owners a quick means to remove sharecroppers whenever they wanted.

Levee board lawyers encountered a problem that had plagued claimants to batture land since Edward Livingston fenced off his batture in 1804—how to define and find boundaries on the ephemeral geography outside the levee. Judge Hall concluded:

> [The levee board] did not provide sufficient evidence to enable the court to determine the location of the property . . . with respect to the present levee or the present mean low water line of the river . . . or the location of any of the defendants' camps with respect to that property. . . . The levee board should come again with a better prepared case.[12]

For the moment, the BDA was victorious. They had won a favorable court ruling, received a public endorsement in the city newspaper from the Catholic Committee of the South, and garnered national attention from the *Life* photo essay. Letters to local newspapers ran heavily in support of their cause. But two days after their setback in court, William Bisso and levee board president Louis J. Roussel struck back, threatening to force utility companies providing electricity, phone, and water service to the batture to remove their lines.

A new trial began in September 1953 in front of Civil Court Judge Louis H. Yarrut. This time the levee board's argument was grounded in legal principles that had emerged from the famous nineteenth-century batture conflict between Edward Livingston and Thomas Jefferson. Public servitudes were enshrined in the Louisiana Civil Code. Similar to easements, they permitted government agencies to seize land for civic purposes. The levee board controlled a servitude on riverbanks to conduct levee work and to protect the city from flooding.

The board's case was straightforward. The Corps had requested the batture to be cleared to accomplish levee repairs essential for public safety. The batture dwellers had no legal right to their homes, and the levee board had the authority and responsibility to take action to remove them. Engineers explained that the camps must be razed so that workers could harvest sand for the project from the adjacent batture.

Attorneys for the batture dwellers responded that demolition wasn't necessary. After all, concrete had been placed on the side of the Southport levee in 1936 without removing the camps there. Just three months earlier, concrete had also been laid on the levee beside Bisso's compound, yet none of the Bisso buildings or camps on the Black batture had been disturbed. George Gebhardt testified that the board had been selling sand from the Carrollton batture between his camp and the sewage and waterboard plant for decades—"they got enough sand in there to top that levee down to Canal Street without moving a camp there."

The Corps insisted it would be less costly and more efficient to raze the settlement. Chief Engineer Willoz estimated the project would finally cost $65,000, or $20,000 less than the amount appropriated, but that hauling sand from a distant site would add 33 percent to the cost. The batture dwellers' attorneys did the math: Even if sand was trucked in, the final cost would still remain within the $85,000 appropriated for the work. However, the Corps and the levee board wanted the camps gone and refused to re-bid the job.

On October 19, 1953, Judge Yarrut found in favor of the New Orleans Levee District. He ordered batture dwellers to remove their dwellings and all property from the Carrollton batture within thirty days or face forcible ejection by the civil sheriff for Orleans Parish. He also ordered electric, telephone, and water companies to remove utility connections to the camps.[13] Judge Yarrut quoted two sections of the Louisiana Civil Code that harkened back to the famous batture conflict of 1804:

> The public has a servitude on the shores of navigable rivers, and for the making and repairing of levees. (Louisiana Civil Code Article 665)
>   Any works built on the rivers or navigable streams . . . may be destroyed at the expense of those who claim them. (Louisiana Civil Code Article 861)

Judge Yarrut addressed the pleas of batture dwellers who questioned the necessity of removal: "The convenience of a group of batture-dwellers on the banks of the Mississippi River . . . must yield to the demands for necessity, economy, or convenience of the state and federal agencies. . . ."[14]

The BDA appealed, and six months later, on April 26, 1954, the Louisiana Supreme Court unanimously upheld the ruling of Judge Yarrut. The remaining batture folks would be served with new eviction notices to vacate their homes. After eighteen months of fighting, the battle of the batture was over.

Arguments of lawyers and speculations of newspaper reporters were easy to find, but I wanted to hear from the people who lived through the fight. It was logical that stories of the last people to live in the settlement would be the easiest to record. I had met and talked to Garfield Beattie and Georgie Dumser, people who lived there decades earlier. Survivors of the batture apocalypse would mostly be younger, and many of their names appeared in news and magazine accounts of the eviction.

I made a list, found scores of corresponding names in the BellSouth directory, and started to call. Eventually, I reached a dozen of those folks who sat on the levee back in 1953, clutching levee board permits and bills of sale and looking for inspiration from their leader, James Kelly. Their response was crushing: "I can't talk about it." "I'm so sorry. Please don't call me again." "I have NOTHING to say." "I don't have anything to say to you." "No." Click. "No." Click. "No." . . .

Some were hostile, others just sounded tired. Not one would speak to me. Fifty years after their eviction, the survivors of the Carrollton Bend apocalypse were still traumatized. What they had on the batture was irreplaceable: The cool air. The wide horizon. The fish. The shrimp. The crazy kids and neighbors. The community. . . . The river.

The last voice to speak to me from the settlement didn't appear in print coverage of the court battle, and he wasn't listed in the phone book. A decade after I first began hunting batture stories, I got word from a friend that a box of documents had turned up in the Louisiana Research Collection at Tulane University. The Batture Dweller Association File had probably been hiding there all that time, neither archived nor catalogued. A librarian had no idea who donated it or when.

The box contained a list of every camp owner on the levee in 1953, keyed to a levee map showing where each lived. Amid deletions indicating people who had abandoned the fight and torn down their camps, attorneys for the BDA scrawled notes that revealed how suspicion and subterfuge invaded the colony: "Levee Board stooge. Don't invite to meeting." "Not part of our group." "Bisso man." "Informant for levee board?"

The heart of the Batture Dwellers Files was material from their last stand, a period from 1955 to 1957, when forty-six of those evicted formed a new organization, the Batture Dwellers Defense Association (BDDA). The BDDA fought to be reimbursed for their ruined homes. The group wrote personal narratives, and from those accounts they created the booklet, "These Were Our Homes."[15] The cheaply printed pamphlet, filled with photographs and testimonials about a lost way of life, was sold for a dollar to recoup legal costs.

George Gebhardt was the honorary historian of the BDDA and the star of "These Were Our Homes." As a child, he worked in his father's shingle-making shop on the Carrollton batture, trapped wild birds for Emile Geisenheimer, and labored at the Fisher Sawmill. He went on to become a lead carpenter on notable buildings around the city before moving onto the batture next to Seymour Geisenheimer after the flood of 1922. Gebhardt couldn't share his stories with me in person. He died shortly after the court rejected his appeal for damages.

Of three personal narratives collected in the Batture Dwellers Files, George S. Kippers's stood out. Kippers hadn't appeared in news accounts of the diaspora because he and his family left the batture after the first eviction notice. He didn't just walk away. George Kippers cut his house in half, hired a shoring company and had it moved to the suburb of Harahan.

In scrawled cursive in the margins and on the back of a "Batture Dwellers and Defense Association Claim Sheet" dated 1955, Kippers related how his house was chopped, loaded, shaken, and then dropped on a vacant lot he purchased in the suburbs. It sat there, open to the elements, for eight months while he borrowed money to pay for the lot, the move, and the renovation.

The biggest cost to Kippers was the life disrupted. He was forced to leave his aged parents, who lived beside him on the river. His friends and family loaned him money, and his son quit school to help support the family. His written account summed up the experience this way:

> I am 50-years old and I borrowed money from everyone who would lend it to me. I am in so much debt, I doubt if I live long enough to

pay it back . . . I am worked to death trying to make a home out of it now. I could <u>never</u> estimate what I lost or how much it cost.[16]

Building a house by hand and then sawing it in half seemed like something a batture dweller might do, but I couldn't imagine moving a torn-up batture camp into the city. As I reread the story and flipped through the Kippers file, a small yellow paper fell out on the library desk. It was an invoice for $750 from a house moving company. At the bottom was a suburban address.

I got in my truck and drove five miles to the address on the invoice and found a small shotgun-style house. No one answered the door, but a magazine poked out of the mailbox addressed to a "Ms. Kippers." I got down on the ground, looked under the house and saw the long cypress beams of an old river barge. I touched its side, a piece of river history in the suburbs.

The final voice to speak from the ruined settlement was the son, George S. Kippers Jr., the boy who quit high school in 1954 to help his family when they were forced off of the batture. At age eighty, George Kippers Jr. bore the tough demeanor of the smallest kid on the playground. His slight body nearly disappeared under an oversize green parka and he scowled beneath a shock of tousled white hair. I looked in his face and saw the same grievances I had heard in angry refusals shouted at me over the telephone.

As the Depression ended, George's father, a self-employed truck driver, was barely getting by. In 1941 he moved with his wife and five-year-old son to the Carrollton batture. A few months later, his parents moved in next door. Their house was built from a barge and it had twenty-eight-foot beams running the length of it. Five-year-old George Kippers Jr. did his small part to keep the family fed.

Daddy had a cow on the batture. We'd milk her and I'd have to sit there on the back porch and churn the freakin' butter. Mrs. Barrileaux had chickens and once or twice a week we got eggs from them and they got the butter. This was how we survived the war. People were suffering and here we were with fresh milk, fresh butter, fresh eggs, and fish from the river.

Like Joe Judd and John Benedict and everyone who lived on the batture as a child, Kippers's fondest memories were of the river itself.

That river has always been like a magnet to me, even today. In the summertime we'd be in the water. We used to swim across and end up way down there past Westwego. In order to get back, we had to walk all the way up past

George Kippers scowls beneath a shock of white hair.
Photo by Macon Fry.

*where we left from, and swim back across. And then we'd get home and get
our ass whipped. When I think about how stupid we were I shake my head.*

Kippers managed to say the things that the people who rebuffed my calls
couldn't. He never stopped scowling, but he looked out at the river and
spoke for many of those people who had their homes destroyed.

*I've been carrying this feeling for the river for a long time. I wish I coulda
raised my kids up here. I had a horse and I had a stable in the yard right
by the house. People used to come out here. Folks would picnic. There was
a Black church in the city, and they used to come right down by the Sewage
and Water Board wharf on Sundays and baptize the people who needed to be
baptized. I didn't want to leave. All my friends were right here in Carrollton.
Whoever was in office robbed everyone. They took the batture away from
everybody. That's why I don't care about the city anymore. They caused my
parents a whole lot of heartbreak. My parents didn't let us know at the time;
all we knew here were good times.*

⚜

Sheriff Scanlon planted a six-by-four-foot eviction notice on the levee.
Photo courtesy of the *New Orleans Times-Picayune*.

The batture dwellers hoped that their settlement mattered to the city. That was the heart of their legal appeal. They hoped that their way of life was valued. They hoped to stir sympathy in their plight. But they weren't fighting elected officials. Their opponents weren't answerable to anyone but their political patrons.

On Tuesday, July 20, 1954, a week before the court-ordered eviction, more residents joined the likes of George Kippers and pulled up stakes. Levee board chief engineer Armand Willoz counted sixty-two camps to be destroyed and reported that most were still occupied. The elderly Dennis Bertrand and George Gebhardt were openly defiant when Sheriff L. J. Scanlon warned them of the coming eviction. James Kelly raged, "I'll never, never move, and they'll never move my house."[17]

Six sheriff's deputies, protected by police, delivered a final notice to each camp. The next day, Sheriff Scanlon returned and planted a three-by-six-foot sign in the middle of the Carrollton Bend. It bore the same warning printed in the sixty-two eviction notices. The board would provide trucks and maintenance workers to haul possessions off the levee on the weekend. Monday would be the showdown.

People began to evacuate in earnest Saturday morning. The levee crown was covered with appliances, furniture, and crates of household goods. Sunday afternoon, the belongings of the dispossessed spilled down the levee side, where eighty-five-year-old Carrie Wood sat on a ladderback rocker in the batture weeds. She placidly awaited levee workers to come pick up her television set, resting on a nearby trunk full of her possessions, and take her to a friend's house.

The eviction began around 7 a.m. on Monday, July 26. It was already nearly eighty degrees. The sun glared over mounds of possessions still stacked atop the levee awaiting transportation. As deputies made a last door-to-door check of the camps, a bulldozer started work, splintering Camp 1 with ease.

Miss Katherine Motta, the music teacher, had spent the night trying to convince her dozen or so cats to abandon her camp before it was wrecked. Next door to Motta, Dennis Bertrand made his last stand, forcing Deputy Sheriff Angelo Fontaine to carry him from the house and out the long catwalk.

Deputy Fontaine had just deposited the old poet atop the levee when he saw a spectator gesturing wildly where the bulldozer was nosing against Camp 2. A woman was still inside. Fontaine halted the machinery and found the aged Mrs. Theodore Miller cradling a disconnected phone, trying to call a moving van to haul her possessions.

Camp 3 belonged to Dorothy Beattie, whose husband, Garfield, had moved onto the batture in 1928. Both their parents lived there, and they had built their first house there. The couple split up about the time the levee board began to threaten the people of Carrollton Bend, and Garfield left the river to raise their son in the city. Dorothy had remained—he couldn't convince her to leave.

I told Dorothy the place would be torn down, but she didn't want to hear this. All of her friends were there. I was working that day and had to get permission to go down at lunch hour. The house was already down when I got there. They had a bulldozer that pushed them over into the river. Bathtubs, toilets, stoves, electric. They had people behind the 'dozers picking up what was left: light fixtures, piping, copper wire. It was women up there crying, I can tell you that.

Shortly after Dorothy's camp went down, a fire consumed three of the structures. Batture dwellers blamed the levee board for setting it; demolition crews blamed the evacuees for leaving gas cans. Smoke lay over the narrow strip of land along the river and a west wind pressed the stench of burning creosote, tarpaper, and damp wood onto a crowd of onlookers.

When evening showers cleared the smoke and turned the silt beach to mud, the first twelve camps were gone. Two days later, the other fifty would be gone. The batture, rutted by heavy machinery and studded with the roots of broken pilings, looked like a forest after a clear-cut.

Dennis Bertrand and Katherine Motta spent two rainy nights on top of the levee, watching thieves pick through piles of possessions left on the crown. The poet slept in a refrigerator crate. Motta sat inside the flap of a tent provided by the Boy Scouts, scanning the ruined landscape for her half-wild cats.

Chapter 15

Keep Your Heads Down

Bureaucrats with bulldozers had gutted the Carrollton settlement. By 1955 a mile of vacant, weedy shore remained between the headquarters of the US Army Corps of Engineers and the Orleans water intake at the Jefferson Parish line. Fresh white concrete armored the levee. The riverside looked naked without the eccentric shapes of self-built river camps.

Two clusters of camps bracketed the hollowed-out landscape. A dozen or so stilt houses clung to the shore upriver in Southport and perhaps three times that many hid in the woods downriver, on Mahalia Jackson's batture beside the Bisso dock. These vestigial colonies survived because their adjacent levees had been resurfaced earlier without disturbing the camps. They were outside the scope of the demolition the levee board approved in 1952.

William Bisso Jr., who complained so loudly about stilt houses beside his private waterfront in 1948, apparently didn't have the will to displace people in those camps without an order from the Corps. Bisso's son, "Cappy," later recalled that most of the residents were Blacks, employed by the family business.[1] For months after the levee work was complete, the Bissos harvested sand from their batture and advertised it for sale in local newspapers. None of the camps were destroyed to accomplish that work.

In 1956 a reporter counted more dogs than residents on Mahalia's batture. Sixty-six mongrels roamed a nest of at least twenty-five occupied camps. Rickety catwalks jogged out toward the shacks, spanning vegetable gardens, chicken coops, goat pens, and piles of flotsam. One pier trifurcated to reach three stilt houses. The homes were covered in cast-off tin, driftwood, tarpaper, and a sign that read WHITNEY BANK: TEMPORARY QUARTERS. The run-down Noah's Ark Baptist Church sat in the middle.[2]

A mile or so upriver in my community of Southport the batture was narrower, and twelve or thirteen camps sat in a neat line along 300 yards of levee. During the Depression, several of those camps had been occupied by Blacks, but refugees from the 1954 batture apocalypse moved in and, by 1957, the Southport colony turned predominantly white. A house painter, riverfront laborers, a fisherman, the families of seamen, and a pack of children called my batture home.[3]

The vestigial batture colonies disappeared from the public eye, dwarfed by the industries that surrounded them—National Industrial Chemical Company, Bisso Towing, The American Creosote Company, National Lubricants Corporation and an asbestos plant. The battle to preserve the line village connecting them had been lost. But soon, more powerful parties on more prominent batture lands awoke to the fight over a different riverfront.

Immediately downriver from the Broadway colony and Bisso Enterprises, the batture at Audubon Park is a place where the Mississippi slows and drops sediment. Landscape architect John C. Olmsted incorporated this gift of the river in his 1899 plans for the park. Frederick Olmsted, John's half-brother, mapped out the riverfront expansion in 1933, describing the park batture as "land from which a park visitor can satisfactorily command inspiring views over hundreds of acres of the Mississippi River and its further shores, where distance can lend picturesque enchantment even to the crudest industrial developments. . . ."[4]

During the Depression, WPA work crews began filling the Audubon batture to create Olmsted's waterfront promenade, but the city lacked money to complete the project. Park commissioners solved that problem in 1941 by allowing the city to use the riverfront as a dump. By the end of the decade, wet garbage was piled on the batture and flies, rats, and wild dogs abounded. The Department of Health blamed children who left picnic scraps on the ground and tossed peanuts to zoo animals. They fogged rodent dens with cyanide gas and applied DDT to the dump to kill fleas. The park batture became an open sore, filled with city's smoking garbage and laced with pesticide.[5]

In February 1961 the Dock Board floated a plan to build a $14 million wharf to stretch from one side of the park to the other. They would put the reclaimed riverfront acres to industrial use. Mayor Chep Morrison and the city council unanimously supported the plan but encountered swift opposition among park commissioners and nearby landholders who didn't want a noisy industrial outpost in the neighborhood.

Opposition to the wharf wasn't just a "not in my backyard" phenomenon. The Park Commission organized a petition opposing the wharf that quickly garnered signatures of 4,500 people—75 percent of whom were from elsewhere in the city. Citizens rose for the first time in over a century to demand a truly public riverfront. Councilman Henry B. Curtis defected and joined the public outcry, pointing out, "Once a park is lost, it is lost forever."[6]

As city council support evaporated, the Dock Board promoted their plan with full-page newspaper ads touting economic benefits and the need for more dock space. They hired an architect to draw a fantastical plan depicting a ski lift gondola that would lift park visitors to a viewing platform on a warehouse roof. Dock Board director Amoss Moses proposed a cocktail lounge on the roof, reasoning that the only non-industrial value of the riverfront was "to see the river and the traffic that moves through the port."[7]

Defenders of the public waterfront were not pacified when Dock Board president Robert Elliot suggested that the "five sets of railroad tracks" between the zoo and the river rendered the Audubon batture "unsafe for recreational use." Using that previously built impediment as an inducement to build new barriers to public access failed to garner support for the wharf. Elliot reassured, "This board is made up of men who are willing and who are able to make decisions for the greater good of New Orleans and Louisiana."[8]

Another piece of riverfront would have disappeared in the name of the public good, but the Audubon Park Commission sued the Dock Board for "illegal seizure" of park property. After a year of wrangling, an appeals court rejected the Dock Board claim. Audubon Park commissioners began planning the riverfront promenade where today people boil crawfish, hold family reunions, fish, toss frisbees, play soccer and baseball, make out, wax their cars—and watch the ships go past.

The Audubon Park dustup was a schoolyard scrap compared to the battle that began when the New Orleans City Planning Commission proposed an elevated expressway along the French Quarter waterfront.[9] The rapid growth of suburbs and the birth of the interstate highway system inspired city planners to unearth a scheme that was first drawn in 1946. In

1958 the City Council, Chamber of Commerce, State Highway Commission, Dock Board, and Mayor Chep Morrison—the same forces that supported a wharf on the Audubon riverfront—all endorsed the expressway.

Advocates of the freeway wanted to speed commuters into the city and capture federal funds to pay for the project. Even a few preservationists believed that a ground-level expressway on the riverfront might ease congestion and reduce harmful vibrations around French Quarter landmarks. In the *Times-Picayune* of November 20, 1958, Martha Robinson, president of the Louisiana Landmarks Society, defined the fear of early opponents: "The automobile is a Frankenstein. We've got to not let it devour or ruin the asset that the Vieux Carré is to the city."

The project would have been a done deal in 1964, when funding for the freeway was approved through the national interstate highway plan. But the power of the river trumped federal dollars. The waterfront at the French Quarter, like my batture in Carrollton Bend, is a cut bank. In 1962 the Mississippi had undercut the wharves and sheds in front of Jackson Square, and forced the Dock Board to begin to raze them. By the time federal funding was approved, the removal of the ugly warehouses was nearly complete. A key barrier between the river and the French Quarter fell.

The debate shifted from highway-induced blight to a more fundamental question. Preservationists, community organizations, and civic groups asserted that the relationship between the French Quarter and the river was paramount. William Ricciutti, a former president of the Vieux Carré Commission, argued, "Any structure which tends to separate Jackson Square from the river will inevitably destroy its historic identification of the Vieux Carré with the river . . ."[10]

The expressway controversy was dubbed "The Second Battle of New Orleans."[11] Like the ragtag fighters under Major General Andrew Jackson who fought back the British in the original Battle of New Orleans, the assembled forces of opposition overcame well-funded and organized institutional support for the freeway. In 1969, over a decade after the fracas began, the federal government withdrew the expressway from inclusion in their interstate plan, effectively killing the project. Visitors now flock to the boardwalk in front of Jackson Square, a place where the public can put their feet in the muddy river.

⚜

The Southport camps during the flood of 1973.
Photo courtesy of US Army Corps of Engineers, New Orleans District.

In the spring of 1973, attention turned from debates in courtrooms and council chambers to the river itself. The Mississippi crested at 18.47 feet at the Carrollton Gauge on April 7. For the first time, water was diverted through the giant Morganza Spillway and into the Atchafalaya Basin to prevent a catastrophic failure at the flood-damaged Old River Control Structure upstream. If the Old River Control had failed, the main current of the Mississippi might have been permanently captured and traveled down the Atchafalaya River, an event that surely would have created a century of new batture lawsuits.

As the river crested in 1973, Vanaan Allen, a Tulane University student, conducted research for an honors thesis at the Southport and Broadway colonies. She found the thirteen camps in Southport mostly vacated in anticipation of the flood. Camp 2 had just been shattered by a runaway barge and was hanging in the river. Four residents remained, busily raising their possessions above the water. One paused to declare, "I ain't talkin' to no stranger."

Despite her difficulty in engaging batture dwellers, Allen made detailed observations of the colonies. Most Southport camps had propane tanks and running water, while the people at Mahalia's batture carried water from the city, used outhouses, and heated their homes with wood or kerosene. The

Children on "Mahalia's batture" during the flood of 1973.
Photo courtesy of the *New Orleans Times-Picayune.*

"dilapidated" camps on the Black batture were covered in tin, tarpaper, and flattened cans. Occupants burned or dumped their garbage in the river.

After speaking with a few people on Mahalia's batture, the young student reached an obvious but important conclusion—one that had eluded observers obsessed with batture dwellers' tax-free and rent-free existence. Allen found that people lived on the river "for not purely economic reasons," but to enjoy a "simpler lifestyle" unavailable in the city itself.[12]

Allen's honors thesis was a fond farewell for the Broadway colony. The elderly and infirm residents were unable to face rebuilding and, according to William Bisso Jr.'s son, "Cappy," the Bisso family destroyed the camps one at a time, as they were vacated.[13] Then the Bissos fenced off the portion of the batture they claimed to own. By the end of the decade all that remained of Mahalia's batture were busted pilings and scattered household junk. Even

Camp 2 (foreground) collapsed in the river.
Photo courtesy of US Army Corps of Engineers, New Orleans District.

those remnants disappeared in the 1990s when a neighborhood group cleared the place that was once home to sixty-six free-roaming batture dogs . . . to make a dog park.

Upriver at Southport, everyone returned from the flood to mop up; residents of Camp 2 found their home collapsed in the river. For the Mitchell family, cleaning up muddy floors was a familiar routine. They had endured floods in 1944 and 1945 and had been washed from their Southport home in 1949 and 1950. Unlike those earlier times when hundreds of homes were affected, no reporters trekked to the levee to report on the returning and rebuilding. There weren't enough people there to notice and the batture dwellers who remained were happy to keep their heads down and stay out of the newspaper.

The batture peace ended in October 1974 when a "notice to vacate" signed by Ashton R. O'Dwyer Sr. was posted on each of the thirteen batture camps. He claimed that the land beneath the homes was purchased from the Texas Oil Company by his uncle George O'Dwyer in 1945.[14] No one I spoke to remembered ever seeing an O'Dwyer on the levee, or recalled any previous claim against their batture, but the O'Dwyer name was familiar to people who lived on the river and to citizens in both Orleans and Jefferson Parish.

Ashton O'Dwyer Sr. was the grandson of E. O. O'Dwyer, who report-edly ran illegal "keno shops" in Jefferson Parish in the 1920s. His father, Rudolph, and uncle, George, operated casinos inside the levee just below the batture camps for decades. These illegal enterprises regularly made front-page news. They shared an uncanny ability to survive though their flashing lights, calls of keno numbers, and packed parking lots were within the daily view of people living on the Southport batture.[15]

Batture residents ignored the vacate notices until a sheriff delivered official summons, then they lawyered-up as best they could. With a suit brewing between the family of a deposed casino magnate and the handful of batture dwellers, newspapers sensed a story, but they came up short on batture residents willing to talk. The most succinct respondent was the retired brewery worker Shoe Gaudet who lived in the camp I would purchase over a decade later—"I love it here. I don't want to move . . . It's quiet and it's peaceful."[16]

The eviction hearing, conducted by a justice of the peace in a hotel ballroom, descended into a shouting match. The river folks had three at-torneys objecting on different grounds, but they coalesced around the fact that O'Dwyer had not demonstrated ownership of the specific land they occupied. Ashton R. O'Dwyer Jr., whose family made their fortune fleecing gamblers, lamented, "This is another case of people wanting something for nothing."[17]

I searched newspapers and court records and talked to my neighbors on the batture, but no one remembered what became of that first eviction attempt. The case disappeared and the colony disappeared from public view for another decade. By then I had found the cluster of Southport river camps and made the place my home.

When I found a letter from Ashton O'Dwyer Jr. on my shack door back in the eighties, I knew little about the history of conflicting claims to the property and nothing about O'Dwyer. Neighbors who were around in the 1950s and '60s had watched the homegrown illegal gambling industry flourish inside the levee, directly below their camps. They were certainly not pleased to see the scion of that family, a wealthy lawyer, claim their homes.

As batture folks again gathered to plan a strategy, some clutched their ownership papers worriedly; others spoke angrily or dismissively about the probability of eviction. But most everyone left the gathering feeling that this threat would pass like the lawsuits and floods of the previous decade—and they were right. The ownership dispute faded from the consciousness of the dozen households, who simply wished to be left alone.

The only people more reticent to talk about the batture than those who were dispossessed in 1954 were my own neighbors. Their only survival strategy had been to keep their heads down. When the river got unusually high and a reporter ventured onto the levee, the artist who lived in Camp 5 emerged in her white cotton nightgown, scowled from the end of her catwalk and screamed at the camera crew, "GO AWAY!" Another neighbor repeated a popular meme from a recent movie about a secret group known as "Fight Club." "Macon, you lived up here long enough to know, the batture is like Fight Club. 'The first rule of Fight Club is nobody talks about fight club. The second rule of fight club is NOBODY TALKS ABOUT FIGHT CLUB!'"

Numerous conflicts sprang up between residents and the Levee Police over small things: vehicles parked on the levee, placement of outbuildings, propane tanks too close to the levee slope, and non-permitted camp renovations. Neighbors themselves sometimes quarreled over the fences between houses and leaky water pipes that sent everyone's bill spiraling. Occasionally someone slashed tires on cars parked in a communal lot beside Camp 1.

The Levee Police didn't have much to do. Their jobs seldom required anything more strenuous than driving back and forth on the miles of levees surrounding the city and ticketing kids partying in the woods or racing mini-bikes, but their bosses on the levee board saw the batture camps as a nuisance. The last straw came one night in 1981 when someone, believed by many to be a guest in Camp 1, towed a 1956 Ford out of the community lot between Camp 1 and 2. A rope with the Ford's bumper attached was found near the top of the levee and the vehicle was found on the city side below, embedded in the rear of a new townhouse on River Road.

The Jefferson Levee Board called a meeting with the batture dwellers to establish a set of rules and accommodations. Residents welcomed the new guidelines, happy to have official sanction and anxious to placate authorities. They were even happier to be granted permits to drive on the levee and build driveways beside their camps. These positive developments smoothed over tensions regarding the wrecked Ford.

The colony became more affluent, not because of an influx of wealthy people or tax dodgers, but because people stayed there, attended school, found better jobs, and were able to save a little money. Newcomers included

French Quarter artists, two aspiring novelists, a young law student, a ballet dancer, a guitar wizard, an office worker with the Corps, and me, a public school teacher.

When a wealthy and powerful businessman purchased the batture camp belonging to the two young novelists in the 1990s, nothing changed. Like everyone else, he loved the river. The well-heeled newcomer created a rustic place with a big deck, adorned it with driftwood and ship rope and invited friends up to enjoy the batture. Our new neighbor came from a family respected for philanthropic and civic contributions in New Orleans; although he didn't make the camp his permanent residence, us batture folks appreciated that if we needed a special tool or a house jack, his posse usually came up with it.

A seminal event for New Orleans and its batture colony came in 2005 when Hurricane Katrina provided a citywide lesson in sea level. It was the moment that everyone learned the elevation of their home relative to the Gulf of Mexico. New Orleans' highest ground is along its edges, especially along the river levee; the batture camps sit even higher. From my camp I look out onto the roofs of houses inside the levees.

I spent the day before the storm building sixteen backyard gardens in the low-lying Hollygrove neighborhood. My volunteer workers begged off throughout the day as their spouses called and pleaded for them to evacuate. Finally, I was left alone at dusk, loading six muddy wheelbarrows, eighteen shovels, and twelve rakes into my truck.

The wind was kicking up off the river when I got back to Camp 6, backed into the driveway, and unloaded. I chained the wheelbarrows to pilings below the house and stuffed the hand tools underneath so they wouldn't become projectiles in a possible tornado. The river was sprouting whitecaps, but sixty feet of silt beach lay between the waves and my house. The weather service put the river height at two feet above sea level, typical of the low water of late summer.

I stripped off my muddy clothes, went in, and washed off the garden grime. I opened a beer and saw my last newscast for three weeks. Katrina had filled the Gulf of Mexico and was heading straight for New Orleans. I made a mental checklist: canoe, life jacket, a hundred bottles of water left over from the garden-build—nothing to worry about. Then the weatherman mentioned, "The Mississippi River is expected to crest at fourteen feet." That meant that the force of Katrina's storm surge would back the river up and cause a twelve-foot rise at my house, 104 river miles above the Gulf of Mexico.

I went back out into the gathering storm and unchained the wheelbarrows, which were about to be covered in four feet of river water. I filled them with tools, rolled them inside my camp and slept through the whole storm. When I awoke and went outside, a giant pecan tree had fallen across my pier; my goat, Sweet Pea, was inside the laundry shed standing wide-eyed atop the washing machine; and the river had retreated, right back to where it had been the evening before.

People inside the levee were less fortunate. After the storm passed, a surge built in the lake and pushed water up drainage canals and waterways around the city. Levees and flood walls built and certified by the Corps failed. The rest of what happened is well-documented history, but a little-known epilogue to the flood played out in the camp of our wealthy neighbor on the Southport batture.

The New Orleans Superdome, home to the beloved New Orleans Saints football team, was badly damaged by the storm and from its use as a shelter for thousands of refugees. Owner Tom Benson moved the team to a temporary base in San Antonio, where he had a ranch and businesses. The rumors began. Benson hadn't gotten the new lease he wanted at the Dome, and it was believed he would permanently move the team. Refrigerators full of rotten food that had been tossed from flooded homes were papered with signs warning, "Caution! Do not open. Tom Benson inside."

The general public was distraught and New Orleans' business community was in shock. Losing a major sports franchise is hard on a city, but in the context of the flood recovery, it would be an economic disaster of far greater proportion. *ESPN Magazine* reported on what happened next:

[Paul] Tagliabue [then commissioner of the NFL] decided to meet businessmen from New Orleans to hear directly from them. He'd heard the Saints complaining that the storm had made the tough economic climate in the city even more difficult. . . . They gathered at the river camp owned by shipping magnate Thomas Coleman, one of a dozen exclusive shacks built on the thin, fragile strip of land, called the batture, running between the levee and the river.

I'm not sure if I was more surprised that such an illustrious group had held a meeting on the lowly river batture, or that our homes were described as "a dozen exclusive shacks." Most entertaining was the assertion that followed: "Generations of New Orleanians have used these shacks, just a couple of miles from Audubon Park and the mansions on St. Charles, for whiskey drinking and holding meetings too secret for the public exposure of an office."[18]

I had to laugh out loud. Generations of "better" New Orleanians had reviled batture dwellers or ignored them for all time. Some of those better citizens had fought to tear down over a hundred batture camps to appease the Corps and save the federal government twenty thousand dollars. Sure there had been clandestine meetings on the batture, but they more often involved bathtub beer or homemade booze and games of chance.

Our new neighbor had barely finished defending the city against the potential loss of its football team when an old threat reappeared atop the levee. A mysterious figure arrived with twenty "No Trespassing" signs and planted the metal posts beside each camp. The signs disappeared that night, and the next day a Mercedes with vanity plates cruised the levee with an angry man at the wheel.

Ashton R. O'Dwyer, the same city lawyer who had claimed the land a decade earlier, was angry at a lot of people. He had remained in New Orleans after Hurricane Katrina despite Mayor Ray Nagin's "mandatory" evacuation. From the street in front of his stately St. Charles Avenue home, O'Dwyer reportedly claimed that he had seceded from the Union, predicted to reporters that the bluebloods would recapture the city, and by one account took delivery of delicacies by helicopter while boasting of his "Lord of the Flies/Robin Crusoe" existence. Then he got busted.

Weeks after the storm, with the city still under evacuation order, O'Dwyer was charged with public intoxication and hauled down to "Guantanamo North," as some locals referred to the chain-link cage that temporarily replaced the city's flooded jail. This was a time when poor citizens who ran afoul of the law could be found shot on overpasses or stuffed in the trunks of torched automobiles, but O'Dwyer didn't think that he got off easy. He sued state and local officials, claiming he had been tortured during his day of internment.

The grandson of casino boss Rudolph T. O'Dwyer also filed a lawsuit naming state and federal agencies, public utilities, and the batture dwellers for illegal occupation of his family's land on the Southport batture. He accused us, "the squatter trespasser defendants," of "conduct so outrageous and extreme in degree, as to go beyond all bounds of decency and to be regarded as atrocious, and utterly intolerable in civilized society."[19] He also complained that someone on the batture stole twenty no-trespassing signs.

The batture folks of 2006 weren't the impoverished urban refugees who faced off with the Orleans Levee Board back in 1954, but most of us still would have struggled to fight a lengthy court case against a lawyer with political connections. When our prominent neighbor entered the fray, what had been a very asymmetrical battle between a wealthy lawyer and a community of river folks suddenly shifted.

O'Dwyer had no more friends in the courthouse than he had on the batture. In 2008, following countless hearings, filings, and heated charges, he was temporarily suspended from practicing law in the federal court in New Orleans. The suspension arose from behavior alleged in an earlier post-Katrina lawsuit. By the time O'Dwyer was fully disbarred in March 2017, he had been accused of "inappropriate language," "name calling," "filing a suit without a factual basis," "engaging in conduct meant to disrupt a tribunal," and "using racial slurs, obscenities and other unprofessional and discourteous language."[20]

After Katrina, Jean Brady Hendrix fulfilled her dream and, at age eighty-four, moved into the most derelict of the remaining twelve batture houses. She was the landlady who had rented out my first batture home for $100 a month. Back then, in 1988, I laughed it off when Jean asserted her desire to add a room to the Shack and move in with me. It seemed like a long way from the uptown rooming house she owned to an unplumbed hut on the river. I couldn't picture the woman who once worked as a B-girl in the French Quarter and sang at the Pink Pussy Patio on Bourbon Street moving into a teetering stilt house. That shows how little I knew about the batture back then.

It may take a jack leg carpenter to keep a batture house standing, but Jean proved that it only takes an eccentric to live in one. She had never driven a car and could be seen daily, pedaling a pink Schwinn bicycle down narrow streets with her miniature poodle, Twee Dee, perched in the front

Jean Hendrix fulfilled her dream and moved onto the batture. Photo courtesy of John Burnett.

basket. Long before Katrina, Jean and Twee Dee had joined a pantheon of New Orleans "characters" with names like "Ruthie the Duck Girl" and "Faith Vader." Jean was recognized as the "Pink Bike Lady."

When Katrina struck, Jean was hunkered down in her boarding house. She reappeared with her flowing white hair, her bike, and Twee Dee a few days later on national TV. Whole Foods Market had opened its doors to donate their stock to stranded residents. Jean got her essentials—a bottle of wine, dog biscuits, and two bunches of flowers. As she departed the store clutching her bouquets, a national audience heard her ask the reporter, "Do you think they will mind that I took two?" I believe many New Orleanians watching her on TV decided at that moment that they would find a way to return.

Jean finally wound up on a bus out of town, evacuated to Denver, a place she hated after repeatedly wrecking her bike on "black ice." Somehow she relocated again to a senior center in Florida, where she made many friends by performing Bourbon Street standards at weekly karaoke nights. But Miami wasn't home. She had no phone, no phone book, and no way to get back until my old pal Rob tracked her down and paid her bus fare back to New Orleans.

Jean quickly connived to swap her burned-down river shack for the dilapidated and vine-covered Camp 11. Minor inconveniences didn't bother Jean, who ignored the leaky roof, the door that wouldn't close, and the patchwork of carpet samples covering the ceiling and walls. She adopted the raccoons and possum that lived in her spare rooms and got neighbors to buy fifty-pound bags of Ol' Roy dog food to feed them. Jean joyously inhabited the place. A perfect latter-day batture dweller.

Every evening I heard the screams of cyclists as they ditched their racing bikes into the grass when Jean pulled her pink Schwinn atop the levee, positioned it perpendicular across both lanes of the bike path, slowly got into the saddle and turned to face downriver. She pedaled a half-mile to Cooter Browns, a bar where she watched the Yankees and crooned ballads for college students who kept her glass full.

Jean died on January 27, 2012, at age eighty-nine. She was remembered in her obituary, and by everyone who knew her, for "a beautiful childlike spirit." I never again said that Jean didn't truly belong on the batture.

Few people ever move from the camps. When a resident drifts off or dies, one of their children will replace them, or some eccentric who feels the pull of the river will connive to get the place the same way I did when Shoe passed or like Jean did after Katrina. Jean's son lives in Camp 11 now. At least I think he's in there behind the vines. Next door, an elderly witness to the 1954 batture apocalypse resides with her daughter. Another camp is home to the river pilot, his wife, and three children. Their eldest son grew up there; like his father and grandfather he will probably attend the maritime academy and guide ships past the colony. If he is lucky, he may raise his own pack of river rats on the Southport batture.

It isn't hard to see the gentrification brought by recent batture arrivals and spread by long-term residents who have saved money, finished school, or otherwise improved their lot. One chronicler of batture life who often bicycles past the camps insists that with the arrival of doctors, lawyers, and well-heeled professionals, "one history has ended and a new one begun." But history, much like a river, rarely stops and starts. True, there may be a new era dawning on the batture, but the newcomers—call them "gentrifiers" if you will—still rounded up odd materials, designed their houses, and oversaw the construction themselves. They brought skills, tools, and determination. They bought onto the batture without insurance or bank loans, then poured love and sweat into their eccentric if grand stilt houses.

Batture kids at play on the silt beach. Photo courtesy of Margot Landen.

They learned to pay attention to a rising river, to secure fences, and to move possessions above an impending crest.

In his first year on the batture, the neighbor in Camp 8 found his propane tank unmoored, bobbing like a fishing cork in the waves. He spent the morning corralling the steel cylinder while his two little girls waded in the yard picking up floating plastic. His beautiful new home had twin salvaged-teak galleries overlooking the river, and the camp resembled a steamboat until he needed office space. In true river rat fashion, he simply slapped siding around the lower deck. On the batture, form still follows function.

Life on the river is no more predictable than it was in the days of batture caves, bird men and levee setback. In 2011 the Corps predicted a river crest with no recent precedent until the Morganza Spillway was opened for the second time in history. The river relented. In 2016 a freak storm sent the Nordbay Tanker against the left bank in front of our camps. In 2019 alone, the Corps opened the Bonnet Carré Spillway for the third time in four years, closed it, and a month later had to reopen it. A flotilla of barges broke loose in Carrollton Bend, a ship struck the Huey P. Long Bridge. and a towboat overturned in the surging river.

The Corps has squeezed my batture between two monolithic construction projects. In 2013 and 2014, they raised the levee four feet and installed

A third-generation batture child. Photo courtesy of Jamie Grue.

a "concrete mattress revetment" extending from the river edge of the batture down to the deepest part of the channel. They removed hundreds of trees along the water edge to anchor woven slabs of concrete to the beach. It was another depredation on the habitat of river shrimp and catfish, but they left our homes undisturbed.

Despite the unceasing battle of engineers to harness its flow, proponents of a public river and batture dwellers clinging to their small holdings have prevailed in the new century. Below the French Quarter, the mile-and-a-half-long Crescent Park opened in 2014. Even further downriver, in the bohemian enclave of Holy Cross in the Lower Ninth Ward, young people have discovered an unreconstructed stretch of batture that was once home to dozens of stilt houses. At night, and especially on weekends a hootenanny with towering bonfires enlivens the water edge.

Father and daughter salvage a river buoy. Photo courtesy of Margot Landen.

On the very edge of Carrollton Bend a brouhaha arose in 2016 when the *Times-Picayune* reported that a sports club had won approval from the Audubon Commission to build a private soccer complex at River View Park, behind Audubon Zoo. The stadium would be built on the reclaimed batture where where, in 1960, the Audubon Commission fought the Dock Board to prevent construction of a wharf and riverfront sheds. The place had become a treasured refuge for locals who call it "the Fly."

The Carrollton Boosters had already built a baseball compound at the Fly a few years earlier, where they operated a concession stand, advertised corporate sponsors, and locked the gate to non-members. When word got out that the Boosters planned another sports complex at the Fly, the outcry to preserve the public waterfront was nearly unanimous. A petition was circulated and, a month after the plan was publicized, it was abandoned.

The skirmish over the Fly was a small event, but along with Crescent Park it gave me hope. Defenders of the Fly shared a vision with the folks who started a dog park on Mahalia's batture, musicians on the Holy Cross shore, opponents of a wharf behind the zoo, and citizens who rose up against a riverfront expressway. Like the Creole rabble who refused to let Edward Livingston fence off the batture in 1804, all of these people saw something other than dollar signs on the willow-draped shore.

Epilogue

There is a quality to the Mississippi River, an irrevocable wildness that flood fighters fear and batture folks love. I realized it when I retreated to my cottage in Virginia after Hurricane Katrina. I returned to the Rappahannock River in 2005 to find powerlines strung across the river. The dirt road winding in had been paved and was lined with "Titans" and "Denalis" and "Yukons" hooked to jet-ski trailers. A two-story brick home with manicured yard stood where woods once surrounded my decaying cabin. Central air-conditioning droned, weed-eaters, lawn mowers, and leaf blowers whirred, whined, and chattered. The place that was my childhood refuge was gone.

People who visit me on the batture now point out the proximity of those same things—powerlines, wealthy neighbors, big cars, and a paved bike path on top of the levee. But wildness has lived beside industry and commerce and flood fighters on the Mississippi River batture for two centuries. River shrimp and blackberries and catfish and batture dwellers have made a deal with the river powerful enough to hold all of that.

In a tribute to the shantyboater and artist Harlan Hubbard, Wendell Berry perfectly captured the bargain that generations of river people have struck with their precarious edge. Berry describes Hubbard as a man who "lived in the rift between wilderness and civilization":

> A man of . . . urban upbringing, living at a time when the wild has survived only on the fringes of the industrial enterprise . . . made himself answer to the old-time American conviction that freedom and independence were to be found in the wilderness. He thus became a man of the margins.[1]

No one knows when the final "dispossess" might happen. Weather maps and river gauges can predict storms and river crests miles away, but they

The twelve camps in Southport, pictured here in 2018, could be gone tomorrow and might be forgotten in twenty years. Photo courtesy of Urban Martinez.

can't divine what year a towering flood will come or foresee when lawyers, government agencies, and industry will conspire to erase our homes. The twelve camps at Southport, the last colony on the lower river, could be gone tomorrow and might be forgotten in twenty years.

But today's batture dwellers, like their ancestors—Georgie, Seymour, Joe and Jean, and countless "river rats"—still look out on a wild and irrevocable frontier, a place on the margins where a sunrise as promising as the first day of spring climbs over the open levee, and melts in the west into a wet horizon big enough to hold generations more dreams and disasters.

NOTES

CHAPTER 1

1. "The Louisiana Civil Code tried to sort . . ." to ". . . how to measure it": A. N. Yiannopolis, "The Public Use of the Banks of Navigable Rivers in Louisiana," *Louisiana Law Review* 31 (1971). Available at: https://digitalcommons.law.lsu.edu/lalrev/vol31/iss4/211.

2. "French colonists who settled . . ." to ". . . berm atop the natural one": Richard Campanella, *Geographies of New Orleans* (Lafayette: Center for Louisiana Studies, University of Louisiana at Lafayette, 2006), 6–7.

3. ". . . a line village that once extended over much of the city's riverfront": *Daily Picayune*, August 4, 1895.

CHAPTER 2

1. "Consult a harbor map . . .": Free digital flood control and navigation maps of the Mississippi River: https://www.mvn.usace.army.mil/Missions/Engineering/Geospatial -Section/MRNB_2007/.

2. "A man can build himself . . ." to ". . . workmen and repairmen upstream.": *Sunday Item Tribune*, October 24, 1937.

3. The phenomenon of squatting and enclosure of frontier lands in America is explored in Steven Stoll, *Ramp Hollow: The Ordeal of Appalachia* (New York: Hill and Wang, 2017).

CHAPTER 3

1. "I don't worry about all that . . .": *Times-Picayune*, June 4, 1985.

2. "If all my dream come true . . .": *Times-Picayune*, March 26, 1989.

CHAPTER 4

1. "engineered wilderness . . ." to ". . . *emanates wildness*": Paul Hartfield, "Engineered Wildness: The Lower Mississippi River, an Underappreciated National Treasure," *International Journal of Wilderness* 20, no. 3 (December 2014).

2. "Mississippi is wild and random": John M. Barry, *Rising Tide: The Great Mississippi*

Flood of 1927 and How It Changed America (New York: Simon and Schuster/Touchstone Edition, 1997), 91.

3. "In the spring the Mississippi can carry . . .": US Army Corps of Engineers document. https://www.mvn.usace.army.mil/Missions/Mississippi-River-Flood-Control/Bonnet-Carre -Spillway-Overview/.

4. National Weather Service river stages and forecasts: https://forecast.weather.gov/ product.php?site=meg&product=RVA&issuedby=ORN.

5. US Army Corps of Engineers river stages and forecasts: http://rivergages.mvr.usace .army.mil/WaterControl/new/layout.cfm.

6. "Billy" William Finch (naturalist and botanist, US National Park Service), in conversation with the author, May 2015.

7. "the days went along . . ." to ". . . tear around till he drownded": Mark Twain, *Life on the Mississippi* (Boston: James R. Osgood, 1883), 82.

8. "There are stories of early river explorers . . .": Keith Sutton, "A Look Back at Mississippi River Catfishing," *Game and Fish*, September 24, 2010. http://www.gameandfishmag.com/ fishing/fishing_catfish-fishing_ar_aao60303a/.

9. "In 2005, a fisherman on the river . . .": Chad Ferguson, "World Record Catfish: The Largest Catfish Ever Caught," *Catfish Edge*. https://www.catfishedge.com/world-record-catfish/.

10. "A dish of river shrimps is easily produced . . .": Thomas Hutchins, *An Historical Narrative and Topographical Description of Louisiana and West Florida* (Philadelphia: printed for the author, 1784), 30. https://archive.org/details/historicalnarratoohutc/page/n5.

11. "considered more delectable . . ." to ". . . for large lake shrimp": *Times-Picayune*, May 14, 1911.

12. "We have always said that . . . we'll be different": *Times-Picayune*, July 22, 1929.

13. "Unworried by the cost . . ." to ". . . on the supper table": John Benedict (batture resident 1932 to 1945), interview with author, September 16, 2000. Harvey Menne (batture resident 1938 to 1945), interview with author, October 4, 2000.

14. "The shrimp are amphidromous . . ." to ". . . five miles a day": Raymond T. Bauer and James Delahoussaye, "Life History Migrations of the Amphidromous River Shrimp *Macrobrachium Ohione* from a Continental Large River System," *Journal of Crustacean Biology* 28, no. 4 (October 2008).

15. "Whether it was because . . .": *Times-Picayune*, June 6, 1947.

16. "Up and Down the Street's readers . . .": *Times-Picayune*, May 11, 1962.

CHAPTER 5

1. "I don't think they're going to be able to rebuild" to ". . . had their own permitting process": *Times-Picayune*, October 4, 1998.

2. "In January 1880, City Railway . . .": *New Orleans Item*, January 20, 1880.

3. "In 1901, a hurricane . . .": *Times-Picayune*, August 18,1901.

4. "The battle simmered . . .": *Times-Picayune*, May 10, 2001.

5. "Camp owners sued . . .": *Times-Picayune*, May 10, 2001.

6. This interpretation of the batture case is informed by Ari Kelman, who details how

the conflict impacted the relationship between the city and the river in *A River and Its City* (Berkeley: University of California Press, 2006).

7. "Today the 'reclaimed' batture . . . the Convention Center": *Times-Picayune*, July 22, 2018.

8. "The river itself had been . . ." to ". . . stop enclosing it": Kelman, 26–27.

9. "The mob apparently recognized . . .": Kelman, 31.

10. "Jefferson declared . . .": Thomas Jefferson to James Madison, Monticello, October 15, 1810, from *The Works of Thomas Jefferson in Twelve Volumes*, Paul Leicester Ford, ed.

11. "Livingston sued Jefferson . . .": James F. Simon, *What Kind of Nation: Thomas Jefferson, John Marshall, and the Epic Struggle to Create a United States* (New York: Simon and Schuster, 2003), 261.

12. "A levee servitude required . . .": A. N. Yiannopoulos, *Louisiana Law Review* XXI, 732.

13. "Later, a commercial servitude . . .": Yiannopoulos, 738.

CHAPTER 6

1. ". . . Bizarre City Along the Riverfront . . .": *Times-Picayune*, March 6, 1932.

2. Descriptions of boatmen and life on the western rivers were found in Michael Allen, *Western Rivermen, 1763–1861* (Baton Rouge: Louisiana State University Press, 1990); Richard Campanella, *Lincoln in New Orleans: The 1828–1831 Flatboat Voyages and Their Place in History* (Lafayette: University of Louisiana at Lafayette Press, 2010).

3. "an unbroken wilderness": Andrew Ellicott, *The Journal of Andrew Ellicott* (1803; reprinted, Chicago: 1962), 119; as found in Allen, 1990, 42–43.

4. "a farm within twenty miles of Philadelphia": Hugh Henry Brackenridge, "To the Inhabitants of the Western Country," *Pittsburgh Gazette*, April 28, 1787; as found in Leland D. Baldwin, "The Rivers in the Early Development of Western Pennsylvania," *Western Pennsylvania Historical Magazine* 16, no. 2 (May 1933): 81.

5. "When pioneers in . . .": George R. Wilson, *Indiana Magazine of History* 18, no. 1 (March 1906): 130, as found in Campanella 2010, 29.

6. "The crews included . . .": Allen, 100.

7. "Flatboats unloaded at . . .": Mathew A. Axtell, "American Steamboat Gothic: Disruptive Commerce and Slavery's Liquidation 1832–1865," PhD diss., Princeton University, 2016. http://arks.princeton.edu/ark:/88435/dsp013197xp44q.

8. "But still from time to time . . ." to ". . . wretched inhabitants": Frances Trollope, *Domestic Manners of the Americans*, Vol. I (Paris: Baudry's Foreign Library, 1832), 2–3. http://www.gutenberg.org/ebooks/10345.

9. "I wasn't convinced that Trollope . . .": Trollope, 27.

10. "Behind other islands . . .": Twain, 9.

11. "a floating armada . . .": Axtell, 130.

12. "Flatboats that hovered . . .": Campanella, 2010, 75.

13. "There were grog shops, hotels . . .": Axtell, 4–5.

14. "Like Daniel Boone . . .": Allen, 6–9.

15. "They are a distinct class . . .": Edward Henry Durell, *New Orleans As I Found It* (New York: Harper and Brothers, 1845), 7.

16. "Commercial boats landing in New Orleans ..." to "... buyers in the city": Emerson W. Gould, *Fifty Years on the Mississippi River: Gould's History of River Navigation* (St. Louis: Nixon and Jones, 1889), 194.

17. "Abraham Lincoln, who ...": Campanella 2010, 90–91.

18. "Hundreds of long, narrow ...": Durell, 7.

19. "The city council passed ...": Campanella 2010, 93.

20. Reporters covering flatboat landings ...": *Daily Picayune*, April 21, 1840; *Daily Picayune*, March 2, 1840; *Daily Picayune*, January 18, 1853.

21. "Flatboatmen referred to ...": Allen, 104.

22. "Steamboat captains used ...": John Habermehl, *Life on Western Rivers* (Pittsburgh: McNary & Simpson, 1901), 26–28.

23. "the dark and fulsome ...": *Daily Picayune*, March 20, 1861.

24. "hundreds of thousands ... weighing 400 pounds": *Daily Picayune*, March 20, 1861.

25. "aptly named after ...": *Daily Picayune*, March 20, 1861.

26. "They nailed wooden ..." to "... the loose planks": *Daily Picayune*, December 23, 1884.

27. "In the morning ...": *Daily Picayune*, March 20, 1861.

28. "In the light of day ...": *Daily Picayune*, January 17, 1874.

29. "The hobo Social Club ..." to "... disappeared from the wharf": *Daily Picayune*, June 10, 1900.

30. "... second only to New York in immigrant arrivals": Richard Campanella, *Geographies of New Orleans* (Lafayette: University of Louisiana at Lafayette Press, 2006), 13.

31. "When you set a rat trap ...": *Times-Picayune*, July 11, 1914.

CHAPTER 7

1. "By far the most interesting ...": Nathaniel Bishop, *Four Months in a Sneak Box* (Cirencester, UK: Echo Library, reprint, 2005), 29.

2. The migration of shantyboats between 1880 and 1910 can be traced in shipping news columns in New Orleans newspapers the *Daily Picayune*, *Times-Picayune*, and *States-Item*.

3. "... put together of odd scraps of material and pieces of driftwood and wreckage": Harlan Hubbard, *Shantyboat: A River Way of Life* (Louisville: University Press of Kentucky, 1953), 2.

4. "If he is patient ...": Ben Lucien Burman, *Big River to Cross: Mississippi Life. Today* (New York: John Day, 1937), 68.

5. "One of the early ..." to "... arrived in New Orleans": *New Orleans States*, April 10, 1922.

6. "Tradesmen hung signs ...": Bishop, 30.

7. "a floating settlement ...": *New Orleans States-Item*, July 19, 1892.

8. "The shantyboat people ...": *Daily Picayune*, October 7, 1898.

9. "One observer of river ...": Burman, 66.

10. "On last Saturday evening ...": *New Orleans States-Item*, November 22, 1884.

11. "They are an unmitigated ...": *Daily Picayune*, March 26, 1890.

12. "Whether this flatboat life produces ...": *Daily Picayune*, August 4, 1895.

13. "Finally, in 1917 ...": Mark Cave, *Saving Wednesday's Child* (New Orleans: Mark Cave, 2008), 108.

14. The story of Patrick and Lottie Morris and Patrick Jr. is based on accounts in the *Daily Picayune*, January 13 and 14, 1896.

15. "Just before the Catfish Hotel . . ." to ". . . swamps of adjacent Metairie": *Daily Picayune*, September 16, 1893.

16. "A posse rounded up . . ." to ". . . friend John Willis": Chris Dier, *The 1868 St. Bernard Parish Massacre: Blood in the Canefields* (Charleston: Arcadia, 2017), 103; *Daily Item*, September 17, 1893.

17. "Terrified black laborers fled . . .": *Daily Picayune*, September 21, 1893.

18. "A negro musician was kept . . .": *Daily Picayune*, January 13, 1896.

19. The lynching of Lottie Morris is commemorated by a marker at the Peace and Justice Memorial in Montgomery, Alabama. The coincident death of Lottie's white husband, Patrick, is not mentioned on that memorial.

CHAPTER 8

1. "A black man who lived . . .": *Daily Picayune*, March 18, 1891.

2. "In 1890 alone . . .": *Daily Picayune*, March 18, 1891.

3. "The prevailing opinion . . .": *Daily Picayune*, March 19, 1891.

4. "Railroads diverted traffic . . .": *Daily City Item*, April 21, 1891.

5. "Across the river . . ." to ". . . from the break": *Daily City Item*, May 17, 1891.

6. "On June 31, 1891 . . .": *Daily City Item*, August 30, 1891.

7. "destruction of property . . .": *Daily Picayune*, August 22, 1891.

8. "A month after . . ." to "And they wept": *Daily Picayune*, September 17, 1891.

9. "Just below . . ." to ". . . floated ashore": *Morning Times*, February 20, 1896.

10. "In 1896 . . ." to ". . . island in Westwego": *Daily Picayune*, August 18, 1896.

11. Most details of this account of Seymour Geisenheimer's life were found in *Times-Picayune* and *New Orleans States*, January 11, 1942.

12. "Brothers Emile, Henry and Simon . . .": *Soards' New Orleans City Directory for 1888–1895* (New Orleans: L. Soards, 1888–1895).

13. "widely known through . . .": *Times-Picayune*, June 25, 1933.

14. "He still has . . ." to ". . . eats his suppers": *Times-Picayune*, June 25, 1933.

15. "the largest and best cypress . . .": Biography of Fischer Lumber and Manufacturing, *Biographical and Historical Memories of Louisiana*, Vol. I (Chicago: Godspeed Publishing, 1892). US GenWeb Archives. http://files.usgwarchives.net/la/orleans/bios/f-000008.txt.

16. "Joseph Bisso, the other . . ." to ". . . steamships in New Orleans": R. Christopher Goodwin and Associates, *Phase I Cultural Resources Survey and Archeological Inventory of the Proposed Carrollton Revetment Project, Orleans Parish, Louisiana, Vol I of II* (New Orleans: US Army Corps of Engineers, November 2004), 91, 102.

17. "We all know that . . ." to ". . . from one state to another": Mississippi River Floods, Hearings Before the Committee on Flood Control, House of Representatives, Sixty-fourth Congress, First Session, on Floods of the Lower Mississippi River, March 8, 9, 10, 13, 14, and 15, 1916, 148.

18. "The City reclaimed the waterfront . . .": Kelman, 122–23.

19. "the process of claiming . . ." to ". . . formerly under water": *Oxford English Dictionary* (Oxford: Oxford University, 2019).

20. "In 1913, Sewage and . . .": Richard Campanella, *Time and Place in New Orleans* (Gretna, LA: Pelican, 2002), 59.

21. "The Finest Houseboat . . ." to ". . . water for bathing": *Times-Picayune*, March 22, 1902.

CHAPTER 9

1. "It was reported . . ." to ". . . four year old paralytic": *Times-Picayune*, March 11, 1920.

2. "The crowd that gathered . . ." to ". . . with intense eagerness": *Times-Picayune*, March 11, 1920.

3. "found that no law . . ." to ". . . a person completely blind": *Times-Picayune*, March 13, 1920.

4. "Watch fires were built . . .": *Times-Picayune*, March 14, 1920.

5. "invoke the law . . .": *Times-Picayune*, March 15, 1920.

6. "It is not my duty . . .": *New Orleans Item*, March 18, 1920.

7. "Their stories transformed . . .": *Times-Picayune*, March 15, 1920.

8. "Six hundred 'crippled and diseased' . . .": *Times-Picayune*, March 27, 1920.

9. "We must do all we can . . .": *New Orleans Item*, April 5, 1920.

10. "Suckers, morons and simpletons . . .": *Los Angeles Herald*, June 23, 1921.

11. "After a dozen long-haired . . .": *New Orleans Item*, January 25, 1922.

12. "On March 1 . . ." to ". . . adoring followers": *Madera Tribune*, March 1, 1922.

13. "After two years in Biloxi . . .": E. Boudreaux, *Legends and Lore of the Mississippi Gulf Coast* (Charleston: History Press, 2013).

14. "Delusions of his immortality . . .": April Hearn, *Hearn's Books Reviews*, 2007.

15. "Brother Isaiah came . . ." to ". . . a hospital bed": *New Orleans Item*, December 20, 1922.

16. "It will interest you . . .": *Times-Picayune*, April 16, 1920.

17. "The mahogany and banana . . ." to ". . . holdings in Nicaragua": Luciano Baracco, ed., *National Integration and Contested Autonomy: The Caribbean Coast of Nicaragua* (New York: Algora, 2011), 111–13.

18. "The following year . . .": Goodwin and Associates, 95.

19. "He was accused . . ." to ". . . Carrollton Bend wharf": *Times-Picayune*, March 13, 1913; October 20, 1917.

20. "When I was a little girl down in New Orleans . . .": Mahalia Jackson, interview with Jules Schwerin, *I Sing Because I'm Happy* (Smithsonian Folkways SFW90002_102, 1979).

21. "Those enterprises . . ." to ". . . Bisso household": Goodwin and Associates, 5.

22. "The houses were . . .": Jules Schwerin, *Go Tell It: Mahalia Jackson, Queen of Gospel* (New York: Oxford University Press, 1994), 21.

23. "The only way that we could . . .": Jackson, interview with Jules Schwerin.

24. "Mahalia sang on . . ." to ". . . Aunt Hannah in Chicago": Laurraine Goreau, *Just Mahalia Baby: The Mahalia Jackson Story* (Gretna, LA: Pelican, 1998).

25. ". . . soundtrack of the civil rights movement": Sonari Glinton, National Public Radio, February 8, 2010. https://www.npr.org/templates/story/story.php?storyId=123498527?storyId=123498527.

26. "Tell them about the dream . . .": *New York Times*, August 27, 2013.

27. "In black and white . . .": Mahalia Jackson's performance of two hymns at the 1963 March on Washington (available on online music sharing sites) is a great place to get acquainted with her more strident style.

28. "too dynamic . . ." to ". . . spiritual qualities.": Kelman, 146.

29. "I used to dream . . .": Jackson, interview with Jules Schwerin.

30. "grew up on . . .": Newton Renfro, "The Batture People," *New Orleans Magazine* (July 1973): 63.

31. "Still others claim . . .": *Chicago Tribune*, May 25, 1966.

32. "After I began to sing . . .": Mahalia Jackson, interview with Laurraine Goreau, April 23, 1971. "Thoughts before Empress," MS No. 19, Lorraine Goreau Collection Series 1, Oral History, Hogan Jazz Archive, Tulane University.

33. "After a memorial . . ." to ". . . section of Carrollton Bend": Goreau 1998, 609, 610.

CHAPTER 10

1. "in fine shape": *Times-Picayune*, March 3, 1922.

2. "Engineers from the Orleans . . ." to ". . . who should pay for it": *New Orleans Item*, October 7, 1922.

3. "Levee maps from . . .": Pontchartrain Levee District planning map # LD5-1071-1, 1924; LD5-1062-1; Louisiana Department of Highways, 1924.

4. For a history of illegal gambling in New Orleans suburbs, see John Edward Appel Jr., "'The Free State of New Orleans': Local Law Enforcement and Illegal Gambling in the 1920s," University of New Orleans Theses and Dissertations, 2010, 1242.

5. "Jefferson Parish Sheriff . . ." to ". . . the Jefferson Courthouse": Miriam Davis, *Axeman of New Orleans: The True Story* (Chicago: Chicago Review Press, 2017), 148–49.

6. "On Sunday afternoons . . .": *Daily Picayune*, December 20, 1897; *Times-Picayune*, July 28, 1907.

7. "Sheriff's deputies reportedly . . .": *Daily Picayune*, July 17, 1912.

8. "One juror, Edward . . .": *Daily Picayune*, July 13, 1912.

9. "O'Dwyers children . . .": Christina Lawrence, "Southport," New Orleans Historical. http://neworleanshistorical.org/items/show/448. Accessed September 6, 2018.

10. "Rowbatham's camp . . ." to ". . . on his deck": *New Orleans Item-Tribune*, November 11, 1928.

11. "'wettest city in' . . .": Samuel C. Hyde, "Prohibition," *64 Parishes Encyclopedia of Louisiana*, Louisiana Endowment for the Humanities, February 7, 2011. https://64parishes.org/entry/prohibition.

12. "He had taken to . . .": Gary Boulard, *Huey Long Invades New Orleans* (Gretna: Pelican, 1998), 183; Goodwin and Associates, 85.

13. "According to testimony . . .": *New Orleans Item*, May 31, 1926.

14. "The sons of Edward O'Dwyer . . .": Christina Lawrence, "Southport," New Orleans Historical. http://neworleanshistorical.org/items/show/448. Accessed September 6, 2018.

15. "In 1921 the Louisiana ..." to "... neighborhoods and parks": History of Orleans Levee District Non-Flood Protection Assets. http://www.nolalakefront.com/about/.

16. The levee board ..." to "... allowed to remain": *Times-Picayune*, November 18, 1922.

17. "On Bayou St. John ..." to "... toward the lakefront": Cassie Pruyn, *Bayou St. John: A Brief History* (Charleston, SC: History Press, 2017), 83.

18. "400 business leaders ..." to "... decent citizenship": *Times-Picayune*, May 9, 1925.

19. "We do not sell to ...": *Times-Picayune*, January 20, 1926.

20. "the mother belonged to ...": *Times Picayune*, April 27, 1926.

21. For more about the Great Flood, see Johnathan Barry, *Rising Tide* (New York: Simon and Schuster, 1997).

22. "New Orleans was run ...": Barry, *Rising Tide.*

23. "Orleans colony pays ...": *Item-Tribune*, November 11, 1928.

24. Anna pronounced ..." to "... the flood of 1927": *Item-Tribune*, November 11, 1928.

CHAPTER 11

1. "Mayor Walmsley reportedly ...": *New Orleans States*, October 11, 1933.

2. "ramshackle shanty town ...": *New Orleans City Guide* (Boston: Houghton Mifflin, 1938), 280.

3. For more on illegal transport, sale, and manufacture of alcohol in Louisiana, see Joy Jackson, "Prohibition in Louisiana," *Louisiana History* 19, no. 3: 277

4. "nothing is left hardly ...": *New Orleans States*, September 28, 1934.

5. "living on his earnings ...": *Times-Picayune*, August 24, 1933.

CHAPTER 12

1. "While spillways prevented ...": J. S. Alexander, R. C. Wilson, and W. R. Green, "A Brief History and Summary of the Effects of River Engineering and Dams on the Mississippi River System and Delta," *U.S. Geological Survey Circular* (2012): 1375, 9.

2. "At the height ..." to "... river's edge": *New Orleans States*, April 5, 1937.

3. "I don't think ...": *Times-Picayune*, March 2, 1939.

4. "The older ones ..." to "... the new house": *Times-Picayune*, May 25, 1944.

5. "The Judd and Skinner ..." to "... the swollen river": *Times-Picayune*, April 15, 1945.

CHAPTER 13

1. "angel of the batture": *New Orleans Item*, February 19, 1940.

2. "nothing to be afraid of": *Item-Tribune*, February 25, 1940.

3. "the city or state must ...": *Times-Picayune*, June 15, 1941.

4. "to prevent epidemic ...": Minutes of Board of Orleans Levee District, June 19, 1945. Book 20, Folio 53.

5. "referred to proper ...": Minutes of Board of Orleans Levee District, July 17, 1945, Book 20, Folio 80.

6. "Insofar as the safety . . .": Minutes of Board of Orleans Levee District, July 17, 1945, Book 20, Folio 80.

7. "Two weeks after . . .": *New Orleans Times-Picayune/States*, March 26, 1944.

8. For information on the development of New Orleans lakefront, see History of Orleans Levee District Non-Flood Protection Assets. http://www.nolalakefront.com/about/.

9. "When Earl Long . . ." to ". . . one-by-one": Michael L. Kurtz and Morgan D. Peoples, *Earl K. Long: The Saga of Uncle Earl and Louisiana Politics* (Baton Rouge: Louisiana State University Press, 1992), 86–88, 137.

10. "I like to get some . . ." to ". . . stacked it outside the fence": *Times-Picayune/States*, January 11, 1942.

11. "Mahalia Jackson scaled . . .": Goreau 1998, 25.

12. "The good neighbors . . ." to ". . . don't want to be bothered": *Times-Picayune*, October 13, 1946.

CHAPTER 14

1. "It was later reported . . .": *New Orleans Item*, September 29, 1949.

2. "a close and thoroughly . . .": *New Orleans Item*, July 15, 1948.

3. "undesirable dwellers . . ." to ". . . fire menaces": *New Orleans States*, October 27, 1948.

4. "People on the lakefront . . .": *New Orleans Item*, October 11, 1948.

5. "We thought it was . . .": *Times-Picayune*, February 9, 1949.

6. "It was moved by . . .": Board of Orleans Levee District minutes, November 17, 1952, File 33, Book 24.

7. "When the Board met . . ." to ". . . river in Algiers": Board of Orleans Levee District minutes, December 15, 1952, File 55, Book 24.

8. "People were buying . . .": *Times-Picayune*, October 8, 1953.

9. The conflict between batture dwellers and public agencies can be traced in hundreds of stories over three years, beginning in December 1952.

10. "The BDA employed . . ." to ". . . be left alone": Batture Dwellers Association Records, File 305, Box 1, Louisiana Research Collection, Tulane University. The Batture Dwellers Association files provide a batture dweller perspective on the legal and public relations battles and personal hardships of the batture apocalypse of 1950–55.

11. "Just before . . ." to ". . . piling from the river": "Waitin' on a Levee for the Dispossess," *Life*, July 13, 1953.

12. "To avoid arguing . . ." to ". . . better prepared case": *Times-Picayune*, July 17, 1953.

13. "A new trial began . . ." to ". . . connections to camps": Batture Dwellers Association Records, File 305, Box 1, Folder 11, 12. "Court Documents."

14. "The public has . . ." to "and federal agencies . . .": *Times-Picayune*, October 20, 1953.

15. "These Were Our Homes," pamphlet, Batture Dwellers Association Records, File 305, Box 1, folder 22, "Printed Matter 1955-Undated."

16. "I am 50 years old . . ." to ". . . how much it cost": Batture Dwellers Association Records, File 305, Box 1, Folder 16, "Batture Dwellers Claim Sheets."

17. "On Tuesday, July . . ." to ". . . never move my house": *New Orleans States*, July 20, 1954.

CHAPTER 15

1. "Bisso's son, 'Cappy' . . .": Goodwin and Associates, 85.

2. "In 1956 . . ." to ". . . sat in the middle": *Times-Picayune*, March 5, 1956.

3. "A house painter . . .": Dennis J. Cipnic, "The Little Land That Isn't There," *Coronet* (April 1960): 84.

4. "land from which . . .": *States-Item*, April 1, 1961.

5. "The Department of Health . . ." to ". . . laced with pesticide": *New Orleans States*, October 25, 1950; November 23, 1950.

6. "Once a park is lost . . .": *Times-Picayune*, May 19, 1961.

7. "to see the river . . .": *States-Item*, June 14, 1961.

8. "five sets of railroad . . ." to ". . . New Orleans and Louisiana": *Times-Picayune*, June 3, 1961.

9. For a history of the riverfront expressway brouhaha, see Richard O. Baumbach Jr. and William E. Borah, The Second Battle of New Orleans: A History of the Vieux Carré Riverfront-Expressway Controversy (Birmingham: University of Alabama Press, 1981).

10. "Any structure which tends . . .": *Times-Picayune*, March 25, 1965.

11. Baumbach and Borah.

12. "As the River crested . . ." to ". . . unavailable in the city itself": Vanaan Barbara Allen, "Comparison of Squatter Settlement integration in Latin America and New Orleans," honors thesis, Tulane University, 1973, 61–97.

13. "according to William Bisso Jr.'s son . . .": Goodwin and Associates, 85, 91; Renfro, 64, 78.

14. "The batture peace ended . . ." to ". . . in 1945": *States-Item*, November 6, 1974.

15. "These illegal enterprises . . .": Appel, 1242.

16. "I love it here." to ". . . it's peaceful": *States-Item*, November 6, 1974.

17. "This is another case . . .": *States-Item*, November 8, 1974.

18. "[Paul] Tagliabue decided to . . ." to ". . . exposure of an office": Wright Thompson, "Beyond the Breach," *ESPN Magazine*, August 24, 2015.

19. "He had remained . . ." to ". . . in a civilized society.": *Times-Picayune*, May 29, 2007.

20. "The suspension arose . . ." to ". . . discourteous language": Olivia Olsen, "Lawyer Disbarred for Instances of Using Racially Charged Language," *Louisiana Record*, April 3, 2017. https://louisianarecord.com/stories/511100362-lawyer-disbarred-for-instances-of-using-racially-charged-language. Accessed September 9, 1018.

EPILOGUE

1. "Wendell Berry described . . ." to "man of the margins": Harlan Hubbard, *Shantyboat: A River Way of Life* (Lexington: University of Kentucky Press, 1977), vi.

BIBLIOGRAPHY

Appel, John Edward, Jr. 2010. "'The Free State of New Orleans': Local Law Enforcement and Illegal Gambling in the 1920s." https://scholarworks.uno.edu/td/1242.

Alexander, J. S., et al. 2012. "A Brief History and Summary of the Effects of River Engineering and Dams on the Mississippi River System and Delta." *U.S. Geological Survey Circular.*

Allen, Michael. 1990. *Western Rivermen, 1763–1861.* Baton Rouge: Louisiana State University Press.

Baldwin, Leland D. 1933. "The Rivers in the Early Development of Western Pennsylvania." *Western Pennsylvania Historical Magazine* 16, no. 2.

Baracco, Luciano, ed. 2011. *National Integration and Contested Autonomy: The Caribbean Coast of Nicaragua.* New York: Algora.

Barry, John M. 1998. *Rising Tide: The Great Mississippi Flood of 1927 and How It Changed America.* New York: Simon and Schuster/Touchstone Edition.

Bauer, Raymond T., and James Delahoussaye. 2008. "Life History Migrations of the Amphidromous River Shrimp *Macrobrachium Ohione* from a Continental Large River System." *Journal of Crustacean Biology* 28, no. 4.

Baumbach, Richard O., Jr., and William E. Borah. 1981. The Second Battle of New Orleans: A History of the Vieux Carré Riverfront-Expressway Controversy. Birmingham: University of Alabama Press.

Bendixen, Alfred, and Judith Hamera, eds. 2009. *The Cambridge Guide to American Travel Writing.* Cambridge: Cambridge University Press.

Bishop, Nathaniel. [1879] 2005. *Four Months in a Sneak Box.* Cirencester, UK: Echo Library.

Boudreaux, E. 2013. *Legends and Lore of the Mississippi Gulf Coast.* Charleston: History Press.

Boulard, Gary. 1998. *Huey Long Invades New Orleans.* Gretna: Pelican.

Burman, Ben Lucien. 1937. *Big River to Cross: Mississippi Life Today.* New York: John Day.

Cave, Mark. 2008. *Saving Wednesday's Child,* New Orleans: Mark Cave.

Campanella, Richard. 2002. *Time and Place in New Orleans.* Gretna: Pelican.

Campanella, Richard. 2006. *Geographies of New Orleans.* Lafayette: Center for Louisiana Studies.

Campanella, Richard. 2010. *Lincoln in New Orleans: The 1828–1831 Flatboat Voyages and Their Place in History.* Lafayette: University of Louisiana at Lafayette Press.

Cipnic, Dennis J. 1960. "The Little Land That Isn't There." *Coronet* 47, no. 6.

Davis, Miriam. 2017. *Axeman of New Orleans: The True Story.* Chicago: Chicago Review Press.

Dier, Chris. 2017. *The 1868 St. Bernard Parish Massacre: Blood in the Canefields*. Charleston: Arcadia.

Durell, Edward Henry. 1845. *New Orleans As I Found It*. New York: Harper and Brothers.

Federal Writers Project of the Works Progress Administration. 1938. *New Orleans City Guide*. Boston: Houghton Mifflin.

Goodwin, R. Christopher, and Associates. 2004. *Phase I Cultural Resources Survey and Archeological Inventory of the Proposed Carrollton Revetment Project, Orleans Parish, Louisiana, Vol. I of II*. New Orleans: US Army Corps of Engineers.

Goreau, Laurraine. 1998. *Just Mahalia Baby: The Mahalia Jackson Story*. Gretna: Pelican.

Gould, Emerson W. 1889. *Fifty Years on the Mississippi River: Gould's History of River Navigation*. St. Louis: Nixon and Jones.

Habermehl, John. 1901. *Life on Western Rivers*. Pittsburgh: McNary & Simpson.

Hatfield, Paul. 2014. "Engineered Wildness: The Lower Mississippi River, an Underappreciated National Treasure." *International Journal of Wilderness* 20, no. 3.

Hiller, Ernest Theodore. 1939. *Houseboat and River-bottoms People*. Urbana: University of Illinois Press.

Hubbard, Harlan. 1953. *Shantyboat: A River Way of Life*. Louisville: University Press of Kentucky.

Hutchins, Thomas. 1784. *An Historical Narrative and Topographical Description of Louisiana and West Florida*. Philadelphia: Printed for the author.

Hyde, Samuel C. 2011. "Prohibition." In David Johnson, ed., *64 Parishes: Encyclopedia of Louisiana*. Louisiana Endowment for the Humanities.

Jackson, Joy. 1978. "Prohibition in Louisiana: The Unlikeliest Crusade." *Louisiana History: Journal of the Louisiana Historical Association* 19, no. 3.

Kelman, Ari. 2006. *A River and Its City*. Berkeley: University of California Press.

Kurtz, Michael L., and Morgan D. Peoples. 1992. *Earl K. Long: The Saga of Uncle Earl and Louisiana Politics*. Baton Rouge: Louisiana State University Press.

Lighty, Kent, and Margaret Lighty. 1930. *Shanty-Boat*. New York: Century.

Miller, Mike (submitted 2001). 1892. "Biography of Fischer Lumber and Manufacturing." In *Biographical and Historical Memories of Louisiana*, Vol. I. Chicago: Godspeed Publishing. http://files.usgwarchives.net/la/orleans/bios/f-000008.txt.

Pruyn, Cassie. 2017. *Bayou St. John: A Brief History*. Charleston: History Press.

Renfro, Newton. 1973. "The Batture People." *New Orleans Magazine* 7, no. 10.

Schwerin, Jules. *Go Tell It: Mahalia Jackson, Queen of Gospel*. New York: Oxford University Press.

Simon, James F. 2003. *What Kind of Nation: Thomas Jefferson, John Marshall, and the Epic Struggle to Create a United States*. New York: Simon and Schuster.

Soards, L. 1896. *Soards' New Orleans City Directory for 1888–1895*. New Orleans: L. Soards.

Speakman, Harold. 1927. *Mostly Mississippi*. New York: Dodd, Mead.

Stoll, Steven. 2017. *Ramp Hollow: The Ordeal of Appalachia*. New York: Hill and Wang.

Thompson, Wright. 2015. "Beyond the Breach." *ESPN Magazine*.

Trollope, Frances. 1832. *Domestic Manners of the Americans*, Vol. I. Paris: Baudry's Foreign Library.

Twain, Mark. 1883. *Life on the Mississippi*. Boston: James R. Osgood.

White, Richard D. 2006. *The Reign of Huey P. Long*. New York: Random House.

Yiannopoulos, A. N. 1970. "The Public Use of the Banks of Navigable Rivers in Louisiana." *Louisiana Law Review* XXI.

Zimmerman, John (photographer). 1953. "Waitin' on a Levee for the Dispossess." *Life*, July 13, 1953.

INDEX

ABOUT THE AUTHOR

Macon Fry is an author, writer, and educator. Fry arrived in New Orleans in 1981 to record and write about the unique culture and folkways of South Louisiana. For the past thirty years he has lived on the watery fringe of New Orleans, occupying a self-built stilt house over the Mississippi River, hidden by the huge levees that keep the city dry.

Printed in the United States
by Baker & Taylor Publisher Services